The Witch's Flight

PERVERSE MODERNITIES   *A series edited by Judith Halberstam and Lisa Lowe*

The Witch's Flight

The Cinematic, the Black Femme,
and the Image of Common Sense

Kara Keeling

Duke University Press
Durham + London 2007

Printed in the United States of America
on acid-free paper ∞
Designed by Jennifer Hill
Typeset in Scala by Keystone Typesetting, Inc.
Library of Congress Cataloging-in-Publication Data
appear on the last printed page of this book.

*Duke University Press gratefully acknowledges the support
of the University of North Carolina, Chapel Hill, which
provided funds toward the production of this book.*

To Chandra

Contents

Without Marcia Landy's support, encouragement, advice, criticisms, patience, sense of humor, and intellectual example, *The Witch's Flight* would not have been written at all. I have not encountered, nor could I imagine, a better mentor and teacher. Though all of the errors herein are my own, this book, if it moves at all, is propelled in large part by my efforts to follow the example set by her intellectual work.

This project has benefited from my engagements over the years with many people, both within academia and outside of it. I am grateful for each person's presence in my life and the ways in which each has informed or challenged the thinking this book conveys. I know that I cannot name everyone, though I would like to do so. I hope that those I may inadvertently have left out will forgive me.

The original readers of this manuscript, my dissertation committee, consisted of Marcia Landy, Wahneema Lubiano, Amy Villarejo, Paul A. Bové, and Colin MacCabe. I am grateful to every one of them for the care with which they

Acknowledgments

engaged with and raised questions about the project. I hope that they will recognize the fruits of that labor in the project's final form. Wahneema Lubiano and Amy Villarejo have continued to provide me with intellectual stimulation and professional advice and support. I believe this project is the better for their continued involvement with it.

D. Soyini Madison and Lawrence Grossberg also generously gave of their time and considerable intellectual abilities by engaging with this project in dissertation form. I am grateful to them for their help with and belief in it as it moved toward completion.

In Pittsburgh an intellectual community helped me to find pleasure in developing and exchanging ideas and theories. I am thankful for the time I was privileged to spend with Brian Broome, Ardene Effatt, Patrick Mullen, Todd Marciani, Alison Cuddy, Joy Van Fuqua, Matthew Tinkcom, Amy Villarejo, Barbara White, Vanessa Domico, Patricia Saunders, Linda Huff, Lisa Coxson, Cherise Pollard, Michelle Elliott, Rich Purcell, Michelle Raitano, Eric O Clarke, and Poppy Cates. I hope that each of them will recognize his or her imprint on my thinking herein.

Though this project was conceived in Pittsburgh, the time of its actual writing corresponds almost exactly with the time I spent in North Carolina. The support of my colleagues in the Department of Communication Studies at the University of North Carolina, Chapel Hill, has been invaluable to me. I am especially grateful to D. Soyini Madison for reminding me over and again about the importance of the work we do. I continue to learn from her almost daily. Lawrence Grossberg and Rich Cante took the time to inquire into and engage with me about the status of this project, and I think that I gained a clearer perspective about it each time I talked with one of them. Bill Balthrop and Julia Wood helped me manage the transition from graduate student to postdoctoral fellow to junior faculty. They patiently offered their time with a grace that always let me know I could ask them for help or advice. The discussions with graduate students in my "Cinema and Social Change" seminar—especially Lisa Calvente, Joshua Smicker, and Miguel Najera—helped me clarify some of the ideas presented here. I also thank Robin Vander and Patricia Harris for their friendship and support throughout this process.

Before I moved below the Mason-Dixon line, I never imagined that I would grow to love the South and discover such complexity in my response to it. The dedicated, thoughtful, and passionate people of the organization Southerners on New Ground (SONG) have helped me to understand the possibilities and challenges of making meaningful change, and they have greatly enriched my life and added texture to my existence in the South, making me proud to have called it "home." Kim Diehl, Akiba Timoya, Rebecca Silver, Annette Shead, Jackie Mirkin, Matt Nicholson, Mandy Carter, Suzanne Pharr, Pam McMichael, Joan Garner, Pat and Cherry Hussain, Holmes Hummel, Stephanie Guilloud, Chantelle Fisher-Borne, Deepali Gokhale, Jessica George, and Robert-John Hinojosa have each taught me valuable lessons, some of which have found their way into this book, about what it means to live, love, and stand for justice in the South. Though I also learned many lessons I thought I never wanted to learn, I am grateful that I had the opportunity to meet and to know each of these individuals. The many other people I have been fortunate to meet through SONG have helped me to sense the yearning that people have for meaningful connections with other living beings. At the Highlander Center in New Market, Tennessee, I had the opportunity to witness how such connections might be forged by working alongside an impressive and vibrant group that included Paulina Hernandez and Caitlin Breedlove. I am grateful and humbled that y'all embraced, nurtured, and challenged me.

Pieces of this project have been presented to various audiences, including those at the University of Minnesota, Stanford University, the University of Illinois, Chicago, the University of California, Berkeley, Bowdoin College, the University of Southern California, Williams College, and Cornell University. This project has benefited from the comments, questions, and suggestions of audience members at each of those sites. I am especially grateful to Joy James and Fred Moten for continuing the conversation after I left their campuses.

This project also profited from the generous support of the University of Pittsburgh, through a Mellon Dissertation Fellowship and a Provost's Development Fund award. At the University of North Carolina, Chapel Hill, the Carolina Postdoctoral Fellowship for Faculty Diversity and a semester's leave granted by the Institute for the Arts and Humanities gave me the time I needed to complete the project. Sections of chapter 6 were published in *The Black Scholar* as an essay with the title " 'Ghetto Heaven': *Set It Off* and the Valorization of Black Lesbian Butch-Femme." They are reprinted by permission of *The Black Scholar*. The journal *Qui Parle* published my essay "In the Interval," which included some material that is presented here in chapter 2. The staff at Duke University Press has been a resource for me. Ken Wissoker has remained committed to this project over several years, and I am grateful to him for helping me to finally see it in print. Two different sets of anonymous reviews provided invaluable feedback on this book in manuscript form.

My thinking about the intersections between race, gender, sexuality, and political economy has been enriched by intellectual exchanges with Judith Halberstam, Chandan Reddy, Roderick A. Ferguson, Jared Sexton, Grace Hong, Barbara Smith, and Jennifer DeVere Brody.

Without my parents, Jane and Rudy Keeling, this book would not have been possible. Their consistent support and presence in my life are invaluable resources that I too often take for granted. I thank my siblings—Tina, Kip, and Cory—and my grandparents—Cedora, Jane and Spalding. It is impossible to explain how much I rely on the fact that they always are there for me. Thank you also to Phyllis Autry and Stanford Ford, who have supported and encouraged me in various ways throughout this project. Nicholas Valadez and Christalynn Ford have been inspirations.

Chandra Ford read every draft of every chapter of this manuscript from its inception to the final copy, commenting on each one meticulously, thoughtfully, and carefully. She is my best critic, my biggest supporter, and my great passion. Huey Pac and Ibo are running a very close second.

To think is always to follow the witch's flight.
— GILLES DELEUZE and FÉLIX GUATTARI, *What Is Philosophy?*

Another Litany for Survival

Little attention has been given to the historical coincidence between the invention of cinema in the early twentieth century and W. E. B. Du Bois's prescient 1903 statement that "the problem of the twentieth century is the problem of the color line." An investigation of the nexus at which the epistemological and ontological mechanisms of racism and the socioeconomic interests that racism serves collide with the mechanisms and interests that animate cinema might open a critical interrogation into the lingering logics of racism and the complex ways in which "race," "gender," and "sexuality" have come both to inform **Introduction** and deform various anticapitalist movements toward Black Liberation. In the name of such an interrogation, the present study takes flight from a set of theoretical explorations of cinema, cinematic processes, and their profound significance to anticapitalist, U.S.-based, Black Liberation movements, and heads toward an examination of black lesbian butch-femme sociality as an exemplary, though imperfect, effort to forge ways of living that enable the survival of expressions of life that, to invoke Audre Lorde, were never meant to survive.

If it can be said, however enigmatically, that "to think is always to follow the witch's flight," then the black femme is the "witch" whose flight the present book pursues in the name of thinking. The black femme is herein crafted as a figure that exists on the edge line between "the cinematic" or "cinematic reality" and what Gilles Deleuze refers to in his study of cinema as a "radical Elsewhere." The black femme thus offers a glimpse into the range of mechanisms whereby transformations within and alternatives to existing organizations of life might be affected. The figure of the black femme orchestrates this book's trajectory because she challenges each of the primary categories that have been constructed in response to racism, sexism, and homophobia ("black," "woman," and "lesbian," respectively) to contend with what is excluded from that category in order for it to cohere as such.

Yet this is not a book about the black femme, or even about black lesbian butch-femme. *The Witch's Flight* is an exploration of the conditions of possibility for their survival, as concepts, as identities, as communities, and, perhaps most important, as problems. It also is an evaluation of what the figure of the black femme in particular and black lesbian butch-femme sociality in general make available to contemporary thought about the connections between visual culture, blackness, gender, and sexuality. In this study the black femme is a figure that exists on the edge line, that is, the shoreline between the visible and the invisible, the thought and the unthought in the critical theories that currently animate film and media studies, African American studies, gender and sexuality studies (including women's studies and queer theory), and critical theory more broadly. Following Avery Gordon, it could be said that the black femme haunts current attempts to make critical sense of the world along lines delineated according to race, gender, and/or sexuality. Because she often is invisible (but nonetheless present), when she becomes visible, her appearance stops us, offers us time in which we can work to perceive something different, or differently.

Because she marks a highly contested and contingent mode of existence—one that, as the Audre Lorde poem referenced in the title of this introduction makes evident, cannot not speak or not appear or not re-member—the black femme sets us to work on questions of survival, including considerations of affective labor, excess, and the (re)production of value. Like the black, the black femme is not but theory and flesh. Following *The Witch's Flight* therefore demands a theoretical scaffolding capable of, or at least calibrated for, framing "the problem of the twentieth century" without reifying the common sense that problem secures. I provide this scaffolding in the first two chapters and continue to build it in subsequent chapters. Each chapter contains a component of the argument that the book as a whole makes, thereby leading the reader into the subsequent chapters or back to the preceding. Nonetheless, each chapter both relies on and is relatively indifferent to the arguments in the other chapters and thus could be read on its own. The readers who choose to skip chapters will miss the overall argument's nuance but still should emerge with something of its substance.

Attending to the lines of flight set in motion by (un)successful attempts to contain or circumscribe the black femme within existing epistemological categories provides an opportunity to elucidate the workings of the cinematic and the cinematic processes integral to contemporary racism, sexism, and homophobic violence.

Follow?

I derive my use of the term *the cinematic* from Gilles Deleuze's elaboration of the word *cinema* in *Cinema 1: The Movement-Image* and *Cinema 2: The Time-Image*. According to Deleuze, film becomes, on its invention, "the organ for perfecting" a "new reality."[1] I insist upon the critical utility of understanding the complex and messy stuff of late-twentieth-century reality within the conceptual frameworks made perceptible by the development of cinema.

My use of *the cinematic* as a term through which to shuttle a complicated aggregate of capitalist social relations, sensory-motor arrangements, and cognitive processes runs the risk of subsuming things specific to other audiovisual media, such as television, under the rubric of *cinema*, a term commonly associated only with film. Yet many of the phenomena with which I am concerned here surfaced with the invention of film technology; thus, it is in the context of a sustained discussion of cinema that Deleuze identifies, characterizes, and engages with those types of images. Following the argument that Richard Dienst makes in the context of considering whether Deleuze's "movement-image might have existed in multiple forms beyond cinema" (and therefore of assessing Deleuze's relevance for Dienst's study of television), what I suggest is "not to say that cinema simply infected everything else with its logic" but to point out that cinematic images surface "in a range of activities sharing the same abstract (acentered, variable) relations of exchange and mobility."[2] Assuming the prevalence since the beginning of the twentieth century of the types of images and processes Deleuze describes —images and processes that are perceptible via film but that can be said to have appeared in other arenas contemporaneous with film—I employ the substantive *the cinematic* to designate a condition of existence, or a reality, produced and reproduced by and within the regimes of the image Deleuze identifies and describes. *The Witch's Flight* is Deleuzian to the extent that Deleuze's work on film provides a theoretical framework and a method for its elaboration and exploration of the cinematic.

The privilege I accord to films as vehicles that circulate "cinematic images" stems from their ability to put particular images into widespread circulation and to package them for various modes of consumption, including

3

intellectual consumption. With this in mind, I have chosen films or other configurations of images whose appearance reveals something within common sense with the potential to unsettle hegemonic conceptualizations of race, gender, and/or sexuality that rationalize, based on a set of conclusions about one or all three of those categories, forms of domination and exploitation.

Because my primary concern is with those images that have found ways of moving with relative ease by affirming aspects of common sense, I focus largely on mainstream and popular films or other images that have achieved broad circulation, rather than on films with a small or limited circulation. The invention of video and the mass distribution of films on video have made the public circulation of images faster and broader while rendering more variable the speed at which the images might be viewed; they might be fast-forwarded, rewound, paused, and reconsidered or re-circulated in a different context. Much of my analysis regarding specific films, for example, is the result of the type of methodical deliberation that is not readily accessible upon a first screening in a movie theater.[3] Assuming the widespread availability of the images that interest me, I consider the formal and aesthetic characteristics of the film or films in which they circulate in an effort to assess the context for the reception of those images.

The context within which each of the cinematic images I discuss was produced, distributed, and exhibited provides a glimpse into that image's journeys and its currency as expressed most crudely, but accessibly, by box-office receipts and other standards of measurement particular to commercial film. (Box-office returns and production budgets are only two among many points of contact between film and money. Not only does filmmaking require a major investment of capital, but, as I discuss in chapter 1, cinema's particular relationship with time binds cinematic images to money.)[4]

Because of my attention to film's role in the circulation of images, certain of the epistemologies and methodologies particular to film studies are invaluable to my analysis of film texts. Scholarly work that probes issues concerning questions of aesthetics, or the dynamics informing the reception or consumption of film images, have been invaluable to my attempts to explore the cinematic itself. But my engagement with film, film studies, and media studies is also an intervention into the manner in which questions of representation, race, and the economic function of media are framed. Deleuze's cinema offers a way of thinking about questions of "race," "gender," "sexuality," and "representation" that challenge demands for "positive," "negative," or "accurate" representations—demands that assume the coherence of an indexical relationship between image and "reality" that has never cohered for blacks and other groups who consistently have claimed to be misrepresented. Deleuze's theories of the cinematic contest these assumptions, allowing for a nuanced and critical understanding of film as part of reality, rather than as a reflection or representation of it, and of the dominance of cinematic processes in making sense of the world for those whose sensory-motor schemata has been habituated by film. In referring to cinematic processes as dominant, I am marking not only the extent to which our knowledges of the world increasingly are mediated by images but also the ways in which our sensory apparatus is accustomed to receiving and forming images according to the parameters and expectations put in place by cinema. For Deleuze, cinema is a mode of thinking, that is, of creating concepts.

Excavating and encouraging alternative ways of knowing and thinking requires the creation and adoption of new concepts and paradigms. Because Deleuze insisted upon creating his own machinery for knowledge production, readers of his work notoriously risk falling into "Deleuzeobabble," a hermetic system of terms and concepts with precise, if at times obscure or obtuse, meanings created by Deleuze in his attempts to challenge and/or break out of existing philosophical systems. While I have attempted not to fall into Deleuzeobabble myself, I have adopted some of Deleuze's terms where I think they might usefully challenge prevalent ways of conceptualizing an issue at hand. Yet Deleuze himself is notorious for having little or nothing innovative to say about race. *The Witch's Flight* is enabled by Deleuze's work but ultimately has to betray Deleuze's commitments for its own. Because of this, it might be understood as working through a set of Deleuzian problems and paradigms in order to emerge with a brain, vision, and soundtrack of its own.[5]

Hear me.

In this volume I examine cinematic images of common sense in an attempt to locate the kernels of perceptions that might be capable of supporting alternate forms of sociality. What I am able to uncover is limited by my own cinematic perception and thus by the common sense(s) that condition it. Nonetheless, risking non-sense in the pages that follow, I have directed some of my own affective labor and channeled the labor I perform in my profes-

5

sional function as an intellectual into a project predicated on the possibility that various hegemonic and official common senses might be exploded, unleashing affectivity's creative, self-valorizing potential, if only in that any-instant-whatever that holds one enthralled by the explosion.

Though the cost of copyright clearances make it unreasonable (remember "reason" itself has economic interests) to think that an actual soundtrack might be sold with this book, each chapter corresponds with a song on the book's soundtrack. In 1971 the R&B group the Undisputed Truth released the enigmatic and haunting cautionary music notes of "Smiling Faces Some-times," the song for chapters 1 and 2.[6] In narratives about the civil rights and Black Power movements, the period between 1968 and 1971 is understood to be the turning point when the conciliatory call for civil rights was replaced by the nationalist-inflected, if often ambiguous, call for "black power."[7] The implications of this shift, as well as its structures of feeling, have exerted considerable influence over the contours of black, radical, and progressive longings today, longings for something better, more just, funky, and inter-galactic than the confining relationships that define the present.

The lyrics to "Smiling Faces Sometimes" caution listeners to be wary of appearances, to look under, above, through, and behind what appears. To turn a smile upside down. I cannot afford the cost of reproducing lyrics here. Go listen to the song. The lyrics are cautionary. They educate. But a consider-ation of the meaning of the song is flat without an account of the music, especially its bass line, which gets caught in an endless repetition. A similar claim can be made about the meaning of *The Witch's Flight*: the words on the page educate, forge lines of flight, and try to engender movement, but what this book is about also can be felt in the movement of its soundtrack. "Smil-ing Faces Sometimes" raises many of the questions the theoretical frame-works elaborated in chapters 1 and 2 have been constructed to address. Indeed, each song referenced in this book comments on the chapter for which it provides the soundtrack, thereby providing *The Witch's Flight* with an affective register that simultaneously exceeds and yearns toward what the book's sometimes dense critical theoretical prose can achieve. As Fred Moten would say, "Words don't go there." Yet both the words on these pages and the music on the soundtrack might propel one into a "lyricism of the surplus" that, while evading currently accessible common senses, still can be felt—like an intuition or premonition, something unseen, but nonetheless present(ly) (im)possible.[8] The end of the world.

"The *forming* of the five senses is a labour of the entire history of the world down to the present."[9]

Work with me.

How can knowledge be forged and shared without being detected by those with the power to prevent that knowledge from exerting a counterhegemonic force? In what ways are subjugated knowledges produced, and how do they survive attempts to incorporate them into dominant regimes of knowledge and their modes of production? How can subaltern common senses that elude consent to domination and exploitation, that create an alternative to existing power relations be crafted? The "slave song" (what Du Bois would have classified as a "sorrow song") "Wade in the Water" is reputed to contain instructions for slaves about how to escape. Such clandestine modes of communication were common during slavery. Frederick Douglass, for instance, notes that " 'Run to Jesus / shun the danger / I don't expect to stay much longer here' was a favorite air and had a double meaning. In the lips of some, it meant the expectation of a speedy summons to a world of spirits; but in the lips of *our* company, it simply meant a speedy pilgrimage toward a free state and deliverance from all the evils and dangers of slavery."[10] The formation of a group of living beings capable of communicating hidden knowledges about how to achieve freedom is at issue in Douglass's account. By necessity, that group excluded those whose perception had been habituated according to interests that dictated the former group's enslavement.

Throughout *The Witch's Flight*, the black femme sets to work on questions concerning the creation of the common under circumstances of domination, exploitation, and oppression. In chapters 3 and 7 I engage with films that seek to reconcile an account opened by the capture, transportation, and enslavement of living beings. But both films—Haile Gerima's *Sankofa* (1993) and Kasi Lemmons's *Eve's Bayou* (1997)—have a different sense of what freedom might require or entail. *Sankofa* valorizes those who died in the struggle for their freedom, while the possibilities generated in *Eve's Bayou* grow out of the common sense of slaves. In chapter 7 Angela Davis's seminal 1971 "Reflections on the Black Woman's Role in the Community of Slaves," written from her prison cell, informs my elaboration of what I refer to as "the black femme function," a potential for self-valorization and creativity that is imminent in and generated by the cinematic itself. Wait. We cannot get there

7

from here. It is too soon. Or too late. Follow me down to Jordan's stream. And onto Eve's Bayou.

"And the traveller girds himself, and sets his face toward the Morning, and goes his way."[11]

As for the witch, she takes flight from the theoretical scaffolding built in chapters 1 and 2, only to find herself fixed in chapter 3 by Haile Gerima's film *Sankofa*, an occasion that allows us to dwell on the narrative of slavery that common-sense black nationalism posits in order to rationalize the subject it constructs and offers as adequate to the task of Black Liberation. The violence with which *Sankofa* expunges femininity and genital sexuality from its revolutionary subject is of particular interest. The figure of the black lesbian femme is among those *Sankofa* renders present impossibilities within the project of Black Liberation and within the common-sense black nationalism that currently solidifies black belonging.

Following a line of flight made available by the interrogation into the terms of Black Liberation *Sankofa* makes visible, I open chapter 4 with the first notes of "Four Women," as sung by Nina Simone. I begin that chapter with an interrogation into the temporality of the cinematic and move through a consideration of the ways in which the cinematic appearance of women in the Black Panther Party became part of the transvaluation that blackness underwent during the 1960s and 1970s. The negotiations around "masculinity," "femininity," and (hetero)sexuality orchestrated by Black Revolutionary Women allow us to glimpse the figures of the black butch lesbian and the black femme lesbian, but not in time to explore the alternative organizations of social life they make available within cinematic reality before they again escape incorporation into common-sense black nationalism.

Such organizations of social life escape valorization via the affectivity expended in order to make sense of the cinematic appearance of Black Revolutionary Women, but they persist as part of what Roderick A. Ferguson refers to as the "multiplications of surplus" generated by capital.[12] In chapter 5 Nina Simone's distinctive voice redefines the optimism of the Five Stairsteps's version of "O-o-h Child," pushing its smooth and reassuring claims that things will get easier in a different direction altogether. Simone thereby sets to work on the psychic dimensions of black life and survival, revealing the "strange blending of love and helplessness" that "O-o-h Child" offers.[13] In chapter 5 I work through Pam Grier's blaxploitation films, highlighting the ways that blaxploitation in general and Pam Grier's blaxploitation films

in particular work to make black nationalism commonly available and productive for capital, even as they generate excess or surplus that might be
invested in subsequent projects. These projects might offer alternative organizations of social life, such as those organized by black lesbian butch-
femme. In Pam Grier's blaxploitation films we glimpse the black butch and
femme before they take flight, only to be caught in the mechanism of visibility as part of the machinery capable of valorizing female bank robbers in
F. Gary Gray's 1996 film *Set It Off*.

In chapter 6 I analyze *Set It Off* in order to articulate the conditions of
possibility for the cinematic appearance of black lesbian butch-femme sexuality. "Ghetto Heaven" by the Family Stand is on the soundtrack for that
chapter. We apprehend the black femme as a figure that exists on the edge
of the visible and the invisible, serving as a portal through which present
(im)possibilities might appear. At the end of the chapter, we encounter "the
black femme function," a capacity for self-valorization that persists as part of
capital's own mechanisms of (re)production. The black femme function persists within capital as that which might offer alternatives to the organizations
of sociality that capital currently sanctions.

In chapter 7 I analyze another commodity, Kasi Lemmon's 1997 film *Eve's
Bayou*, which itself illustrates the black femme function. In this final chapter
of *The Witch's Flight* my analysis of *Eve's Bayou* returns to the questions
Sankofa opened up, those regarding the past, memory, gender, and the present (im)possibilities of and for liberation. *Eve's Bayou*, like *Sankofa*, raises
questions of survival, (re)production, and the valorization of alternative organizations of social life within the cinematic; unlike *Sankofa*, it allows one to
dwell upon forms of labor that enable the survival of those who, like the black
femme and the black butch, were never meant to survive.

What did Erykah Badu say about "my cipher"? It keeps movin'. Like a
rolling stone.

The coincidence between the invention of cinema and W. E. B. Du Bois's
proclamation that "the problem of the twentieth century is the problem of
the color line" reveals the importance of a politics of visibility to struggles
against racism in the United States and to the related struggles against
sexism and homophobia. Efforts to resist U.S. racism were varied and sustained during the twentieth century, and those trajectories of resistance that
aimed for reform of existing structures and institutions, rather than radical
or revolutionary change, more successfully deployed a politics of visibility,

9

which bore fruit with the reforms achieved by the civil rights movement. One of the implications of the analyses I present in *The Witch's Flight* is that a politics of visibility conducted on the terrain of the cinematic is inevitably reformist unless it breaks free from this world, the cinematic, itself. A radical politics must necessarily liberate itself from the world of the cinematic and the common senses that animate it, as I argue in chapter 2, wherein I turn to Frantz Fanon's thinking about the parameters of black ontology and the relevance of that analysis for theories of film and other aspects of visual culture.

The significance ascribed to colonialism and decolonization by most world-historical narratives of the twentieth century is undeniable. Yet, as debates within postcolonial studies concerning the *post* in *postcolonial* indicate, progressive histories that posit a "before" and an "after" of colonialism obscure how colonialism's violences, excesses, logics, economies, and common senses continue to inform and affect in fundamental ways existing organizations of life and activities of living. The perceptual mechanisms whereby living beings are ordered into "races" and "sexes" are essential materials for *The Witch's Flight*, which takes the nexus of cinema, racism, and sexism as its critical starting point and as the crucible in which cinematic reality takes form and maintains itself.

10

Indeed, I seek in *The Witch's Flight* to make those perceptual mechanisms visible to a critical common sense even as I both point out the extent to which cinematic regimes of the visible participate in struggles for hegemony and valorize other ways of knowing. Yet, an elucidation of the problems of visual representation and how they continuously are (re)constituted might strike a blow to the existing hegemonies of racism and sexism by (once again) undermining their claims to the inevitability of their rationalism and might assist, however minutely, in ongoing projects of decolonization and, yes, still liberation.

Before the witch takes flight, however, I turn in the next chapter to a sustained consideration of the theoretical scaffolding that allows one to perceive the cinematic and the perceptual processes that organize and maintain it. The work I perform in the next two chapters generates the witch's flight, because the witch—the black femme I desire and pursue throughout this study—takes her raison d'être from the very mechanisms and conditions that sustain the cinematic, even as her existence is part of a collective will to destroy it.

An appeal to the visual is not uncomplicated or innocent. As theorists we have to ask how vision is structured, and, following that, we have to explore how difference is established, how it operates, how and in what ways it constitutes subjects who see and speak in the world. This we must apply to the ways in which black women are seen and not seen by the dominant society and to how they see themselves in a different landscape. But in overturning the "politics of silence" the goal cannot be merely to be seen: visibility in and of itself does not erase a history of silence nor does it challenge the structure of power and domination, symbolic and material, that determines what can and cannot be seen.

—EVELYNN HAMMONDS,
"Black (W)Holes and the Geometry of Black Female Sexuality"

The Image of Common Sense

In *The Witch's Flight* I seek to carve out alternative ways of thinking about how communicative technologies "not only express, but also organize the movement of globalization."[1] To provide a way of demonstrating the perceptual (and cognitive) processes demanded and engendered by globalizing capital, I interrogate how "we" (late-twentieth-century subjects within capitalism and its global structures of command who are geographically located —and/or intellectually constituted—within the "belly of the beast," particularly in the United States but also in other so-called developed countries) might make

1 | *"Smiling Faces Sometimes"*

sense of films. Processes of "cinematic perception" enable us to consume cinematic images wherever and however such images are found.

Cinematic perception is not confined to interactions with moving-image media such as film and television. Involved in the production and reproduction of social reality itself, these perceptual and cognitive processes work to order, orchestrate, produce, and reproduce social reality and sociality. In other words, in addition to operating in and through the variety of technological apparatuses for the "mechanical reproduction" or "electronic transmission" of objects as images, cinematic processes govern (in the sense of exercising continuous sovereign authority over) the selection of which im-ages can appear and of what is likely to be perceptible in their appearance.[2] They designate a specific perceptual schema that is adequate to the task of perceiving those images and that corresponds to a "matter" that is itself cinematic. Neither cinematic perceptual schemas nor cinematic matter pre-cedes the other. Together they constitute the cinematic, an assemblage that might also be referred to as "twentieth-century reality" because we neither posit nor access "reality" except via these processes, which were perfected by film.[3]

A film starts. A viewer creates various circuits between the present percep-tion of the set of images that the film comprises and past memory-images available to make sense of the film. Although these circuits are open, at-tentive recognition seeks to conform present perceptions to past memory-images by pummeling the fullness of each into the molds of the other. Clichés will come to predominate perceptions under conditions wherein one's set of memory-images is already a set of clichés or, speaking more broadly, when that set consists of collective images, experiences, traditions, knowledges, and so on, and when the bodily habituation that determines perception has been made common through "affectivity."

Henri Bergson's understanding of "affection" informs my thinking about the centrality of affect to cinematic processes. In *Matter and Memory* Bergson takes "pain" to be paradigmatic of "affect." He claims that when a thing acts on one's body, the division of labor in one's body is such that certain ele-ments are sensory and immobile while others are mobile, functioning to move the body as a whole. The job of the sensory and immobile elements is simply to transmit stimulation to the body's motor elements that execute the reaction. The sensory elements must do so and remain immobile because the body can move as a whole only through the labor of the mobile elements. As Bergson explains, pain (or affect more generally) is "a kind of motor tendency in a sensitive nerve," an unavailing effort of the sensory apparatus to recoil from the stimulation.[4] He suggests that "every pain is a *local* effort, and in its very isolation lies the cause of its impotence, because the organ-ism, by reason of the solidarity of its parts, is able to move only as a whole" (ibid.). Affect intervenes in the movement of the body when "the interested part" of the body, "instead of accepting the stimulation, repels it" (ibid.).

That effort marks the body's power to absorb stimulation or movement.

Affect, understood as the intervention of the interested part of the body, is a form of labor that is intrinsic to the body's self-constitution. While one's perception measures the possible or virtual action of a thing on one's body, affection can be understood initially as the moment in which one's perception ceases to measure an object's potential action upon one's body and begins to sketch out the object's actual action. Affection is the point at which the body to be perceived is one's own body; it thus locates the emergence of a real action. The difference between affection felt and image perceived is thus one of degree, not of kind. Bergson explains, "Between the affection felt and the image perceived there is this difference, that the affection is within our body, the image outside our body. And that is why the surface of our body, the common limit of this and other bodies, is given to us in the form both of sensations and of an image" (234).

If pure perception exists in the aggregate of images, affection is the activity whereby one's own body is adopted as a privileged image around which other images arrange themselves according to their possible actions upon that body. Through affection, each living image comes to define its own body by differentiating it from other images in the fact that it can be felt from within, by affective sensations caused by the body's actual effort on itself.

It is therefore through affection that pure perception is made into individual perception. An affection posits one's skin as the boundary between the inside and the outside of one's body. In so doing, it necessarily modifies the pure perception that exists in things by positing one's body as a center of indeterminate action around which are grouped all the other images which might affect it. "Affection is, then, that part or aspect of the inside of our body which we mix with the image of external bodies; it is what we must first of all subtract from perception to get the image in its purity" (58). In matter, there is "something more than, but not something different from, that which is actually given" (71).

That affection results in the constitution of one's own body suggests that the body is able to store actions of the past in the form of "motor contrivances." Such motor contrivances determine the variety and complexity of one's body's reaction, depending on past experiences. The fact that one's body is capable of habituated responses points toward the existence of the past in the form of motor mechanisms. If this were not the case, one could not differentiate one's body from the aggregate of images because each affection would be simply a singular present sensation.

13

Clichés provide a way of continuing movement because, in the face of a present perception that affects the sensory elements, they reestablish a relation between the sensory and the motor elements of the sensory-motor schema, allowing for recognition to occur and present movements to continue.[5] Were the sensory-motor apparatus to be overwhelmed by a present perception, were motor movement not to be continued by recognition, a different kind of movement could occur.

In Deleuze's terms, that different kind of movement is thinking. Deleuze's interest in cinema's time-image lies precisely in its potential for thought—in cinema's ability to tear a "real image from clichés"—an operation that breaks the sensory-motor link and extends a perception not into a motor action, but into thought. In his work on cinema Deleuze relies upon Bergson's arguments about attentive recognition in order to explain how the movement-image might give way to the time-image. Where attentive recognition fails is, therefore, most important for Deleuze: "Bergson constantly circles around the following conclusion, which will also haunt cinema: attentive recognition informs us to a much greater degree when it fails than when it succeeds. When we cannot remember, sensory-motor extension remains suspended, and the actual image, the present optical perception, does not link up with either a motor image or a recollection-image which would reestablish contact."[6]

The time-image designates an "optical and sound situation" that corresponds to a perception invested by those senses which have been liberated from their duty to the motor schema, a duty to which the body's division of labor had sentenced them. In order to enter into relation with thinking, cinema's images have to confront that state to which they constantly sink: cliché.

A cliché can be understood as a common memory-image directed onto a perception prepared according to a common sensory-motor schemata. A cliché is a type of common sense that enables motor movement to occur. *Common sense*, in my usage of the term, refers simultaneously to a shared set of motor contrivances that affect subjective perception *and* to a collective set of memory-images that includes experiences, knowledges, traditions, and so on and that are available to memory during perception. Within the framework I will be developing throughout *The Witch's Flight*, common-sense memory-images may enable another type of mental and/or motor movement to occur, thereby enabling an alternate perception. But, more often, common-sense memory-images provide, in the form of clichés, a way of continuing present movements.

Deleuze defines a cliché as "a sensory-motor image of a thing." But his definition implies a weak sensory-motor connection that might be broken in any instant whatever.[7] Deleuze argues that "we . . . normally perceive only clichés." That clichés are what "we" normally perceive is the outcome of adaptation and survival: "We see, and we more or less experience, a powerful organization of poverty and oppression. And we are precisely not without sensory-motor schemata for recognizing such things, for putting up with and approving of them and for behaving ourselves subsequently, taking into account our situation, our capabilities and our tastes. We have schemata for turning away when it is too unpleasant, for prompting resignation when it is terrible and for assimilating when it is too beautiful."[8]

As living images, our senses are conditioned to accommodate oppression and exploitation, even our own. For Deleuze, the time-image reveals a "purely optical and sound situation," thereby providing an opportunity for a sensory perception wrenched from a habituated motor response to create a new perception. For this reason, according to Deleuze's analysis, film retains the potential to manifest an alternate perceptual schema that could perfect a different social reality.

Walter Benjamin wrote explicitly about the role of film in training the senses to meet the demands of "modern life" and to grasp film's potential for transforming reality.[9] The differences between Deleuze's "cinema" and Benjamin's "mechanical reproduction" are substantial and, in some respects, fundamental. In contrast to Deleuze's insistence that there has never been anything behind the image, Benjamin's work on film—in particular, "The Work of Art in the Age of Mechanical Reproduction"—is shot through with, if not a nostalgia for, at least a belief in, an original object before its mechanical reproduction into an "image" that lacks the "aura" or the uniqueness of the original object.

In "The Work of Art in the Age of Mechanical Reproduction," Benjamin advances the theory that film corresponds to the masses' desire to transform property relations. The fascists, however, "violated the apparatus" by pressing it into the production of "ritual values."[10] For Benjamin, mechanical reproduction is the fundamental operation of film technology. For him, film, an industrial art that brings objects closer to man, is the vehicle through which "man" might "become the object of sensuous consciousness."[11] In

15

positing film technology as an inherently revolutionary tool "violated" by the fascists, Benjamin differs fundamentally from Deleuze who, in seeing cinema as "the organ for perfecting the new reality," locates the interests of cinema within capital. Deleuze states his disagreement with Benjamin baldly: "What defines industrial art is not mechanical reproduction, but the internalized relation with money."[12]

These fundamental differences between the two men's presentation of film are indicative not only of the differences between the philosophical traditions on which each draws, but also of the historical context within which each sets out to consider film. Benjamin, for his part, was writing during the time period that Deleuze identifies in retrospect as marking the shift from the regime of the movement-image to that of the time-image. Benjamin's identification of film's role in training the human sensorium to accommodate the demands of "modern life" provides valuable insight into the historical conjuncture which saw the proliferation of clichés as the hallmark of an emergent reality.[13]

Benjamin distinguishes between contemplation, which is the mode of reception adequate to the traditional work of art (a painting in a museum, for instance), and film spectatorship, which is characterized by "reception in a state of distraction." In his analysis film is the "art form that is in keeping with the increased threat to his life which modern man has to face. Man's need to expose himself to shock effects is his adjustment to the dangers threatening him."[14] Part of modern man's adjustment to the shocks constitutive of modernity involves numbing his sensory-motor apparatus in response to the shocks so that their reception becomes a function of habit, a matter of course: "For the tasks which face the human apparatus of perception at the turning points of history cannot be solved by optical means, that is, by contemplation, alone. They are mastered gradually by habit, under the guidance of tactile appropriation."[15]

Shock, according to Benjamin's formulation, "should be cushioned by heightened presence of mind," a mental state in which the viewer becomes a critic. Benjamin's analysis of the shock effect of film renders the critical faculties of "the masses" automatic, requiring no attention. It is through man's (a term meant to include women and children) exposure to shock effects that his sensory-motor schema (what Benjamin calls "the apperceptive apparatus") becomes capable of responding to the threats and dangers of "modern life." In Benjamin's terms film is a training ground for man's survival, for his adjustments to the dangers threatening him. Film "corresponds to profound changes in the apperceptive apparatus—changes that are experienced on an individual scale by the man in the street in big-city traffic, on a historical scale by every present day citizen."[16]

Benjamin relies upon a formulation of film as a "mass art," and he claims that "the growing proletarianization of modern man and the increasing formation of masses" are "two aspects of the same process." Because Benjamin's focus is on film as a mass art, he looks at film through a different lens than that employed by Deleuze. While Deleuze's focus on "masterpieces" leads him to isolate exceptional images, images capable of "tearing a real image from clichés," Benjamin is concerned primarily with how film consolidates collectivities capable of producing and surviving in such modern conditions as assembly-line factory work, big-city traffic, and war.[17] For Benjamin, film provides a way of making man's sensory-motor apparatus adequate to the tasks confronting him in the modern world. His account provides a way of understanding cinema's role in making each sensory-motor schema common. Cinema's images "constantly sink to the state of cliché" because cinema (film technology) is a privileged participant in making each living image's apperception a function of a common sensory-motor schema or, in other words, of a "common sense."[18]

What interests are most readily served by such a system? Certainly, Benjamin provides fascism as one answer. But, in order to claim that his response describes the interests of all of cinema, fascism would have to be wrenched from its specific historical manifestations so that it might be better articulated as a general condition of existence throughout film's history. I will leave that project to others. Deleuze's work suggests the basis for a related but more generalizable response: cinema and "cinematic perception" serve money's interests.

Film and Money

During a discussion of Bergson's theses on movement, Deleuze asks, "what is the interest" of a system that reproduces movement by relating it to any-instant-whatever? Deleuze argues that as an industry and an art, as an industrial art, film is defined by its "internalized relation with money," stating that "money is the obverse of all the images that the cinema shows and sets in place."[19]

In this respect, one might argue that the movement-image corresponds to Guy DeBord's "spectacle." DeBord claims that "the spectacle is another facet of money, which is the abstract general equivalent of all commodities."[20] But I would qualify any reading of Deleuze's work on cinema in relationship to DeBord's argument about the society of the spectacle by pointing out that for DeBord, "the spectacle" is all there is, while for Deleuze, images "appear" in their fullness and cinematic perception retains from them only what interests it. Deleuze argues that there exists not a civilization of the image, but "a civilization of the cliché where all the powers have an interest in hiding images from us, not necessarily in hiding the same thing from us, but in hiding something in the image."[21]

The political challenge for filmmakers, according to Deleuze's analysis, is to reveal that which has been hidden in the image by rediscovering "everything that has been removed to make [the image] interesting" or by "suppressing many things that have been added to make us believe that we were seeing everything."[22] Both operations are important political processes because the realm of visibility—what can be retained from each image's appearance to an eye—is conditioned in advance by common sense. For filmmakers involved in aesthetic projects having to do with representing identities that have been negatively or un-represented, this means that merely placing in front of a camera an image presumed to be identical with the category needing to be represented is not enough to challenge the forces that deny that category representation. The filmmaker also must interrogate the very constitution of that image as representative.

Deleuze is less explicit about the way that the "reception" of a film participates in the consolidation or the destruction of clichés than he is about the participation in those processes of filmmakers, particularly those he considers to be "the great directors of the cinema."[23] My argument that common sense can be understood as a collective set of memory-images available for memory to direct onto a perception carved out according to a collective motor habituation augments my reading of Deleuze's cinema.

When considered within the context of the relationship between film and money, my understanding of common sense underscores Bergson's acknowledgment of the "effort" or labor involved in "attention" (wherein motor movement is inhibited). The colonization of the senses by the forces of production is not something that is turned on only when a living image is interacting with a film image. One of the training grounds for the sensorium of living beings, film perfects a sensorium that already was becoming cinematic and functioning according to a common sense.[24] Moreover, that sensorium normally perceives only clichés not simply when looking at films' images, but whenever it interacts with other images. My use of *cinematic perception* therefore is particular not to film spectatorship, but to the reception of images whenever they appear to a sensory-motor schema capable of memory and affect. This includes watching a film, but it also includes, for instance, interacting with one's neighbor.

Antonio Gramsci and Common Sense

My understanding that common sense is a collective set of memory-images recognizes that a mental movement is involved in cinematic perception and that this movement, no less than the motor movement involved, can become habituated or "common." I use the word *common* to mean "of or relating to a community at large" and not as an intellectual judgment wherein it is counterposed with a higher form of rationality. I insist on thinking about common sense not as a moment in the teleology of Reason, but as the condition of possibility for the emergence of alternate knowledges that are capable of organizing social life and existence in various ways, some of which might constitute a counterhegemonic force.[25] My approach to common sense is closest to that of Antonio Gramsci, for whom the category is an integral part of his effort to understand how certain groups are able to direct social life and maintain consent to their rule.[26] Gramsci's political allegiance to the Communist Party, however, links his conceptualization of common sense to a discourse of rationality that makes the party the logical result of the unification of a properly proletarian philosophy and practice. Nonetheless, of all the thinkers on common sense, Gramsci probably did the most to wrench it from its rationalist predication, and his attention to the category signals an impulse to think "mind" and "body" together.

In his thinking about intellectuals, Gramsci insists that "all men are intellectuals," but not all "have in society the function of intellectuals."[27] Gramsci points out that non-intellectuals do not exist because "each man . . . outside of his professional activity, carries on some form of intellectual activity, that is, he . . . participates in a particular conception of the world, has a conscious line of moral conduct, and therefore contributes to sustain a conception of the world or to modify it, that is, to bring into being new modes of thought."[28]

19

Common sense is the name Gramsci gives to "man's conception of the world." In his thinking about how such new conceptions (and, hence, new strata of intellectuals) might surface, Gramsci highlights the connection between what he calls "muscular-nervous effort" and "intellectual activity." For Gramsci, the two are inextricable: "The problem of creating a new stratum of intellectuals consists . . . in the critical elaboration of the intellectual activity that exists in everyone at a certain degree of development, modifying its relationship with the muscular-nervous effort towards a new equilibrium, and ensuring that the muscular-nervous effort itself, in so far as it is an element of a general practical activity, which is perpetually innovating the physical and social world, becomes the foundation of a new and integral conception of the world."[29]

By claiming that common sense is a shared set of memory-images and a set of commonly habituated sensory-motor movements with the capacity to enable alternative perceptions and, hence, alternative knowledges, I am challenging narratives of political struggle that reify Reason, such as that of traditional Marxism, many of those underpinning nationalism, and those that support models of political organizing based on consciousness raising more generally. I am also insisting on a conceptualization of common sense in which shared conceptions of the world are inseparable from sensory-motor functions.

Gramsci understands that the culture, society, and modes of thinking that are characteristic of subaltern groups contain in embryonic form the basis for a new organization of social life and political economy.[30] At the same time, those very aspects of subaltern life that contain the potential for supporting movements toward radical socioeconomic transformations currently lend "spontaneous consent" to the "general direction imposed on social life by the dominant fundamental group."[31] An investigation into the common sense of subordinated or oppressed and exploited groups can reveal both how common sense provides consent to the groups' domination and how it might support a viable alternative to their domination.

Marcia Landy, whose readings of Gramsci's writings are attentive to their complexity and occasional contradictions, points out that "Gramsci's notion of common sense and good sense is the linchpin in his analysis of existing and future hegemonic formations, which brings together his discussions of politics, economics, and culture."[32] Common sense contains elements that consent to dominant hegemonies, as well as to aspects that are antagonistic to them. It can be understood as a record of a group's survival, incorporating compromises to dominating and exploitative forces while retaining challenges to those forces.

There is not just one common sense, but various common senses—as many as there are groups of living beings with brains. I pay attention to black common sense and, later, to butch-femme common sense in an attempt to reveal where these conceptions of the world and the modes of sensory-motor habituation through which they are supported and expressed harbor viable alternatives to white bourgeoisie North American common sense. While much of Gramsci's attention and, consequently, much of the attention of his readers (including myself) focuses on the common sense of subaltern or marginalized and oppressed groups, dominant groups operate according to common sense as well. Their conception of the world provides the official common sense of a society, one that garners the spontaneous consent of many subaltern groups. Like subaltern common sense, "official common sense" contains elements "borrowed" (or, more likely, stolen or appropriated) from other groups, particularly those exploited by the dominant group. These "appropriated" elements provide a record of concessions made in the struggle for hegemony and a strain within official common sense that renders it vulnerable to further transformations.

Throughout the *Prison Notebooks*, Gramsci argues for the need to challenge received ways of thinking and seeing, including assumptions about which forms of knowledge are most valuable. As does Gramsci, I insist that "culture" and "politics" must be thought together, particularly during this time of ongoing decolonization in the midst of a global restructuring of capitalism. Further taking my cue from Gramsci, I attend to common sense in an effort to understand how what "we" see in an image participates in the struggle for hegemony involved in capitalist exploitation.[33]

Following the work of thinkers such as Lisa Lowe and David Lloyd, for whom alternatives to "capitalist modernity" form "in conjunction with and in differentiation from" the modernizing forces of capitalism over time, I attend to the consolidation of common sense and its circulation via various media in order to explode common sense from the inside—an operation whereby common sense might issue something new or, at least, send forth a different perception corresponding to a different set of socioeconomic relations.[34] By examining particular arrangements of cinematic images, I seek to reveal those aspects of common sense that are becoming perceptible and that

21

might support alternate forms of sociality, forms that are not necessarily predicated on familiar modes of exploitation and domination.

Gramsci's thinking provides a way to understand common sense as a radically historical category without reifying a narrative of progress that tramples everything in its way once and for all on its march toward victory. According to Gramsci, common sense is "a product of history and a historical becoming."[35] It is composed of various sediments of philosophy, religion, institutional practices, superstitions, and other forms of knowledge derived from lived experience. In depicting it as a record of a group's historical becoming, Gramsci is recognizing its role in the constitution of that group; it is a record of that group's responses to "certain specific problems posed by reality" over time.[36] "Strangely composite," common sense contains "traditional" and "modern" forms, in addition to "superstitions" and other forms of wisdom and knowledge.

To the extent that my work with common sense seeks to reveal elements that might support the elaboration of alternatives that exist within the cinematic, my thinking is similar to Gramsci's, which asserts that common sense contains the seeds of good sense. For Gramsci, good sense is that part of common sense that might be elaborated into a conception of the world that is critical and coherent and thus capable of elevating to leadership the collective it consolidates. Thinking about common sense in terms of collective memory-images reveals that one can "belong" to several groups simultaneously; the mass production and global diffusion of images has created a commonly available set of memory-images that includes news footage, music videos, television programs and broadcasts, and films. To claim, therefore, that common sense is what is perceptible in each cinematic image's appearance is to remark on the extent to which whatever appears to an eye is a document of one's historical becoming and to suggest that one's historical becoming is part of a collective: "In acquiring one's conception of the world one always belongs to a particular grouping which is that of all the social elements which share the same mode of thinking and acting. We are all conformists of some conformism or other."[37] Wedding Deleuze's Bergsonian account of cinema with Gramsci's Marxist version of common sense reveals the inherently political implications of any discussion of visuality, visibility, and/or cinema, and it responds to Evelynn Hammonds's call for black feminists to interrogate the very terms and mechanisms of visibility.

In his analysis of the cliché Deleuze highlights the collective valence of common sense, but stops short of clearly revealing the cliché's political implications. When directed onto a perception, a cliché, as a subset of common sense, continues an arrested movement. During perception, memory retrieves from the past what is useful to the present. What appears to an eye is precisely what remains useful to the maintenance of the present. It is what allows for the living image's survival in the present. Even when the present and the past are incommensurate, common sense in the form of a metaphor can "furnish us with something to say when we no longer know what to do."[38]

In common sense, as Landy points out, "traditional elements co-exist with modern formations and continue to play roles in making the world appear reasonable and expedient to individuals and groups whose interests might be better served by challenging these structures."[39] Gramsci is interested in "locating where and how change and resistance can be identified," and common sense is a particularly stubborn form to transmute because it is predicated on survival.[40] It contains what has worked in the past to enable survival in the face of the new, and it therefore can appear in a present perception to accommodate another new situation, even when that situation's contours could be more accurately perceived in time.

When thinking about common sense's role in cinematic perception, it is important to note that, insofar as memory and perception become indistinguishable during perception, "the image has to be present and past, still present and already past, at once and the same time."[41] When common sense (as memory-image) and a present perception are incommensurate and the present image cannot be recognized so that an arrested movement can continue, something has become too strong in the image and the sensory-motor link collapses. In such situations, as Deleuze explains, one becomes a seer or a visionary. Common sense explodes, revealing that its fundament is time, "non-chronological time" or "the present split in two heterogeneous directions, one of which is launched towards the future while the other falls into the past."[42] In this operation, motor common sense delinks from mental common sense, the movement-image gives way to the time-image, and the cinematic "confronts its most internal presupposition, money."[43] In the cinematic, time is money, but the exchange is unequal; the relation between time and money is an impossible equivalence.[44]

Common sense accommodates unequal exchanges, but it also might give way to something different. When something in the image becomes too

23

strong, the sensory-motor connection collapses, and one becomes a vision-ary, staring at the new. Movement still occurs, but it is an internal movement, an affective labor wherein the visionary sees himself or herself (or any varia-tion of a gendered self's formation) inside time, dividing in two as affector and affected. The movement that results, including whatever action erupts outward when and if the motor relinks with the sensory, will become a component in the consolidation of a hegemony capable of using what was just new, "and the film will be finished when there is no more money left."[45]

Affectivity

In delineating cinematic processes I insist upon the importance of forms of labor, effort, or activity to the production and reproduction of cinematic real-ity. Gramsci, in his formulation of common sense, identifies the "muscular-nervous effort" involved in fashioning one's conception of the world, an effort inseparable from "intellectual activity." Effort is involved also in the production and reproduction of cinematic reality via affection.

Wedding Bergson's "affection" to Gramsci's notion that the production and maintenance of common sense is a sensory-motor intellectual activity, I rely upon the term *affectivity* to mark the way that a living being's interactions with other images involves a form of labor that has to do with affect, with those sensations and feelings that carve out a subjective perception in things, but that cannot be divorced from the mental operations required to make sense of the world. I also borrow from Landy's thinking about the reception of film images, wherein *affectivity* defines "a form of labor expended in the consumption of cinematic images, in the enterprise of voluntarily offering up our lives 'as free contributions to capitalist power.' "[46] For Landy, affec-tivity offers a corrective to those theorizations of cinematic reception (the activity of watching films) that consider only "the profit nexus of the media" as the point of convergence between media and capital. She argues that what is often missing from such accounts is "the labor invested on the part of the consumer, a labor that is intrinsic to all forms of commodity production."[47]

While it might be tempting to condemn mass cultural productions, see-ing them only as forces colonizing the sensorium from above, Landy's invo-cation of affectivity in the context of its role in "the dissemination of modern folklore" is a reminder that the consumption of cinematic images is often a pleasurable, rewarding activity that always requires an investment on the

24

part of the spectator, not only of time and money but also of affect and labor. Moreover, because films must "compensate the different audience members for voluntarily offering their time and money," Landy's formulation of affectivity highlights precisely the way that, as a form of labor, interacting with film images is a process wherein surplus labor is extracted in the form of attention and directed toward the further consolidation of cinematic reality.[48]

My use of the term *affectivity* also carries within it the very process Deleuze describes as constitutive of the three "material aspect[s] of subjectivity."[49] My embrace of a notion of affectivity is meant to signal just how deeply capitalism's drive toward globalization strikes. The directly economic valence that Landy grants affectivity inheres even in the very process whereby one becomes oneself via affection. Because cinematic perception is employed not only when consuming film's images but often when interacting with other of the images that comprise the material world (I call this world "cinematic reality," following my reading of Deleuze and Bergson), affectivity must be understood as designating a form of labor necessary to survive in that reality and integral to that reality's (re)production. As such, affectivity names a form of labor that is a "natural condition of the producer's existence."[50] In order to survive, living images offer up their lives as contributions to capitalist power via affectivity, becoming like slaves whose productive labor is useful primarily to another's acquisition of wealth.

The socioeconomic and cultural dynamics of globalization must be understood not only in spatial terms that designate capital's relentless march to exploit the globe, but also in terms of its ability to reach into those processes whereby one comes to be oneself and even to make that violation feel good, an ability that has both spatial and temporal implications. The temporality of globalization is not chronological, linear, or progressive. Accordingly, while the drive of global culture or mass culture is toward homogenization (or, in other words, the consolidation of a type of global common sense), this goal cannot be achieved; to be perceptible, mass culture relies on existing common senses, and common sense is a heterogeneous form, containing past images that may infect any attempt to forge a homogeneous global common sense.

Insofar as Bergson and Deleuze are correct in their assertion that affect plays a definitive role in carving out perceptions, affectivity is the labor that holds cinematic reality together. As Deleuze points out, under the regime of the movement-image, affect is a spatial category that differentiates between interiority and exteriority. Under the regime of the time-image, it becomes a temporal category, the very operation of time wherein presents pass and pasts are preserved. Affectivity is a form of labor that does not yet register in the economic sense as labor. At the same time as it is that which maintains cinematic reality, affectivity locates the productive, creative power of groups of living images. Affectivity generates the movements and temporalities of cinematic reality. It is labor expended not only in the consumption of cinematic images, but also in the production and reproduction of cinematic reality itself.

In the Interval

Current thinking about and studies of race and representation customarily acknowledge that theories and assertions premised on any assumption that racial categories neatly and predictably organize living beings are problematic. Yet those studies fail to interrogate the mechanisms that authorize their own embrace of racial categories to describe that which they presume is represented via visual media. On one hand, they admit, almost perfunctorily, that the way they frame their subject matter is problematic, while, on the other hand, they reproduce the logic through which that subject matter becomes a problem. By so doing, they reproduce the hegemony of (neo)colonial discourse, blinding themselves to that within their subject matter which might produce challenges to hegemony and limiting their inquiries to the range of possibilities existing only within the realities that colonial and neocolonial discourses organize.

2 | *"Smiling Faces Sometimes"*
(Just Press Repeat)

"How Does It Feel to Be a Problem?"

Colonial and neocolonial discourses rely upon the rhetoric of "the black problem" as one way of ascribing "race" to black bodies while ostensibly rendering "white" bodies nonraced, universal, and, hence, nonproblematic. Yet, as revealed by the question that W. E. B. Du Bois posits as emblematic of liberal white engagements with black existence—"How does it feel to be a problem?"—the formulation of the black problem in colonial and neocolonial discourse is also a delimitation of the black's being.[1] As such, Du Bois's question demonstrates that the structure of the black's identity is presumed to proceed according to the equation "black" = "problem" so that white identity and white being might be constituted unproblematically.

Yet claims to an unproblematic white existence have been called into question, just as other anti-essentialist arguments reveal that claims to blackness are always "problematic."[2] To understand that neither "the Black" nor "the White" can be or exist unproblematically, it is salutary to recall that the Greek etymology of *problem* is "a thing thrown or put forward."[3] The Greek term *problema* can "signify projection or protection, that which one poses or throws in front of oneself, either as the projection of a project, of a task to accomplish, or as the protection created by a substitute, a prosthesis that we put forth in order to represent, replace, shelter, or dissimulate ourselves." The term also means "shield . . . behind which one guards oneself in secret or in shelter in case of danger."[4]

As Du Bois made clear through his description of himself as "bone of the bone and flesh of the flesh of them that live within the Veil" that separates the black world from the white, in the colonial world the realm of representation and of visibility is primarily a province of whites in which any individual black is a projection of all blacks.[5] In the context of current work on race and visual representation, the etymology of *problem* raises the possibility that the Black and the White each are problems in the sense of a prosthesis or of projections of a project thrown forth in order to dissimulate or to provide shelter. In chapter 5 of *Black Skin, White Masks*, which bears the English title "The Fact of Blackness," Frantz Fanon reveals what these problems—the White and the Black—are thrown forth in order to shelter. Fanon thus uncovers the hegemonic assumptions that inform contemporary discussions of race and visual representation. Most extant considerations of Fanon's relevance to film theory fail to grasp the degree to which his thinking provides a series of suggestive ruminations about the existence of the Black, the status of the Black's body, and the Black's experience of his body. Many adaptations of Fanon's work by film theorists have tended to overlook the fact that he engages critically with both Maurice Merleau-Ponty and Jean-Paul Sartre, in addition to Jacques Lacan and G. W. F. Hegel. Most important, they ignore the radical nature of the challenges Fanon poses to European humanism, especially to the Freudian and Lacanian psychoanalysis on which much of film theory, especially feminist film theory, continues to rely. Any serious consideration of Fanon's dialogue with psychoanalysis must contend with the extent to which his work, like Bergson's (at least according to Deleuze), marks a crisis in psychology.

Fanon engaged aspects of Freud and Lacan's thought in *Black Skin, White Masks*. Fanon accepted many of pyschoanalysis's premises and worked not to reveal its inadequacies, but to detect where and how the Black deviated from its tenets. While Fanon recognized that the psychopathologies of colonialism converged with the sicknesses of the project of European man (a.k.a. "the

28

human"), even in his later work *The Wretched of the Earth* he understood that conundrum to be fundamentally a human crisis; Fanon's emancipatory call was, as Lewis Gordon and others have pointed out, precisely for the emergence of "a new (hu)man." I later orchestrate a break with Fanon's humanism in order to pursue some of that which has been expunged from "the human" in order for him to cohere, but for now I offer an alternative reading of Fanon, a reading that produces a cinematic Fanon.

The lacunae in previous film theorists' readings of Fanon occur in part because "The Fact of Blackness" often is considered in isolation from the rest of his anticolonialist project. It is understood, moreover, as simply an analysis of the experience of the "man of color," instead of as an interested delineation of the set of constraints and limitations that colonization places on epistemological and ontological projects more generally. When considered as part of Fanon's attempt to "set afoot a new man," "The Fact of Blackness" poses a set of fundamental challenges to existing notions of black identity and cinematic representation and thus to existing notions of identity and representation more generally. I refer to *Black Skin, White Masks* in order to reframe the "problems" of cinematic representation and call for thinking differently about the set of socioeconomic and cultural relations that cinematic representation currently orchestrates. I argue that "the black image" and "the white image" are inherently problematic and that the black image might best be understood in terms of the spatiotemporal relations it makes visible.[6]

My use of the term *image* follows Gilles Deleuze's appropriation of Henri Bergson's definition: "a certain existence which is more than that which the idealist calls a 'representation,' but less than that which the realist calls a 'thing'—an existence placed halfway between the 'thing' and the 'representation.'"[7] Like Deleuze's embrace of Bergsonian images in his work on cinema, my arguments regarding images carry repercussions for the study of film's images in particular and of the images claimed by visual studies more generally. Yet, insofar as the conception of "image" that I borrow from Bergson via Deleuze is also a conception of "matter" as "image," my thesis has implications for contemporary understandings of the mechanisms whereby racist and neocolonialist material relations (and the various violences that sustain those relations) continue to be orchestrated and maintained, even after the official defeat of colonial rule across the globe and the achievement of black civil rights in the United States.

Insofar as it can be argued, as Deleuze argues, that Bergson's 1896 book

29

Matter and Memory was "the diagnosis of a crisis in psychology," the correspondence between Fanon's theorization of the temporality of blackness and the acquisition of black subjectivity and Bergson's attempt to reconcile movement as physical reality with the image as psychic reality is especially relevant to a study that takes as its primary point of departure questions of blackness and the cinematic.[8] Deleuze's adaptation of Bergson's work as a way to theorize the cinematic allows one to grasp the socioeconomic and temporal transformations cinema orchestrated, bringing the biopolitical component of the cinematic into stark relief. Fanon's work raises the possibility that the phenomenon of "blackness"—its temporalities, subjectivities, and the mechanisms of its (re)production—is paradigmatic of those transformations. Taken together, Fanon's and Bergson's thinking (when read through Deleuze's adaptation of it in the context of cinema) produce a theory of the biopolitics of the cinematic that is attentive to the micromechanisms through which power relations are (re)produced and rationalized. I dwell at some length on Fanon and Bergson's theories in order to provide an account of these mechanisms.

For Fanon, the Black imago has been equated with sin, rape, the genital, badness, ugliness, immorality, evil, and so on. Because of this, when the Black imago serves as a locus of identification through which to establish the *Innenwelt* (inner world) of the black, the black recognizes that sin, rape, ugliness, and evil is himself, as Fanon points out in *Black Skin, White Masks*.[9] Revising Lacan's account of the mirror phase in order to render it adequate to the black's experience of it, Fanon points out that for the black, the jubilant assumption of his specular image, which he experiences as a child, is rendered inaccessible to him when he achieves a socially elaborated "I." The socially elaborated self instead feels "shame. Shame and self-contempt. Nausea" (116).[10] Affect and "historicity," or the set of past images of blacks that come to reside in each appearance of the Black, are the only accessible content of the Black. For Fanon, the historicity that inheres in the Black includes "tom-toms, cannibalism, intellectual deficiency, fetishism, racial defects, slave-ships, and above all else, above all: 'Y A Bon Banania'" (112).[11] This appearance of the past in the present—what Fanon calls historicity—limits the present expression by binding it in a closed circuit with the colonial constructions of the past.

The process I am describing here in Fanon's language of historicity can be understood also in the terms used by Henri Bergson to describe "attentive

30

recognition." The consistency between Bergson's formulation of attentive recognition and Fanon's description of the historicity that confines the Black is strikingly relevant to an understanding of how cinematic processes work to secure and maintain hegemonic political economies.

In *Matter and Memory* Bergson observes that memory preserves "past images," an observation that leads him to hypothesize that "the past survives under two distinct forms: first, in motor mechanisms; secondly, in independent recollections."[12] Recognition, or "the utilizing of past experience for present action," must occur in at least one of two ways. Sometimes, it lies in the action itself and the habituated motor response. At other times, recognition "implies an effort of the mind which seeks in the past, in order to apply them to the present, those representations which are best able to enter into the present situation" (78).

Bergson argues that the sensory-motor apparatus of a living being enables a process of perception and adaptation that results in "the record of the past in the form of motor habits" (84). That operation can be called "memory" because it prolongs the useful effects of past actions into the present (82). Projecting oneself into the perceived object in a process that Bergson calls "affection," one retains a memory-image of situations and objects through which one "has successively traveled, and lays [those images] side by side in the order in which they took place" (84).

Insofar as perception is prolonged into movement, an effort is necessary to discover "the known, localized, personal memory-image which is related to the present" (95). This effort requires pulling away from "the act to which perception inclines us" (an act which would propel us into the future) in order to go into the past. The whole series of memory-images remains present to a living image, but "the representation that is analogous to the present perception has to be *chosen* from among all possible representations" (95). As Bergson explains further, "Movements, accomplished or merely nascent, prepare this choice or at the very least mark out the field in which we shall seek the image we need. By the very constitution of our nervous system, we are beings in whom present impressions find their way to appropriate movements: if it so happens that former images can just as well be prolonged in these movements, they take advantage of the opportunity to slip into the actual perception and get themselves adopted by it" (95–96).

In this process of recognition memory-images play an accessory role, merely slipping into the present situation in order to complete the movement. Such is the process of inattentive recognition, which implies a habituated movement. Memory-images are not stored in the body, but slide into it in order to assist in the execution of the relevant movements away from the object perceived.

When the recognition is not habitual, but attentive, movements return to the object, "to dwell on its outlines." In the case of attentive recognition, motor activity ceases to continue perception by prolonging it into useful reactions and instead allows "the images which are analogous to the present perception" to come regularly into the mold carved out of the object by perception.

An analysis of attentive recognition leads to the question Bergson poses: "In those cases where recognition is attentive, i.e., where memory-images are regularly united with the present perception, is it the perception which determines mechanically the appearance of the memories, or is it the memories which spontaneously go to meet the perception?" (99). Bergson answers that it is the latter—what appears in a present perception is not determined in advance by a mechanistic movement; rather, an element of spontaneity is at work in attentive recognition.

32 Implying a backward movement of the mind, attention entails "an arresting action" because it requires a retreat from the sensory-motor present. In the case of attentive recognition such an inhibition of movement simply prepares the body for a series of more subtle movements that will be grafted on it. Memory continues the work of recognition by directing "upon the perception the memory-images which resemble it and which are already sketched out by the movements themselves. Memory thus creates anew the present perception, or rather it doubles this perception by reflecting upon it either its own image or some other memory image of the same kind" (102). The process of recognition is centrifugal; memory-images are directed outwards from the living being, or what Bergson refers to as a "center of indetermination," toward analogous present perceptions whose molds they fill. It is diffusive, not unifying.

Attentive recognition fills perceptions with analogous memory-images to the extent that perception and memory become indistinguishable. It involves an inhibition of movement—an arrest of the present action wherein movement that "naturally" would be away from the object is directed outward back toward the object perceived. The inhibition of movement is simultaneously a mental movement away from the present, which is sensory-motor, and into the past, the open set of memory-images.

It is important to note that the set of memory-images is open because, even though the number of images contained therein is finite, each image exists there in its fullness and, therefore, contain aspects and contours that are not perceived. Like a present image, memory-images when brought to perception might yield unforeseen elements. Bergson explains that "an act of attention implies such a solidarity between the mind and its object, it is a circuit so well closed that we cannot pass to higher states of concentration without creating, whole and entire, so many new circuits which envelop the first and have nothing in common between them but the perceived object."[13] For recognition to occur and for motor movement to continue, the memory-images must be made commensurate with, not merely analogous to, the perceived object.

In situations wherein what is to be perceived is incommensurate with what has been perceived previously, attentive recognition makes them commensurate by whittling an analogous memory-image into a cliché in order for movement to continue. Or, in other words, an image perceived will be a cliché when the memory-image sent out to meet the perception has to be mutilated in order for recognition to occur (i.e., for it to fit into the mold prepared for it by perception). In order for motor movement to continue responding to the sensory stimulus that occasioned it, the analogous memory-image must be made commensurate with the perceived object; memory therefore directs memory-images in their fullness onto the present perception where, so that recognition may occur, they must "give up much of their detail" in order to "flow into the mold" sketched out by the present perception (98).

According to Fanon, a colonized and civilized society marks a condition of existence in which the black's being is precluded by his perceptible "blackness" because past images, stories, and the like constantly overwhelm perceptions of his present. Under these circumstances, the black is a cliché; the preponderance of commonly available past colonial images of blacks (tom-toms, cannibalism, etc.) flow easily into any present perception of a black and become indistinguishable from it. The circuit thereby created seems to be closed—there is no possibility of a conception of a future that could be different from the colonial past. Although this circuit is always only artificially and tenuously closed, for the living being who is recognized a priori as black according to a collective conception of blackness, the present is simply affect, a sensory perception that is the arrested action of the past on the present.[14] In Fanon's day the range of affect that was the black's present

33

included "shame," "self-contempt," "nausea," and so on.[15] In such a society the ontological interrogation into the black's being can be answered only via a description of the black's affective constitution: how does it feel to be black?

"I Wait for Me"

Fanon's understanding of the role and importance of culture, and of film as a privileged cultural form for the production and circulation of the Black imago, provides one context for understanding the vehemence and persistence with which attention has been given to "representations of Black people" in American mass culture. For, within Fanon's thought, it is the historicity carried in and provided by the images in current circulation that condition the Black imago and, hence, the black himself. But, for Fanon, a reformation of cultural images of blacks (e.g., more positive images) merely makes the black feel better about himself. It does not destroy the problems of visual representation, because the violent event of colonization and enslavement that is the foundation of colonial society ensures that, as soon as they appear as such (and they always already appear as such), the Black and the White are problems. As long as an antinomy is projected onto the world as a way to organize and rationalize life, the spatiotemporal coordinate that Fanon revealed to be colonial reality's condition of possibility remains present as the violent imposition of a horrifying past. The colonial mode of representation, many of whose mechanisms Fanon exposed, is a projection of this coordinate. The colonial mode of representation still strives to assert itself as a rational and natural expression of existing socioeconomic relations, even though the specific political system characterized by European colonial rule over African and Asian territories has been defeated and its economies reorganized.

The explication of the lived experience of the black that Fanon provides in chapter 5 of *Black Skin, White Masks* is aimed at extricating or unfixing the black from the "hellish cycle" to which he has been confined, a cycle set in motion by one's recognition of the Black. For theorists of visual culture, taking Fanon's thought seriously means acknowledging the coordinate from which the closed and limiting trajectory of this cycle is projected and contending with the temporal structure within which that cycle becomes the only one possible. Once the recurrent violence of colonization and enslavement and the configuration of (neo)colonial temporality authorized by that violence have been acknowledged, studies regarding race and representation will be relieved of their quest to locate and identify more accurate (somehow less problematic) representations of blacks, whites, and so on, and charged with the daunting task of understanding, articulating, and challenging (in ways that must hold open the possibility of the impossible) the socioeconomic relations and the spatiotemporal configurations made visible by images. The latter project requires that every recognition of the Black and the White entail an acknowledgment of the violence that authorizes such recognition. Each appearance of the Black and the White conserves that violence. Yet, if the Black conserves the originary violence of colonialism and redeploys it, it might function simultaneously (as Fanon explains about "the native" in *The Wretched of the Earth*) as "the corrosive element" within colonial and neocolonial reality.

In order to grasp how the black might function to conserve and to corrode the authorizing violence of colonial and neocolonial reality, it is important to explore Fanon's explication of the temporality of colonial existence. In the introduction to *Black Skin, White Masks*, Fanon makes it clear that "the architecture of this work is rooted in the temporal" (12). Articulating an understanding of colonial temporality is fundamental to Fanon's attempts to extricate the black from the anomalies of affect that are characteristic of the colonial mode of representation of otherness because, metaphorically speaking, the black's cage is itself temporal: the past traumas of colonization and slavery continue to affect and shape the present at the expense of the black's future liberation. *Black Skin, White Masks* begins, in fact, with a statement that invokes a cycle characteristic of colonial existence: "The explosion will not happen today. It is too soon . . . or too late" (7). The temporal structure of the colonial mode of representation of otherness that Fanon describes is that of a closed cycle of anticipation and explosion wherein the black's explosion, because it is merely what has been anticipated, always occurs "too late," and "the explosion," decolonization, is impossible ("too soon . . . or too late").

Yet Fanon recognizes that the black's explosion is an integral component of the problematic production of the Black and the White on which colonialism's mode of representation of otherness relies. Because the black's explosion has been anticipated within the terms of the hellish cycle to which he is confined, it does not liberate him; instead, it fulfills and initiates the infernal circle.

David Marriott has discussed the description Fanon gives of himself: "If I

35

were asked for a definition of myself, I would say that I am one who waits" (120). Fanon's use of the term *wait* has a double signification. The first, that of "lying in wait," can be understood to be part of what Marriott recognizes as Fanon's reliance upon the language of war. In Fanon's self-description the anticipated object is the Black "imago that is already there, lying in wait for him."[16] But waiting, in a more general sense of suspended anticipation, is "a moment of suspension, one that delays, perhaps permanently, the timely expression of anything that might be called one's own. It is as if the black is permanently belated."[17]

In addition to signaling watching with hostile intent, the English word *wait* also carries a sense of constant attentive observation that includes the body's posture and attitude and that keeps the mind ready. It is this latter sense that comes to the fore as Fanon continues his description of himself: "I investigate my surroundings, I interpret everything in terms of what I discover, I become sensitive" (120). While Fanon interacts with his environment according to the sensory-motor processes of his sensitive body, the temporal configuration he describes is that of an interval before an anticipated event and after an event that has precipitated the waiting. Under such circumstances, to exist as one who waits is to exist in an interval.

In Fanon's case it is to exist in an interval wherein the terms of waiting have been preordained. What ends the wait is what has been anticipated, even when it is the black's explosion, and so the cycle continues and the interval endures. Fanon explains: "Too late. Everything is anticipated, thought out, demonstrated, made the most of. My trembling hands take hold of nothing; the vein has been mined out. Too late!" (121). The hellish cycle wherein the past constricts the present so that the present is simply the (re)appearance of the past, felt as affect, restricts by anticipating in advance the range of the black's (re)actions to his present experience. Fanon makes this point when he states that "the Negro is a toy in the white man's hands; so, in order to shatter the hellish cycle, he explodes" (120).

The black's explosion is a violent (re)action that shatters the cycle of anticipation, yet conserves colonial reality's foundational violence by reinstating its temporal structure. While the black's explosion must be understood as an always present possibility within colonial reality, "the explosion" to which Fanon refers in the first sentences of *Black Skin, White Masks* must be differentiated rigorously from the black's explosion because it is in excess of any black's explosion. The explosion itself is best understood as the absolute violence of decolonization. Significantly, the explosion is an always present impossibility within colonial reality wherein it is always "too soon" or "too late" for it. Yet, like the always present spirits of the African ancestors who incessantly presage the coming community in Haile Gerima's *Sankofa*, the singular violence of decolonization permeates colonialism's violent foundation.

The black's explosion shatters the cycle of anticipation only to reinstate it as the interval between that explosion and the next one. In excess of any black's explosion, the explosion, decolonization, is, as Samira Kawash points out, "neither a means to something else nor a condition for its own sake; outside means and ends, this violence shatters the very world that has determined the value and distinction of means and ends."[18] The impossible possibility of the explosion marks, for Fanon, decolonization. Kawash explains that "Fanon's absolute violence of decolonization . . . [is] an uncanny violence in excess of any instrumentally conceived ends, a violence that cannot be contained or comprehended within social reality. The absolute violence of decolonization is outside agency or representation; rather, it interrupts and erupts into history and wrests history open to the possibility of a justice radically foreclosed by the colonial order of reality."[19]

While decolonization as such cannot be anticipated, it might be awaited as the impossible and unanticipatable content that will shatter its expression, rendering that expression suddenly unrecognizable and incomprehensible.

In Fanon's account film and its reception play decisive roles in finessing, challenging, or quite (im)possibly exploding colonial reality's cycle of anticipation and violence. In the English translation, Fanon's statement, well-known among film theorists, "I cannot go to a film without seeing myself. I wait for me. In the interval, just before the film starts, I wait for me" directly follows, without so much as a paragraph break, his reference to the black's explosion ("in order to shatter the hellish cycle, he explodes"). Previous considerations of the oft-cited passage "I cannot go to a film without seeing myself" have overlooked the importance it attributes to the relationships of time made visible by cinema, as well as the statement's significance to Fanon's insights into the black's explosion and its excesses. The statement can be understood as both an articulation of the temporal structure of colonial reality and of cinema's importance to that reality. When considered within the context provided by the claims that precede and follow it, Fanon's description of sitting in a theater waiting for himself to appear opens up questions regarding time, the image, and the possibility of the impossible, that is, the possibility of exploding the lingering logics of colonial reality.

Fanon treats film, like literature (as in his reading of Richard Wright's

37

Native Son), as sensory data; he interacts with its sounds and images. At the end of chapter 5 of *Black Skin, White Masks*, film, or, more specifically, the cinematic Black image, is anticipated. Fanon describes the experience of sitting in a movie theater, anticipating "the Negro groom" who is "going to appear," as one in which "my heart makes my head swim" (140). In his description, anticipation involves a sensory phenomenon that establishes a present connection between body ("heart") and mind ("head"). Fanon presents that connection in terms of an experience that, because it can be perceived only in terms of what is projected out of it and thus only according to the terms of a project or the contours of a path that already have been given, comes too late.

Yet, as Deleuze has argued via his reading of Bergson, there is always more in a present image than commonly is registered in the perception of that same image.[20] Deleuze's articulation of what is perceived allows for cinematic images to be discussed in terms of Antonio Gramsci's notion of common sense. Though marrying Gramsci and Deleuze in this way is not without conflict, their union opens up an understanding both of how cinematic images become part of the struggle for hegemony in a globalizing capitalist economy and of the role of excess and affect in that struggle.

38   In order to glimpse the potential that resides in the excesses of what commonly is perceived in an image, it is necessary to consider another sense in which Fanon can be described as "one who waits." Waiting can connote not only expectation or anticipation but also a sense of enduring without something expected or promised, as well as a type of service-oriented labor where one is indefinitely bound to meet the needs of another. All of these senses of *wait* foreground the temporal configuration within which one waits, which, in these cases, is that of an interval. But the sense of enduring also foregrounds the way that the time Fanon posits in the interval, just before the film starts, is open. In the interval Fanon is exposed to and endures the examination and expectations of the people (whose color is not specified) in the theater, who are also waiting, perhaps anticipating the appearance of the Negro groom and thus, quite possibly, his explosion. On the other hand, perhaps they simply are enduring, surviving the interval. For the one who waits (the black), colonialism in general, like now, is an interval punctuated by a hellish cycle of appearances in which one must survive.[21]

Although Fanon provides a description of what is anticipated in the interval ("a Negro groom"), the time just before the film starts is nonetheless a time swimming with possibilities and, less perceptible but no less immediate, impossibilities. In his account of "film spectatorship" Fanon limits the range of possibilities and impossibilities felt in the interval, just before the film starts, to an exchange that occurs at the end of *Home of the Brave*, a "racial problem film" released in 1949. Limiting the sensations of the interval to *Home of the Brave*'s explicit statement on "the race problem," Fanon privileges the film's ideology over the range of possible meanings communicated by its images. The exchange in the film to which Fanon refers is between a black American GI, Peter Moss, and a white American named Mingo, who had lost an arm during the same mission in which Moss had temporarily lost his ability to walk. Referring to that exchange, Fanon laments, "The crippled veteran of the Pacific war says to my brother, 'Resign yourself to your color the way I got used to my stump; we're both victims'" (140). At the end of chapter 5 of *Black Skin, White Masks*, the range of (im)possibilities sensed in the interval is limited to the film's insistence that the black resign himself to the restrictions placed on his existence by adopting what Fanon calls "the humility of the cripple."

Yet it seems that Fanon also senses that many of the film's images resonate on the level of affect in ways that might exceed the film's ideological address. What exceeds the film's ideological address authorizes Fanon's own refusal to accept *Home of the Brave*'s "cure" for "the black problem," that is, adopting "the humility of the cripple."[22] To this prescription, Fanon emphatically asserts, "With all my strength I refuse to accept that amputation" (140). More than simply an ideological stand, Fanon's refusal to accept the film's delimitation of his existence is also an insistence, however fleeting, on the (im)possibility of a different perception when confronted by that film's images.

Still in the interval, Fanon claims that "I feel in myself a soul as immense as the world, truly a soul as deep as the deepest of rivers, my chest has the power to expand without limit" (140). In the interval that Fanon describes, one punctuated by "the film," the content of the present, the affect, exceeds its expression as an "I" who waits for a "me" that can be only a projection of the past.[23] Fanon feels the utterly naked, unprotected, disarmed freedom of a limitless, open, and opening existence, one that knows no boundaries and that certainly is not locked into an infernal circle. Liberation, if there is such a thing, is possible in the interval as a present impossibility, an expansion that explodes even the interval in which we wait.

Throughout *Black Skin, White Masks*, Fanon advocates for nothing short of "the end of the world," the death of the Black and the White, and the creation of new (hu)mans. To hold colonial reality open to the (im)possibility of decolonization, however, Fanon must explode the formal legitimacy and veracity of the colonial mode of representation of otherness. He seeks to do so by prodding and destabilizing its epistemological, ontological, and temporal structures, describing how they support and perpetuate inhuman relations, and by insisting on the existence within colonial reality of a temporal structure in which the impossible possibility, justice, perhaps, is yet to come.

The interval most often conforms to (neo)colonialism's temporal structures, which sustain themselves by pummeling the fullness of the present into knowledges fashioned in the exigencies of the past, thereby completing and initiating an infernal circle. Nonetheless, the temporality of the interval is not necessarily that of (neo)colonial reality. Instead, the temporality of the interval in which (neo)colonial existence is stuck is an opening—in the interval, waiting happens without protection, exposed to the examination and expectations of others. The challenge that the experience of the interval provides entails opening thought to "the unforeseeable, the unanticipatable, the non-masterable, non-identifiable."[24] Perhaps a whole other reality—one that we do not yet have a memory of as such—opens up.

A film starts . . .

Cinematic Machines and Representation

The assumption that underpins debates about representations of minorities in American film is that film can adequately represent populations, such as, for instance, black people or queer people, that are presumed to be easily identifiable by visual attributes and more-or-less coherent as a collective.[25] But such debates rest on a further assumption: that the quality of film's representations of the collective matters politically.

A sense that cinematic machines conflate two different significations of "representation" has informed those sectors of film and television theory and of filmmaking and television programming that are concerned with addressing the sociopolitical (and, less often, economic) situation of "marginalized populations."[26] In some cases a sense of the political stakes involved in aesthetic portrayals of such populations has led to demonstrations against films and television programs that have been deemed to have failed in their responsibility to adequately represent those populations.[27] While it is clear that there exists a widespread acknowledgment that film and television images are politically important, it is less clear why these images, which seem to be simply aesthetic portraits, are also political proxies.

In her influential essay "Can the Subaltern Speak?" Gayatri Chakravorty Spivak discusses the distinction between the two senses of *representation*.[28] She engages critically with the "much publicized critique of the sovereign subject" that is integral to the work of the French poststructuralists, particularly Deleuze and Foucault. Spivak's concern is to point out that the French poststructuralists inaugurate a Subject (of Europe) that is an accomplice in the consolidation of the global division of labor.

Spivak points out that "two senses of representation are being run together" in Deleuze's pronouncement of the death of representation, "'representation as 'speaking for,' as in politics, and representation as 're-presentation' as in art or philosophy."[29] An effect of Deleuze's dismissal of representation is that it fails to register that the sense of representation that has to do with state formation and the law is at work in his evocation of "the oppressed," even if the sense of representation that has to do with "subject predication" seems to have been displaced through his critique of the sovereign subject and, particularly, via his insistence on himself as "a multiplicity" (and, therefore, incapable of functioning as a representative). As Spivak explains, "The banality of leftist intellectuals'. lists of self-knowing, politically canny subalterns stands revealed; representing them, the intellectuals represent themselves as transparent."[30]

In order to maintain the possibility of a radical, politically responsible, and non-elitist pedagogy, Spivak insists that "the shifting distinctions between representation within the state and political economy, on the one hand, and within the theory of the Subject, on the other, must not be obliterated."[31] To illustrate the complicity and the difference between those senses of representation, Spivak reads the passage in Marx's *The Eighteenth Brumaire of Louis Bonaparte* wherein he claims that "the small peasant proprieters 'cannot represent themselves; they must be represented,'" and she highlights the distinction between Marx's use of the German verbs *vertreten* ("to represent" within the state and political economy) and *darstellen* ("to represent" within the theory of the Subject).[32]

Spivak insists that a "developed theory of ideology" must accompany the poststructuralist critique of the sovereign subject. She points out that "reality" is accessible only through forms of "re-presentation" (portraiture, or *Darstellung*) and that those forms actually disguise the selection and deployment of "representatives of hegemonic formations" (in the sense of proxy, or *Vertretung*). Spivak thus advocates for theories that "note how the staging of the world in representation—its scene of writing, its *Darstellung*—dissimulates the choice of and need for 'heroes,' paternal proxies, agents of power—*Vertretung*."[33]

In her critique of Deleuze and Foucault's essentialist, utopian appeal to the concrete experience of "the oppressed," Spivak diagnoses a primary aspect of the regime of the cinematic image. Concrete experience, or "the reality" that Deleuze argues "is what actually happens in a factory, in a school, in barracks, in a prison, in a police station," is perceptible only via forms of common sense, where common sense designates a collective conception of the world and a generally habituated sensory-motor schema.[34] What's more, common sense plays a role in the very choice of what will be selected from the plane of immanence and designated "reality." Common sense, for its part, is related intimately to the struggle for hegemony and thus to the workings of economic exploitation, including the "extraction (production), appropriation, and realization of (surplus) *value as representation of labor power.*"[35]

Insofar as common sense consists of memory-images in their fullness that subsequently are perceived to be representations of past events, experiences, and situations, cinematic perception involves the mental activity of projecting a "problem" onto a perception prepared according to a common sensory-motor schema. Common sense is the general form of a collective historical endeavor or, to speak specifically of its mental aspect, of a set of collective historical endeavors that is necessarily "disjointed and episodic" because it consists of several sediments of past images that themselves provide a record of the success of past philosophies and situations. These past images are called forth by a present (image's) appearance to an eye.

Working to make sense(s) common to the broadest range of living images (within the target market) in the interests of capital and its dominant hegemonic forces, film and television conflate the two valences of representation. An aesthetic representation (portrait) is also a proxy in the eyes of those forces (not necessarily each force all the time) because common sense is imbricated with the consolidation of hegemonic forces. This is not because film or television "reflects" reality or imposes itself on "real life." It is because the labor (affectivity) required to make sense of the images that cinematic machines select, cut, frame, and circulate is the same kind of labor required to live in and make sense of the world organized by the cinematic.

In presenting a collective enterprise characterized by affectivity (a sort of general labor time) in the form of images of common sense (in order to reach the broadest possible market), cinema conflates the two senses of representation and presents a proxy under the guise of a portrait.[36] Cinematic representation is inherently problematic in at least two senses. To describe the first sense, one can take the appearance of the "black image" to be paradigmatic of the cinematic image. Each appearance of a black image to an eye is an appearance of every black insofar as "black identity" is a historical project predicated upon a substitution that implies an aporia. A present perception of a black tends toward cliché because each appearance of a black to an eye is recognized as an appearance of the Black, a memory-image commonly available to memory during perception. The problem that the Black *is* is common sense. Cinema and cinematic processes make this historically unprecedented mode of subject predication, that of the Black, into a general condition of existence. Each appearance of an image to an eye is a "problem," perceptible as common sense. In this case, the problem is that of re-presentation (Darstellung).

Second, in rendering every image's appearance to an eye a re-presentation, cinema and cinematic processes dissimulate the political and economic determinants of common sense, that is, what is retained from that image's appearance. In the case of film and television, political agents (representatives) appear to be simply aesthetic portraits (re-presentations). Taken to the extreme, the situation finds its converse, as when political agents appear (for instance, on television at the 2000 and 2004 Republican National Convention) and the interests they serve are masked by calling forth the perception that sees them as re-presentations. (The success, power, and visibility of Condoleeza Rice, Colin Powell, and Clarence Thomas, for example, are invoked as evidence of the success of blacks, even though the interests those figures serve continue to rely upon racism to maintain their hegemony, as was particularly evident during the 2000 election when thousands of people of color were systematically disenfranchised in Florida and elsewhere.)

The situation I am diagnosing here is something like what Richard Dienst describes when he claims that " 'winning time' on television now becomes the most crucial stake in group politics, an acceptance of the cynical assump-

43

tion that enregistration by the machine will succeed where the politics of representation failed."[37] Dienst seems to recognize that "representation has not withered away."[38] But he fails to register that "the politics of representation," as he obliquely puts it, insofar as it has been practiced by groups excluded from (or included unsatisfactorily in) the realm of representation (both senses) based upon their appearance, already is predicated on cinematic processes. For those identity-based groups that traditionally have been denied access to the mechanisms of representation, the politics of representation is primarily a politics of visibility. That this form of politics has been televised means only that it has been intensified. On the other hand, if it is measured by its capacity to effect reform, then the battle for "enregistration by the machine" seems likely to be a success because it is a battle over common sense.

If it is measured by its capacity to support substantive transformations in the political economy of race, the politics of representation as enregistration by the machine might hold promise only if a transformed critical engagement with its images wrenches those images open to the force of what they currently hide within them.[39] In order to hold images open to the possibility of the impossible, we must change our basic "image of thought" and reframe questions that we heretofore have framed primarily in terms of representation (Darstellung), even as we keep in our view the extent to which, as Spivak points out, those re-presentations continue to dissimulate the choice of and need for representatives (Vertretung). The intensification of the politics of representation as various "minority groups" vie for enregistration by cinematic machines signals the need for a transformed approach to cinematic images, one that recognizes the work of such images as representatives while remaining open to what each image of common sense harbors as a productive potentiality within it.

Something terrible has happened. A "horrible exhibition." It is happening still. Through "the blood stained gate," we take flight. Follow. . . .
— SAIDIYA HARTMAN, *Scenes of Subjection*, and
DOUGLASS, *Narrative of the Life of Frederick Douglass*

[*Sankofa* fixes us,] in the sense in which a chemical solution is fixed by a dye.
— FRANTZ FANON, *Black Skin, White Masks*

"In Order to Move Forward"
Common-Sense Black Nationalism and Haile Gerima's *Sankofa*

Haile Gerima's construction of a revolutionary black nationalist subjectivity as advanced in his 1993 film *Sankofa* is exemplary of common-sense black nationalism's negotiations with what it considers to be versions of "black femininity"; it dramatizes the violence with which common-sense black nationalism tends to confront black femininity, and it provides a set of images through which to explore the ways common-sense black nationalism secures consent to dominant conceptualizations of gender and sexuality and thus to the forms of domination and exploitation those conceptualizations rationalize.[1]

3 | *"Wade in the Water"*

Writing in 1997, in the innovative essay "Black Nationalism and Black Common Sense: Policing Ourselves and Others," Wahneema Lubiano points out that "black nationalism is significant for the ubiquity of its presence in black American lives—in those lives' conventional wisdom."[2] Lubiano describes nationalism as a "social identification," and she provides a context for its production as a political praxis for black Americans by reminding her readers that understanding nationalism in this way "draws on various nineteenth-century black intellectuals' descriptions of their group's political imperatives."[3] Counterposed to those forms of white American nationalism that solidify official narratives of U.S. history, black nationalism in its broadest sense is, according to Lubiano, "a sign, an analytic, describing a range of historically manifested ideas about black American possibilities that include any or all of the following: racial solidarity, cultural specificity, religious, economic, and political separatism. (This last has been articulated both as a possibility within and outside of U.S. territorial boundaries.)"[4] It is, further, "a constantly reinvented and reinventing discourse that generally opposes the Eurocentrism of the U.S. state, but neither historically nor contemporaneously depends upon a consistent or complete opposition to Eurocentrism."[5]

In its current manifestations, black nationalism is, in other words, the form of common sense that has become hegemonic among those who understand themselves to be "black." As such, it explains and secures that group's cohesion as black, giving the notion of "belonging" to that group a political force that is antagonistic to those forms of racist domination and exploitation that assist in the consolidation of white bourgeois hegemony in the United States.[6]

Yet, as a form of "subaltern" common sense (as opposed to "official" common sense), the expressions of black nationalism in circulation today provide various loci of consent to existing modes of domination and exploitation. For instance, as Lubiano points out, common-sense black nationalism "reinscribes . . . in particular places within its own narratives of resistance" those aspects of official common sense that rationalize state sovereignty. Lubiano contends that such "reinscription most often occurs within black nationalist narratives of the black family," pointing out that "black feminist cultural commentators across two centuries have developed critiques of this familial narrative."[7]

Lubiano's discussion of common-sense black nationalism illuminates the ways that it contains elements in embryonic form that, under certain circumstances, might be elaborated into a "critical and coherent conception of the world" which would correspond to the ascent of a sensory-motor schema necessary to an alternative movement against U.S. white bourgeois hegemony.

The LA Filmmakers, the Black Arts Movement, and Questions of Third Cinema

Sankofa is an Akan word that can be translated into English as "return to the past in order to move forward."[8] Haile Gerima's film *Sankofa* tells a story of Mona, an African American fashion model who is visiting Ghana on a photo shoot. *Sankofa* introduces its viewers to Mona, with her blonde wig and seductive clothing, as she prances in front of a white photographer's camera while he makes sexually suggestive sounds of agreement about what he is seeing through his long camera lens. While Mona is posing for this photo shoot at Elmina Castle, a well-known former slavehold on the Ghanaian coast, an elder, the Sankofa linguist, indicates that Mona has been chosen to be sent into the past. After wandering into the castle, Mona is transported to the past to live as Shola, a slave on the Lafayette Plantation, which is located somewhere in the Americas. Over the course of her time there, Mona-Shola joins the secret rebel slave organization with which her lover, Shango, is associated. After Shola is killed (presumably) during a rebellion, she is carried back to Africa and thus back to the present on a buzzard. When Mona-Shola emerges from the castle reborn into the present, she is transformed, no longer the willing object for the white man's camera. She heeds the call of Sankofa's drum and gladly takes her place among other diasporic Africans who have been called by it.

Gerima spent twenty years researching, writing, and producing *Sankofa*, which was released in the United States in 1993.[9] While the twenty-year production schedule certainly spanned much of the historical becoming of the "post-60s" diasporic African identity that the film seeks to enable, the film's lengthy production also complicates attempts to contextualize the film historically. *Sankofa* is a product of the "New Black Cinema," a term Thomas Cripps used in 1982 to refer to the then most recent wave of black independent filmmaking.[10] New Black Cinema was a politicized movement related to "the New American Cinema" that was emergent in the early 1970s and that continues to reinvent itself. As part of the New Black Cinema, *Sankofa* can be understood within the context of the sociopolitical and film-industrial trends of the early 1970s for three reasons.

First, Gerima began working on the film during the early 1970s. Although it is inadvisable to historicize the film by situating it solely in the period of its inception, *Sankofa* should be understood within the context of black diasporic cultural and political trends of the early 1970s, trends that continue to exert a direct influence on American culture and politics. Second, Gerima started film school at UCLA in 1968, becoming part of the first wave of university-trained filmmakers, a group that has been referred to as "the film generation" and that would come to exert a tremendous influence on the American film industry.[11] Although Gerima and his black classmates at UCLA would define themselves and their work in opposition to Hollywood (what Gerima refers to as "conventional cinema"), they enrolled in film school around the same time as filmmakers such as Francis Ford Coppola and George Lucas were finishing film school and entering the industry.[12] As a university-trained filmmaker, Gerima creates work that is in contentious dialogue with the blockbuster productions that hail from the New American Cinema industry. Moreover, the global economic, technological, and social transformations that led to the reformation of Hollywood during the 1960s and 1970s cannot be separated from the forces that enabled Gerima and his colleagues to access and experiment with the film medium in innovative and often oppositional ways.

Third, while *Sankofa*'s production history places it in an uneasy relationship to the corpus of "African American films" (the film notes "USA/Germany/Ghana/Burkina Faso" as its national affiliations), its political and aesthetic project places it in alliance with aspects of "black film" and Third Cinema. Insofar as the designation "black" came into widespread usage in the United States in the late 1960s and early 1970s and marked the (re)creation of a diasporic black identity, *Sankofa* can be considered to belong to black film's project. *Sankofa*'s inclusion in the corpus of Third Cinema films is more clear cut, if only because the rubric of Third Cinema carries an international connotation that the category of black film, with its institutionalized bias toward North American racial politics and production processes, threatens to obscure. A notion first advanced by Latin American filmmakers, Third Cinema has come to designate an international project that includes films, filmmakers, and critics for whom cinema is a political activity that cannot be divorced from its potential role in effecting social and cultural transformations.[13]

In short, even though *Sankofa* was released in the United States in 1993, it is crucial to place the film within the historical context of its inception and to understand it as a product of several interrelated historical narratives. These include the transformations that the American film industry has undergone since around 1960; the influence that the film generation subsequently exerted in Hollywood and the auteurist inflections of that influence; the systematic exclusion of black filmmakers from Hollywood during this same period, coupled with Gerima and his colleagues' collective refusal to train for inclusion in Hollywood; and the cultural and political philosophies and practices circulating in black America and throughout the black diaspora at that time. Contextualized in this way, *Sankofa* provides an opportunity to examine the possibilities for the production of a black cultural nationalist subject presented in a female body. Insofar as the terms of this subject's production inform present hegemonic black common sense(s), my engagement with *Sankofa* seeks to unearth those terms in an effort to lay bare the assumptions and exclusions they rationalize.

Gerima, an Ethiopian native, entered UCLA's film school in 1968, the same year that *The Hour of the Furnaces*, a foundational film of Third Cinema, was released in Argentina and that Larry Neal's trenchant statement "The Black Arts Movement" was published in the United States. Along with the theory of revolutionary nationalism (as elaborated by the Black Panther Party), both texts and movements exerted a tremendous influence on Gerima and his black colleagues' philosophy and practices while studying filmmaking. Neal's characterization of the Black Arts Movement (BAM) supports my claim that *Sankofa* takes BAM's project to the limits of what it can do, even though it employs a familiar "Hollywood" style and aesthetic to do so. *Sankofa* elides Third Cinema's and revolutionary nationalism's emphasis on the necessity of developing a praxis rooted in a critique of racist political economy, a critique Gerima advances elsewhere in his work, in favor of developing BAM's black cultural nationalist project and putting it into circulation as a dominant sediment in black common sense.[14]

At the heart of BAM is a set of questions and prescriptions about the political and ethical responsibility of the black artist to his or her community and about the relationship between art and politics. Neal begins his acclaimed "The Black Arts Movement" with the following assertion.

> The Black Arts Movement is radically opposed to any concept of the artist that alienates him from his community. Black Art is the aesthetic and spiritual sister of the Black Power concept. As such, it envisions an art that speaks directly to the needs and aspirations of Black America. In order to perform this task, the Black Arts Movement proposes a radical reordering of the western cultural aesthetic. It proposes a separate symbolism, mythology, critique, and iconology. The Black Arts and Black Power concept both relate broadly to the Afro-American's desire for self-determination and nationhood. Both concepts are nationalistic. One is concerned with the relationship between art and politics; the other with the art of politics.[15]

Although questions about the black artist's political and ethical accountability to his or her community have been intrinsic to African American cultural production and criticism since its very inception, the most pointed and decisive articulation that the black artist has an inherent and authoritative responsibility to "his community" finds its voice in the BAM of the 1960s.[16] Neal's 1968 statement on BAM is exemplary of the philosophical underpinning of the movement, but one must keep in mind that, like any dynamic cultural movement, BAM was diverse and varied, and the philosophies and tenets I present were debated and revised over time by the artists who contributed to it.[17] The emphasis on cultural nationalism remained, however, a significant organizing principle of BAM.

The artists in BAM asserted that the black artist had an intrinsic responsibility to speak to the "black community" (as opposed to speaking to white people for that community). Such an understanding of the artist led Neal to condemn the Harlem Renaissance as "essentially a failure" because "it did not address itself to the mythology and the life-styles of the Black community. It failed to take roots, to link itself concretely to the struggles of that community, to become its voice and spirit."[18]

That some BAM artists rejected the possibility of reading the Harlem Renaissance as a historical predecessor to their own movement—as a part of a tradition out of which their project grew or as a component of a historical narrative into which they wrote themselves as actors—opens onto a series of observations about BAM's project itself (at least as that project has been described by Neal). Significantly, according to the BAM artists represented in Neal's statement, the rejection of the Harlem Renaissance as a cultural antecedent is not a rejection of tradition. It is the assertion of a prior, more "pure" tradition to which the Harlem Renaissance proved woefully and irretrievably irresponsible. According to many of BAM's artists, by failing to recognize "the idea that Black people, however dispersed, constitute a *nation* within the belly of white America"—an idea that Neal traces back to Marcus Garvey but that can be traced back even further—the Harlem Renaissance is simply a diversion from the inevitable "flowering of a cultural nationalism that has been suppressed since the 1920s."[19] That cultural nationalism relies upon an authentically "black aesthetic," the basis of which already exists.

To make the point that the basis of an authentic black aesthetic already exists, Neal quotes Don L. Lee (who later changed his name to Haki Madhabuti): "We must destroy Faulkner, dick, jane, and other perpetuators of evil. It's time for DuBois, Nat Turner, and Kwame Nkrumah. As Frantz Fanon points out: destroy the culture and you destroy the people. This must not happen. Black artists are culture stabilizers, bringing back old values, and introducing new ones."[20]

The purification of "old" forms and values is explicitly an element in the formation of a black aesthetic. Neal quotes Brother Knight: "The Black artist must create new forms and new values, sing new songs (or purify old ones); and along with other Black authorities, he must create a new history, new symbols, myths and legends (and purify old ones by fire). And the Black artist, in creating his own aesthetic, must be accountable for it only to the Black people. Further, he must hasten his own dissolution as an individual (in the Western sense)—painful though the process may be, having been breast-fed the poison of 'individual experience.' "[21]

The trouble in the designation "black authorities" notwithstanding, the creation of a black aesthetic is described by Neal as a "natural reaction to an alien sensibility," one that "informs the cultural attitudes of the Black Arts and the Black Power movement." Ultimately, "the Black Arts Movement believes that your ethics and your aesthetics are one."[22] As an "ethical" movement that calls for the purification of "old"—that is, contaminated by alien sensibility, forms, themes, and values—BAM is engaged explicitly in policing the range of affective identificatory possibilities carried by the term *black*. Indeed, insofar as *black* was experiencing a revaluation in the United States during the time that BAM was formulating its theories, it was a particularly contested term.[23]

For BAM artists, the Black is who one is. For them, it is an ontological designation (or at least it can become one via the process of its recovery), but one that has been violently obscured as a result of the African's insertion into the West. Culture, governed by the Black aesthetic, is the purifying vehicle through which black people come to be themselves. The Black emerges at the nexus of culture and politics; it is a cultural achievement whose (achieved) blackness is inherently revolutionary because it is authentic and, significantly, not white.

Within the doctrine of cultural nationalism is a call for self-determination. At the heart of BAM's challenge to artists is nothing less than to take responsibility for the unfolding of a collective, authentically black self. Neal quotes Maulana Karenga: "Without a culture Negroes are only a set of reactions to white people."[24] With a culture based on a "pure" Black aesthetic, a black person is more authentically himself, that is, Black, part of a collective identity, and finally awakened to the meaning of his life. As a collective identity, "Black" is capable of self-determination and poised to achieve nationhood.

The philosophy of cultural nationalism that undergirded much of BAM also informed the work of students attending UCLA's film school in the late 1960s and early 1970s. Gerima's appearance at UCLA, along with Charles Burnett's one year earlier, inaugurated the first wave of the black independent-film movement.[25] The training of this school of filmmakers lasted approximately a decade and included Gerima, Burnett (*Killer of Sheep* [1977], *To Sleep with Anger* [1990]), Larry Clark (*Passing Through* [1977]), John Reir, Ben Caldwell, Pamela Jones, Abdosh Abdulhafiz, and Jama Fanaka in the first wave, and Bill Woodberry, Julie Dash, Alile Sharon Larkin, and Bernard Nichols in the second wave.

The theories about film these students elaborated collectively are inseparable from the cultural and political movements of the sixties, both in the United States and globally, particularly the emergent international Third Cinema movement.[26] The students articulated a declaration of independence from business as usual at the UCLA film school, which included among its tenets the positions that accountability to the black community is more important than training to be incorporated into a racist film industry; that the destiny of black people is the proper concern of this group's work, not "self-indulgent assignments about neurotic preoccupations"; and that among their tasks is that of recreating cultural memory, a task that leads them to unearth and re-present suppressed black literature, lore, and history.

Like BAM artists, the LA filmmakers set forth an understanding of the artist that stressed responsibility and accountability to the black community, a commitment that they saw as including the willful creation of a film form and content adequate to the particularities of black life and distinct from white models. As did BAM artists, the LA filmmakers addressed their films to a black audience. (In this respect, they unwittingly conform to the logic of the New American Cinema, which operates according to a notion of a market differentiated along, among other characteristics, racial lines).

The cultural and political context out of which *Sankofa* was born is thus one of intentional opposition to Hollywood's historical role in representing blackness on-screen. Inseparable from the projects of BAM and the declarations of the LA filmmakers, *Sankofa* retains BAM's assertion that the designation "black" is the result of an ontological unfolding toward a pure, natural, and authentic self poised to achieve self-determination in the form of an African nation. It takes BAM's assertion further by encouraging blacks to recognize themselves in "the African," thereby returning to their source.[27] But, where BAM stressed the need to create a black aesthetic, *Sankofa* deploys a Hollywood aesthetic with which its viewers already had become habituated to interacting and infuses it with an Afrocentric content.

The film posits a relationship between black identity and cultural images that is consistent in many ways with Fanon's elaboration of the Black imago's role in the formation of black identity in *Black Skin, White Masks* and with Fanon's theories about violence in *The Wretched of the Earth*.[28] The construction of black identity on which *Sankofa* relies is consistent with Hegel's master-slave dialectic as elaborated by Fanon. *Sankofa* taps into this dialectic in order to attempt the project for which Fanon seems to call: remembering and experiencing the original traumatic violence of slavery. For Fanon, though, the point is not to elaborate a black past, but to liberate the black man from himself by extracting "a human" from the Black, thereby destroying the Black.[29] In *Sankofa* a body that is perceptibly black and female—the character Mona—mediates the film's unfolding of a diasporic African identity.

However, *Sankofa*, like black cultural nationalism in general, fails to adequately factor into its analysis of racism the imbrication of the ongoing production of black and white racial categories with those of systemic economic exploitation. While Fanon calls in *Black Skin, White Masks* for the liberation of the black man from himself, *Sankofa* calls for the extrication of the Black from the White and the achievement of a hypothetical prior African purity. Gerima sees film as a cultural medium adequate to the task of (re)staging an original encounter between the Black and the White in order to disentangle one from the other. Sending Mona back into the past to live as Shola, a slave on the Lafayette Plantation, *Sankofa* seeks to decolonize Mona's mind and body. In so doing, it wants to decolonize the mind and the sensorium of the contemporary cinema audience as well.

A Colonized Sensorium

In his writings Gerima has given a critical voice to the sense that the commercial motion-picture industry (usually, Hollywood) fails to represent black people in any but the most reductive, exploitative, and insulting ways. Writing in 1986 to set forth his recommendations for the tasks that Third Cinema must set for itself, Gerima states,

> As we approach the 21st century, the ideological mystification and domestication of society by the commercial motion picture industry has come to be accepted by the mass of human beings around the world. The escapist world outlook pre-

53

sented by this dominant medium finally conventionalized its language, establishing itself as the universal standard. It parades itself unabated, presenting the most unnatural as natural; a colonial language invented only to benefit in all its aspects the Eurocentric world order. . . . In order for this glamorous commercial cinema successfully to colonise, imperialise, and lobotomise the minds of millions of people all over the world, it must reduce the world population to little children. In this uneven struggle for ideas, these [film] stars, these models, these toys, daily insensitively trample around the world in a seemingly silent battle, dementing and at times replacing any kind of national or cultural identity.[30]

In his depiction of the commercial motion-picture industry as an ideological tool of "the Eurocentric world order," Gerima posits an audience that is a passive vessel for an ideology beamed into it from a Eurocentric above. In addition, Gerima asserts that the motive for the commercial cinema's imposition of Eurocentric "cultural toys" onto Third World countries and peoples is "the subjugation of our labour, our land, and our raw materials."[31] In seeing Eurocentrism and white supremacy as "ideologies" that are simply enabling tools used to ease the exploitation of the so-called Third World, Gerima overlooks the way that ideology is itself a product of the mode of production, less a tool that can be removed than a necessary component that cannot be eradicated without drastically changing the entire system that produces and uses it.

54

Furthermore, Gerima's conceptualization of commercial cinema does not register the complex and contradictory ways that black audiences actively participate in and, often, actively resist the Eurocentricism of commercial cinema. Finally, the very fact that he can critique mainstream cinema's pervasive ideology indicates that he conceives of an outside to it. He stands somewhere on the outside of the Eurocentric, escapist "world outlook" or "ideology" promulgated by commercial cinema, probably in an Afrocentric above, looking down on the mass audience he laments while urging others who share his perspective to create films capable of correcting the damage inflicted upon the masses by commercial cinema.

The formulation of common sense I offered in the previous chapter provides a more nuanced and flexible approach to questions of reception and spectatorship and of the role (potential and actual) played by spectator(s), filmmaker(s), film critic(s), and film theorist(s) in the collective enterprise of constructing a film's "meaning."[32] Gerima's theory of commercial cinema's "ideological mystification" of the masses cannot explain the existence of "alternative readings" of that cinema's images nor can it continue to hold much explanatory value in an increasingly differentiated global market. But an anti-elitist formulation of common sense enables one to recognize where hegemonic forces such as Eurocentrism have been unable to achieve total consensus, despite their apparent pervasiveness in mainstream movies. In addition, as Gramsci's perspective on common sense's role in the struggle for hegemony makes clear, thinking about film in terms of common sense means that one is always aware that capitalist relations are inherent in the production, circulation, and consumption of film's images.

Gerima is keenly aware, however, of one element of common sense: "It is in this epoch that the cultural toys have made a drastic inroad into our central nervous system, governing and fashioning our behaviour—our minds are occupied territory."[33] Highlighting cinema's ability to make common the sensory-motor schemas of living beings, Gerima advocates for a Third World cinema wherein "every frame and every take, every shot and every sound must be able to enter into the different compartments of our brains the way a guerrilla engages in hand-to-hand combat."[34] Gerima explains that film's images must "enter into our brains" in order to "erase and eliminate" all the "colonial models occupying our optic nerve."[35]

Though its aesthetic traverses already well-worn pathways in the brain, *Sankofa* puts Gerima's theory into practice on two levels. Within the film, Mona is decolonized, sent to experience the violence of slavery so that she can be reborn as an African. For the film's spectators, a similar operation is carried out. The spectators must be made to experience Mona's experience of slavery in such a way that the colonial models occupying the spectators' optic nerves can be extricated so that their minds can be returned to their supposedly original African state. For spectators who feel themselves to be white, Gerima's film enables them to recognize the humanity of the enslaved Africans. Restaging the master-slave confrontation, the film's project, like that of BAM, whose cultural nationalism it embraces, is premised on achieving recognition of the black's humanity.

To accomplish these feats, *Sankofa* redeploys a film form and style that is familiar to the commercial motion-picture audience. In *Sankofa* Gerima attempts to utilize formal and aesthetic techniques familiar to audiences of Hollywood cinema and the spatiotemporal relations that those techniques orchestrate—those same aspects of the commercial motion-picture industry that he identifies as responsible for colonizing the sensorium of the mass

55

audience—in order to reverse the colonization process that he believes those techniques carry out.[36] In other words, he uses the same tools to decolonize the audience of commercial cinema that he believes were used to colonize that audience in the first place.

The sequence in which Mona is branded in Elmina Castle provides an illustration of *Sankofa*'s reliance upon familiar filmic narrative devices and visual cues. That sequence uses continuity editing to establish the spatial dimensions of the dungeon where Mona is branded and to direct attention to the site of Mona's branding. The sequence begins when Mona follows a group of tourists into the dungeon. As their voices grow distant, the doors to the dungeon slam closed. Mona's journey into the past begins. Under the stares of chained blacks, she attempts to escape. Throwing open the doors, Mona discovers that the space she left to enter the dungeon has been transformed into a past version of that space. She attempts to run, but white slavers drag her back, as the music on the soundtrack changes from an African drum–inflected rhythm to a Negro spiritual. The slavers rip Mona's shirt off violently, leaving her naked from the waist up. As Aretha Franklin's voice wails Thomas A. Dorsey's "Take My Hand," the slavers brand Mona's bare back with a red-hot iron, leaving her to fall, her arms spread apart, recalling Christ's crucifixion—a deftly orchestrated metaphor of Mona's martyrdom. She suffers for those blacks who, like her, have lost their way and become Westernized. She suffers so that they might be saved and brought back home to Africa. Like the practice of branding, whereby a socially recognizable sign is imprinted violently onto one's physical body, the filmic metaphor can bear a "social judgement" insofar as it elaborates "a circuit which includes simultaneously the author, the film, and the viewer."[37]

As in the system of continuity editing on which most of the film relies, the effect of the filmic techniques in this scene is to organize the audience's attention and to direct its understanding.[38] Given the racial dynamics that inform cinematic perception and the process Fanon describes of recognizing oneself in the Black, spectators who already feel themselves to be black will most likely recognize themselves in Mona or in the Africans in chains. Mona's frightened assertion—"I'm not an African. I'm an American"— implicates even those blacks who feel themselves to be simply Americans (as opposed to black Americans or African Americans) in the identificatory logic that the film (re)authorizes through its style. While I can only speculate as to the precise affect that each spectator will access in this scene, it is clear from the film's narrative logic and from the shots that follow the branding that the intended effect of this sequence is to drag the spectator into slavery with Mona.[39]

Relying upon and reinforcing a sensory-motor schema made common by its prior interactions with Hollywood cinema, *Sankofa* merely effects a reversal: blacks are capable of a range of emotions, actions, and attachments and are free to move in and to organize a variety of spaces, while whites are one-dimensional, stereotypical, and confined to one or two locations, always appearing only in relation to the dramatic action that involves the Africans. (*Sankofa* thus turns the question "How does it feel to be a problem?" back onto the white man. While such affective manipulation might be satisfying, while it might drive home the point that being rendered one-dimensional and caricatured is damaging, insulting, painful, crippling, and nauseating, while it has a capacity to evoke white guilt, it is hardly the stuff of a transformed sociopolitical landscape or image-scape, as it reifies rather than challenges racism's categories.) Working via a common sensory-motor schema, *Sankofa* defies its audience's habituated perception of slavery by offering an alternative set of images that correspond closely enough to existing images of slavery to be recognizable to the audience as "images of slavery."

Working via the aspect of common sense that has to do with sensory-motor habituation, *Sankofa* dares its audience to recognize slavery differently, and it enables the audience to do so. At the same time, however, the film advocates for what the mental aspect of common sense, by virtue of its "strangely composite" character,[40] makes an impossible political task: the erasure of memory-images deposited through the struggle to survive slavery, especially when survival meant "being" a slave.

If the common sense of oppressed and exploited groups is, as Gramsci suggests, a record of the groups' survival, then it is clear that the black common sense that enabled individual and collective survival during slavery contains nodes of consent to slavery. Because *Sankofa* is unable to conceive of a slave existence that does not remain stuck in the preconscious state of the thingness of the bondsman in the Hegelian struggle for "Lordship," it is unable to contend with the extent to which the experience of slavery itself provided both a sensory-motor schema and a set of memory-images common to those enslaved—a slave common sense. Locked within a Hegelian ontological framework that denies humanity to the slave, *Sankofa* must ignore the common sense of the slave, aspects of which remain active sediments in black common sense, complicating its ability to elaborate a critical and coherent black cultural nationalism. In order to unfold a Black human consciousness, *Sankofa* must deny the humanity of the slave as slave (if there is such a thing) and ignore the aspects of slave common sense that continue to inform present black common sense.

The experience of slavery, especially that of surviving it, consolidates a collectivity that shares a habituated sensory-motor schema and a set of memory-images, a common sense that continues to inform perceptions within our present hellish cycle.[41] Seeing its spectators as vessels for ideology and fulfilling a project that depends upon the erasure of memory-images, *Sankofa* ignores what exists in the present, reaching instead into the past in an attempt to erase the difficulties and complacencies, the nodes of common-sense consensus to present modes of domination and exploitation. The narrative logic of the film's framing device—a Europeanized and eroticized black American woman is sent into the past so that she might realize how she is being exploited and oppressed in the present—itself is predicated on a dismissal of the complexities of the current situation. The questions Saidiya Hartman asks about "whether the image of enslaved ancestors can transform the present" are relevant.

58

> If the goal is something more than assimilating the terror of the past into our storehouse of memory, the pressing question is, Why need we remember? Does the emphasis on remembering and working through the past expose our insatiable desires for curatives, healing, and anything else that proffers the restoration of some prelapsarian intactness? Or is recollection an avenue for undoing history? Can remembering potentially enable an escape from the regularity of terror and the routine of violence constitutive of black life in the United States? Or is it that remembering has become the only conceivable or viable form of political agency?[42]

Returning to the (Cinematic) Past

By re-presenting slavery as a site of cultural contamination in order to unearth a prior cultural purity, *Sankofa* takes BAM's black cultural nationalist project to the limits of what it can do. With *Sankofa*, Gerima sets out to undo mainstream cinema's "problematic" representations of slavery, but he does so by constructing another problem, perceptible as Mona-Shola at the end of the film, that dissimulates a different agent of power. The subject that emerges in Mona at the end of *Sankofa* is a masculine diasporic African cleansed of the impurities deposited by colonization and slavery, especially any form of sexuality that would threaten to align the Black with "the genital." That "impurity" so troubling to Fanon, his blackness, remains.

With *Sankofa* Gerima recognizes the mechanisms of Darstellung at work in mainstream depictions of slavery, but ignores those of Vertretung, which are equally important in providing contemporary forms of racist domination with their economic articulations and justifications. Accordingly, he seeks to dismantle the objectionable and insulting depictions of slaves, but he overlooks the role such depictions play in consolidating hegemonic racist relations. Gerima's particular reinscription of the Black according to his specular predication, authorizes a "new balance of hegemonic relations."[43]

Moreover, while Fanon questions the adequacy of representational schemas, including memory, in achieving the event of experience, *Sankofa* deploys film, a representational medium, in order to provide an experience of slavery. Striving to make a Black human by returning to the past in order to re-image the confrontation that creates "Lord" and "Bondsman," and in order to give that experience to Mona and to the film's spectators, *Sankofa* seeks to provide the Black with a different, more authentic, past. Fulfilling the call of BAM, the film presents itself as a vehicle through which the Black might move forward by returning to the past.

Turning to the Black's past, *Sankofa* finds cinematic images, among them, *Gone with the Wind* (1939), *Band of Angels* (1957), *Mandingo* (1975), and *Roots* (1977). The film's return to the past is fundamentally a confrontation with existing cinematic (memory) images that are widely available as part of a perception of any black according to an official common sense.

Sankofa releases a cast of characters capable of doing battle with those through whom slavery had been narrated previously. Prissy screams stupidly for a doctor in *Gone with the Wind*, claiming "she don't know nuthin' 'bout birthin' no baby," but *Sankofa*'s powerful Nunu, who is rumored to have killed "a cracka" just by staring at him, rallies her warriors around her, cuts a runaway down from her whipping post, and delivers the dead runaway's baby while the slave community protects the birth. The happy, singing slaves of *Band of Angels* are no match for the watchful, angry slaves on the Lafayette Plantation, who silently witness each atrocity of slavery, recording it for future generations. Where *Mandingo*'s black buck pleases a plantation mistress "or else," Shango and Shola (Mona) lovingly and tenderly place leaves

59

and weeds on each other in the river. The countless black hussies who seduce the slave master in the hopes of getting into the big house are revealed to be the stuff of white fantasy when the slave master on the Lafayette Plantation repeatedly and brutally rapes Shola just as he might a dog. And, perhaps above all, the moment the black man's inferiority comes into being through the other never happens: Kunta Kinte never gives in and says his name is Toby. *Sankofa*'s enslaved Africans would rather die first.

Returning to the past, *Sankofa* finds not the aporetic experience of slavery, but a slew of problems that plague any cinematic appearance of a slave. *Sankofa*'s return to slavery is, above all, a revision of existing mass cultural memory-images that are capable of affecting the formation of the Black. In this respect, *Sankofa* provides an alternative set of images for memory to access and thus an alternative perception of slavery and, ultimately, of the Black. By so doing, *Sankofa* broadens the range of possible affects available in a black's appearance to an eye and, hence, of the quantity and quality of possible identifications with the Black. It is most likely (almost certainly) the case that the registers of affect the film provides for a black's self-identification are more affirming of a black self than are those provided by, say, Butterfly McQueen's Prissy.

The film presents slavery as that which must be exorcised in order for the African to continue the process of his historical progress, which was interrupted by slavery. In the film the enslaved Africans resist and rebel against slavery in every possible way. Except for Joe, the film's impure and tainted mulatto conceived during a rape, none of those enslaved actually become slaves in the sense of capitulating to the superiority of the master. Shola, who begins as a house slave who "never knew anything else," stakes her life for her freedom and dies rather than remain a slave. Shango resists in the same manner. Their resistance and, above all, their willingness to die rather than live as slaves guarantees each African his or her humanity.

Gerima explains in an interview about the film: "I brought out the individual identities and motives of the characters, transforming the 'happy slaves' into an African race opposed to this whole idea, by making the history of slavery full of resistance, full of rebellion. Resistance and rebellion—the plantation school of thought believed it was always provoked by outsiders, that Africans were not capable of having that human need."[44] In *Sankofa*, as in Hegel, being a human is inconsistent with being a slave. Apparently, innovating ways in which to survive under exploitative, oppressive, and violent conditions is inconsistent with being a human if it includes aspects of consent to those conditions.[45]

Providing a way for the black to feel better about himself is not the extent of *Sankofa*'s project. Presenting rebellious and resistant Africans who find themselves enslaved, the film purports to portray slavery more authentically and accurately (i.e., less "problematically"). *Sankofa* makes a representational claim to historical accuracy and cultural authenticity in an effort to install a past that is capable of unfolding a collective identity different from that represented by Mona at the beginning of the film. The identity it unfolds is built on a different regime of identification, that of the film's diasporic African, purporting to belong to a more "natural" state of being black.

Through its mulatto character, Joe, through its sustained meditation on Christianity via long takes of Euro-Christian paintings and iconography and via Joe's doomed quest to become pure and Christian, and through the attention it gives to the African culture, traditions, and language of the newly enslaved field slaves, especially Nunu and Shango, as opposed to the compromised but sometimes innovative sociocultural formations of the house slaves who have by and large accepted their lot, *Sankofa* posits that "slavery" (as re-presented by the film) is an originary site of cultural contamination that the constitution of the dichotomous categories "black" and "white" precedes.[46] Instead of marking the emergence of black subjectivity, slavery in *Sankofa* indexes its contamination.

Rather than demonstrate how film's images are invariably political proxies by questioning the basis for those images' constitution, by elaborating a different conceptualization of the image regimes currently understood under the rubric of "representation," or by revealing the inadequacy or unreliability of the knowledge to be gained from those images, *Sankofa* keeps intact cinema's predilection toward camouflaging agents of power, even as it recognizes the political importance of challenging existing representations.

The Black Is a Black Man

By purporting to issue a more authentic, revolutionary Black subject at the end of the film, *Sankofa* reaches the limits of what a black cultural nationalism can do.[47] The formation of a black subject capable of being expressed by a nation is predicated on a process of exclusion. In *Sankofa* among those who must be excluded are those who survived slavery by refusing to stake their

61

lives and those who are perceived to remain "inhuman" according to the epistemological framework of colonialist racism, which *Sankofa* embraces in order to subvert, especially those who do not challenge colonial racism's equation of the Black with the genital. *Sankofa* dramatizes each of these exclusions.

Sankofa illustrates the first by portraying a process wherein the sensory-motor schema of the enslaved Africans becomes habituated. At several points throughout the film, including the branding sequence, enslaved Africans silently witness the action, but are unable to react themselves. They are seer-slaves, the silent characters who are always watching from the sugar fields. They are most closely aligned with the film's spectator, who likewise is capable of seeing the intolerable present images *Sankofa* frames, but unable to react to them within the space and time of the viewing situation. The activity of the film's seer-slaves is survival; they endure by mutely witnessing an intolerable present perception, which becomes an unassimilated part of the set of memory-images that they share with those who survive in a similar fashion.

Sankofa's seer-slaves dramatize a process, described by Deleuze, whereby the sensory delinks from the motor mechanism and, in this case, arrests the film's movement toward the production of a black nationalist subject. The delinking occurs in order to ensure the slaves' survival, which would be jeopardized by their motor movement in the face of the brutality confronting them. The seer-slaves have no ready-made rationalizations into which their present perception might fit. Yet, instead of seizing the opportunity provided by the irrationality of the present perception in order to reveal what is new within the slaves' perception, *Sankofa* establishes a linkage for its viewers, continuing their movement toward receiving *Sankofa*'s images in simple black-versus-white terms by pressing it into the common sense of a dialectic of struggle for recognition by the Other. The present perception of the seer-slaves arrests movement, both within the film and possibly in the film's viewers, thereby providing the opportunity for an alternate conception of slavery to emerge. In order to move forward, *Sankofa* ignores the possible alternatives of and for "the human" that exist in both its slaves' and its audience's present perception. Instead of directing the spectators' attention toward those alternative conceptions, *Sankofa* chooses to pursue a Black humanity that relies upon rendering the slaves inhuman.

I am not arguing for a project wherein the slaves are humanized—to humanize slaves by portraying them staking their lives for freedom *is San-kofa*'s project. I am arguing instead for a sustained and careful engagement with the modes of existence that must be purged from the epistemological and ontological frameworks that give rise to the human in an effort to reveal what alternatives to the human exist. Within a Hegelian or a Freudian framework, the slave or the other is a potential site of such alternatives.

The seer-slaves in *Sankofa* share the sensory-motor schema of the film's spectators, who also are confronted with something intolerable in the world, a graphic depiction of slavery, but are unable to react except to see it and to feel it, thereby arresting the movement of the film's action upon them. The seer-slaves in *Sankofa* do not stake their lives in a struggle for self-consciousness, preferring to remain hidden and alive in the sugar-cane fields. If those who recognize themselves in the slaves of the seventeenth century can do so because some of those slaves survived as slaves, black common sense contains not only an account of black rebellions and resistance to slavery but also a record of the slaves' survival achieved precisely by consenting to aspects of their enslavement. *Sankofa* seeks to erase that aspect of common sense by positing a set of memory-images corresponding to those who did risk death to escape slavery and to those who did die. But, in so doing, it posits that those who did not risk death, those who survived as slaves, must be expunged in the process of unfolding the collective African the film presents as adequate to the present need for liberation. 63

The slaves in the fields who watch and survive are like the film's spectators who have been dragged into slavery with Mona-Shola. The spectators must survive the film, working to make sense of it, then get up and walk (or move via whatever means are available) into a world that continues to operate according to a hellish cycle and attempt to survive it. In the moment that Shola "dies" asserting her humanity, dying for freedom is an option that is foreclosed to the spectator, who is asked not to die, but to live to see the end of the film.[48] Not only are the slaves who survive slavery expunged from the African who unfolds at the end of the film, so are the spectators who survive the film and remain oppressed and exploited. Neither attain the status of Black human.[49]

Other categories that the film posits and expunges as inhuman or not human in order to prolong a perception of slavery into "forward" movement are constructed in relationship to genital sexuality. Fanon's observation that within colonialist representational schemas "the Negro is the genital" is relevant to understanding the difficulties that *Sankofa* poses for itself by using a perceptibly female body to mediate the unfolding of the Black human.

To the extent that the perception of the female body commonly carries a notion of femininity in the sense of passivity or receptivity to sensations from the outside or in the sense of being an object for desire, the female body poses a series of difficulties for any attempt to be recognized as human. *Sankofa* addresses the difficulties posed by its choice to unfold the Black human in a body that is recognizable as black and female by wrenching "femininity" from its customary association with the female body. Shola must refuse to be feminized in order to claim her humanity. Because the equation between the Black and the genital precludes the black's humanity, Shola also must refuse to be sexualized in any manner. *Sankofa* argues that the notions of femininity and genital sexuality that commonly inhere in perceptions that posit a "black female body" are Western conceptions deposited in common sense as part of the colonial mission. These elements have to be purged from Shola before she can represent the Black (hu)man.

The love sequence between Shola and Shango is informative in this regard. The lovers bathe each other in the river, gently caressing each other with leaves and weeds. They are not shown engaging in sexual intercourse. What they do to show their affection and mutual attraction for one another demonstrates that neither character can be equated with the genital. The perceptible biological differences between the male body and the female body are insignificant as the couple engages in an erotic play that ostensibly has been stripped of the power differentials of "active" and "passive." Each is active, placing plants on the other, and each is passive, having plants placed on his or her body. This scene is a purifying one for Shola. In the sequence that follows, Shola kills her white rapist.

In both the love scene with Shango and the scene in which Shola claims her humanity with her death, what is expunged from Shola is a notion of femininity as designating passivity or receptivity to sensations from the outside and one's currency as an object for desire. The notion of sexuality as genital sex also is expunged from Mona-Shola. *Sankofa* features several images of Mona-Shola's body being violently penetrated or otherwise violated. Mona's body is branded. Shola's body is raped repeatedly and whipped. *Sankofa* does these things in the name of returning her to her source in order to unfold a collective Black human. Shola stakes her life and finds her humanity when she refuses to be raped again by the slave master. During a rebellion, Shola, by now "demoted" to being a field slave, is working in the cane fields when the white slave master approaches her, removing his belt. Shola flashes back to being raped by him, resists his advances, then stabs him several times with a machete before running away with head slaves in close pursuit.

To confront the prevalent portrayal of female slaves as sexually available to the slave master for consensual sex, *Sankofa* understandably depicts those sexual encounters as violent rapes. The immediate context within which Shola stakes her life is when she is again threatened with rape by the slave master. Not only does Shola have to resist being raped again in order to be recognized by the spectator as a human and not an animal, but she must refuse any association with passivity, and she must, even with Shango, be distanced from any affiliation with the genital. She actively must reject any attempt to constitute hers as a feminine, sexual body because, as *Sankofa* makes clear, the constitution of the black body as feminine and sexual has been the work of colonization.

In its quest to produce a black nationalist subject, *Sankofa* might be said to "assume that the female subject serves as a general case for explicating social death, property relations, and the pained and punitive construction of black-ness."[50] Rather than disregard sexual injury, *Sankofa* dramatizes its redress, but it does so by making it an individual, rather than a collective or a sys-temic, responsibility. Rather than opening onto an analysis of sexual violence against slaves as inscribed and sanctioned systemically in ways that might have complicated present common-sense understandings of gender differ-ences and the causes of sexual violence, *Sankofa* insists that Shola herself must redress the violence perpetrated against her. By doing so, the film implies that such violence is individuated, rather than systemic, and even sanctioned by Shola herself, because, until she (finally) fights back to put an end to a feminizing violence, she tolerates rather than resists being raped.

In Shola's experience of slavery, feminization, genital sex, and slavery are coextensive, each functioning to organize a colonized and civilized sociality that continues to hold black bodies enslaved. Whereas Mona is feminized, sexualized, and Westernized, Shola rejects all three of those characteristics, preferring "death" over feminization, genital sexuality, and enslavement. Defeminized, Shola marks a profound transformation in Mona who, at the beginning of the film, gleefully seduces the white man's (phallic) camera, subjecting herself to what is figured in *Sankofa* as a violation of her Africanity, wearing a blonde wig and fake fingernails in order to be widely circulated and consumed, presumably in some fashion magazine.

Femininity, sexuality, and slavery must be expunged from the image of a perceptibly black female body in order for that body to stand in for the so-called humanity of the Black. Femininity, genital sexuality, and slavery are unable to inhere in "the human" that _Sankofa_ upholds. A similar type of erasure does not occur for masculinity or for blackness; both persist according to a specular logic of identification. While it is difficult to describe the "Black human" who emerges at the end of _Sankofa_ without lapsing back into the categories that the film has demonstrated to be the stuff of colonialism, it is crucial to recognize that the violence unleashed in the name of decolonization is leveled most frequently at those who are recognizable as women and/or as feminine. With these difficulties in mind, it remains possible to say that the Black human that emerges at the end of the film is a "problem" that dissimulates a paternal proxy in a recognizably female body. It is black, yet unable to represent the audience that has witnessed the unfolding of its humanity, because _Sankofa_ has constituted that audience as a passive vessel for ideology, as seers who recognize themselves in the film's slaves, but who are unable to react to the present perception of racialized violence by staking their lives, and who as a mass, feminized audience are affected and formed by sensations from the outside.

Sankofa's mass audience is the present that the film strives to unchain by propelling it into the past. By doing so, _Sankofa_ chains the present to the past. Instead of freeing the black from the problematic representations that constitute his imago and thus determine his self formation, _Sankofa_ links the black ever more closely to the authority of past appearances. Every cinematic appearance of a black is perceived according to a past perception. As Fanon puts it, "The Negro, however sincere, is the slave of the past."[51] Chaining the black to the past, _Sankofa_ reifies the black's slavery—his role within the infernal temporal circle that continues to authorize racist oppression and exploitation. It does not liberate him from it.

The film inherited Fanon's Hegelianism, but not his sense of the temporality of revolutionary change. Fanon asserts, "I am not a prisoner of history. I should not seek there for the meaning of my destiny. I should constantly remind myself that the real leap consists in introducing invention into existence. In the world through which I travel, I am endlessly creating myself."[52] Fanon's call to introduce invention into existence relies upon a different temporal schema than that which informs Gerima's project with respect to Mona in and the spectator of *Sankofa*. For invention to be introduced into existence and for one to be "endlessly creating" oneself, time and space must be open, capable of allowing time and making room for change to occur. In reaching into the cinematic past in order to uncover a hidden history of resistance to slavery, *Sankofa* recognizes that the past appears with each present. But it fails to allow for the creativity of the present, which launches itself into the future. Chaining the present to the past, *Sankofa* restricts the future, directing it into a black cultural nationalism that is the expression of an exclusive and violently exclusionary "humanity."

Fanon's injunction to introduce invention into existence is a call for an embrace of a space and a time that might be unknown. It is a call for a theory of real movement, a theory that complicates how film theorists and other theorists of visual culture approach the set of questions that is currently theorized under the rubric of "representation." It is a call for an understanding of history and "the whole" as the Open, not as the teleological unfolding of progressive instants. It is a plea for a cease-fire in the aporia, for a respite from things thrown forward in order to dissimulate, for the emergence of an any-instant-whatever without recognition. The final prayer with which Fanon closes *Black Skin, White Masks* is an entreaty for a cinematic perception attuned to the appearance of alternatives hidden in the Open. It is a call for a motor tendency on a sensitive nerve of a slave that does not continue a present movement, but instead creates a different future movement: "O my body, make of me always a man who questions!"[53]

Leaving the Hegelian Fanon and the problems he throws forward to the nationalists and the humanists, visionaries, not without problem, retain a shared memory-image, the cinematic Fanon, in order to look at the temporality of cinematic perception, the complex interplay of race, class, gender, and sexual differences, and the possibility of introducing invention into the black's existence.

67

"We'll Just Have to Get Guns and Be Men"

The Cinematic Appearance of Black Revolutionary Women

Technological cinematic machines, especially television, figured promi-
nently both in the political strategies of leftist activists and organizations
and in the international circulation of U.S. politics and culture throughout the 1960s and 1970s. For this reason, a formulation of black identity
that recognizes that identity as a cinematic phenomenon is indispensable
to my attempt to understand how the strategies of the Black Power Movement, the Black Panther Party in particular, became part of the conditions

4 | *"Four Women"*

of possibility for what has been referred
to as "perhaps the greatest irony of the
post-1968 period"—the coexistence of a vi-
sual cultural terrain wherein "Black aesthetic commodities" figure promi-
nently and an ethicopolitical terrain wherein "Black citizenship is increasingly devalued."[1] In order to arrive at an understanding of how the praxis of
the Black Power Movement contributed to this situation, I describe an operation that is perceptible in the praxis of the early Black Panther Party (BPP). At
the same time as the international circulation of the image of "armed
Negroes"—or, as I put it, "blacks with guns"—garnered for the BPP the
support of thousands worldwide, it also became part of a diffuse effort to
harness and direct the processes of transvaluation blackness was then undergoing and to set those processes to work in the service of a globalizing capital
contending with decolonization movements across the globe.

Seize the Time

The spatiotemporal schema of a whole that changes had been given philosophical elaboration near the beginning of the twentieth century by Henri
Bergson. Bergson's theory of real movement is the basis for Gilles Deleuze's
elaboration of cinema and it provides Deleuze with the model of spatiality
and temporality that underpins cinematic reality. Where Bergson begins by
positing a relationship of equivalence between movement and image, Frantz

Armed members of the Black Panthers Party stand in the corridor of the Capitol in Sacramento today, May 2, 1967. They were protesting a bill before an Assembly committee restricting the carrying of arms in public. Associated Press photo by Walt Zeboski. Reproduced by permission of AP/Wide World Photos.

Fanon foregrounds the relationship between time and image. For Fanon, the Black, an imago, is the visual index of colonial time; the black's existence is a generalized effort to evoke a past disaster whose specificity and uniqueness the black's appearance does not call forth.[2] For Fanon, the black is a passing, present preservation of a general past that keeps reappearing. The black might reveal time's differentiation into presents that pass and pasts that are preserved. In other words, the Black is a direct image of time or, to employ Deleuze's language, the Black is a time-image.[3]

Certainly, my reading of Fanon follows, at the expense of a faithful delineation of the point where Fanon's thought actually arrives, a direction to which he only tends in certain places in his writing. Yet, even though he did not follow the trajectory of this line of his thought and although he does not employ Deleuze's language, Fanon thinks of the Black as a time-image in order to argue that change is immanent to the black's existence. According to this tendency in Fanon's argument, in any present perception of the black there exists the possibility for an alternative organization of sociality to appear, one that would not support the black's appearance and that, therefore, would break the chains which bind the black to the past (as a slave), freeing the black man from himself by revealing that one's present perception of him (a perception of the past) is inconsistent with the black's new situation. Fanon's formulation of the temporality in which the black exists corresponds to Bergson's understanding of temporality, which Deleuze reveals as cinematic.

Yet, where Bergson argues that the present is sensory-motor because the past is perceived (sensory) and the future is action or movement (motor), Fanon contends that, in the case of one who is a slave of the past (the Black and the White), the present is confined to the past, so the past infects the future toward which the present tends.[4] Hence, the black's present is characterized solely by sensation (or feeling—self-contempt, shame, nausea), and those sensations are simply the past's action on the black's body. But it is an arrested action that is *felt* as the affect, an internal arrested movement ("a motor tendency on a sensitive nerve") whereby the black comes to be himself: black. For Fanon, the black marks an interminable present characterized by an affect that results from the black's encounter with images of the past, an encounter that is repeated indefinitely.

In the conclusion to *Black Skin, White Masks* Fanon initially argues that the liberation of the black man from himself entails a break with the past: "Both [the white man and the black man] must turn their backs on the inhuman voices which were those of their respective ancestors in order that authentic communication be possible."[5] Fanon suggests that such communication will enable the black man and the white man to "create the ideal conditions of existence" for a better world. This communication must occur in the present and tend toward a future that has broken from the past of colonization.

"Freedom," as Fanon figures it here, entails an effort to "leap" out of the contingency of History, not in the sense of transcending History, but in the sense of going "beyond" the narrative of the past that has heretofore determined the contours of his existence: "The body of history does not determine a single one of my actions. I am my own foundation. And it is by going beyond the historical, instrumental hypothesis that I will initiate the cycle of my freedom."[6] Fanon's version of "freedom" is immanent to the Black's existence.

Each present, or any-instant-whatever, contains the possibility for the black's liberation because that present tends toward an indeterminate action, the future. While Fanon at first seems to explain the possibility for liberation solely in idealist temporal terms, the last line of the book, the oft-quoted prayer "O my body, make of me always a man who questions!" makes it clear that he considers matter to be integral to his liberatory temporal schema. The action that is the future relies upon the present, the body, which is sensory-motor. The future is a function of the body's sensory-motor apparatus and therefore cannot entail a break with the past, but it can spring from a present presentation of a different "sheet of past."[7] Fanon invokes a future in the form of a prayer, an indication that "always a man who questions" exists only as a possibility, a plea, a longed-for future action. That man is not the outcome of a present whose contours are given. Nor is he the outcome of a past in which "tom-toms and cannibalism" characterize a body that is perceived to be black and on that basis expelled in order to consolidate "Mind" and "Reason." He will emerge from a different past, one that has yet to be uncovered.[8]

Implicit in his prayer for his body to make of him "always a man who questions" is a conception of the past as the coexistence of what Deleuze refers to as "sheets of past." In Deleuze's Bergsonian formulation, "The past appears as the most general form of an already-there." The past is a "pre-existence in general" which our recollections presuppose and of which our perceptions make use.[9] What of this preexistence is accessible from the present is arranged into "regions, strata, and sheets," each of which is characterized by its own "dominant themes," "tones," "singularities," "aspects," and so on. All of the regions and sheets of the past exist alongside of, within, or connected with one another. There is not one past, but sheets of past.

Fanon's prayer is for one who questions and thus for a situation wherein nothing is given or givable, everything is open to interrogation, and the body exists as that which chooses what is to come. Fanon's final prayer indicates that, for him, the possibility for liberation lies in a cinematic reality wherein the whole is the open, change is possible, and there exist, as Bergson puts it, "actions that are really free, or at least partly indeterminate."[10] That Fanon must posit a Bergsonian understanding of movement, of time, and thus of change as the conditions of possibility for wrenching an alternative socio-economic situation from the Black reveals the extent to which he conceives of black identity and subjectivity, both of which equate the black with his imago, as cinematic phenomenon.

The Whole World Is Watching

On 2 May 1967 a group of armed Black Panthers, female and male, entered California's capitol building amid "movie cameramen, still cameramen, regular cameras" as "bulbs were flashing all over the place."[11] Prior to this protest, Huey Newton and Bobby Seale had determined that, as co-founders and leaders of the BPP, one of them should remain in Oakland while the other took a group of Panthers to Sacramento. Newton mowed the lawn at his mother's house while Seale and several other party members traveled to Sacramento to protest the Mulford Bill, legislation under consideration at the time that eventually made it illegal for the Panthers to carry weapons. Because he was not actually at the California state-capitol building during the demonstration, Newton's experience of that event was in and through mass media. Newton recalls his experience as follows: "About noon a bulletin interrupted the radio program. It told of brothers at the capitol with weapons. My mother called out to me that all channels were showing the event. I ran into the house, and there was Bobby reading the mandate."[12]

Newton's narrative of his experience of the Panthers' protest in Sacramento emphasizes the variety of media—radio and television in particular—through which the event circulated. Likewise, Seale's description of entering the California state-legislature building with "bulbs flashing all over the place" draws attention to the event's spectacular context of production, an aspect of the protest that enabled Angela Davis to find the image of "the leather jacketed, black-bereted warriors standing with guns at the entrance to the California legislature" in a German newspaper while she was in Frankfurt studying with Theodor Adorno.[13] In the United States, *U.S. News and World Report, Life, Time,* and the *New York Times Magazine* all carried photographs of the Panthers "as a disciplined and tough-looking cadre of militant and macho revolutionaries."[14]

In addition to print media, television news broadcasts included "live foot-age" of the protest at the California legislature and information concerning the resulting arrest of over twenty Panthers. The widespread circulation of the image of the Panthers at the legislature building in Sacramento enabled the BPP to establish itself as a vehicle through which the revolutionary theories and sentiments of young black Americans nationwide might be expressed. As Newton put it, "In a matter of months we went from a small Bay Area group to a national organization."[15] The cinematic appearance of the BPP via their circulation in newspapers and on television played a crucial role in establishing them as a national organization.[16] As is the case with every cinematic appearance, however, that of the BPP was predicated on a set of omissions that are now becoming perceptible primarily as a result of the repackaging and recirculation of the BPP in books and films marketed to academics and political activists.[17]

On 2 May 1967, even though Seale read "Executive Mandate No. 1" as planned, the weapons that the Panthers displayed at the California legislature occluded the message he and the other Panthers had traveled to Sacramento in order to deliver. According to Newton, the main purpose of the protest was "to deliver the message to the people."[18] The mandate that Seale read stated that the Black Panther Party for Self-Defense (as they were named at their inception) "call[ed] upon the American people in general, and the Black people in particular, to take careful note of the racist California Legislature now considering legislation aimed at keeping Black people disarmed and powerless while racist police agencies throughout the country intensify the terror, brutality, murder, and repression of Black people."[19]

Newton recalls, "The message was definitely going out. Bobby read it twice, but the press and the people assembled were so amazed at the Black Panthers' presence, and particularly the weapons, that few appeared to hear the important thing. They were concentrating on the weapons."[20] Yet the visual message conveyed by the weapons rendered the protest a "success": "We had hoped that after the weapons gained their attention they would listen to the message. . . . Sacramento was certainly a success, however, in attracting national attention; even those who did not hear the complete message saw the arms and this conveyed enough to the Black people. . . . From all across the country calls came to us about establishing chapters and branches; we could hardly keep track of the requests."[21]

The Panthers' admonition against the racist California legislature was not what was retained from the cinematic appearance of the BPP: "Few appeared

to hear the important thing." In most of the available accounts, the perceptible content of the cinematic image that circulated as a reference for the
BPP's protest at the California state legislature was "armed Negroes." From
the fecundity of images available that day, "blacks with guns" was retained as
the content of the BPP's cinematic appearance.

Blacks with guns was a new appearance of the Black, not his destruction.
It made visible a sheet of past different from that to which Fanon argues the
black had been enslaved, the sheet of past which had been harnessed by
cinematic perception in order to authorize the black's appearance. Consistent with Fanon's injunction to introduce invention into existence, this appearance of the BPP short-circuited a sensory-motor schema habituated to
recognize the black according to the colonialist, racist common sense that
Fanon so astutely pathologized. Newton thus describes "the press and the
people assembled" staring in amazement "at the Black Panthers' presence
and particularly the weapons." It might be argued that those assembled were
"amazed" and "unable to hear the important thing" because they were confronted with an appearance of the black that confounded their ability to
recognize him according to habit.

74   Unable to force blacks with guns into the common memory-images that
they habitually called forth in order to recognize a black as the Black, the
press and those assembled had to stop and think: If the civil rights movement had secured the black's full citizenship, why did he pick up the gun?
How could slavery, share-cropping, silent suffering, gospel singing, Aunt
Jemima, Uncle Tom, Topsy, "We Shall Overcome," cotton picking, illiteracy,
"massa lovin'," cannibalism, watermelon-seed spittin', white-woman chasing, nonviolent resisting, Mammy, and Jezebel give way to blacks with guns?
If "shame and self contempt," "nausea," and the soul-stirring sadness of
Negro spirituals pervades the black's being, from where did the Afros, guns,
and "black pride" spring?

The appearance of American blacks with guns revealed that those commonly shared memory-images which previously supported perceptions of a
black were inadequate to a present perception of blacks with guns because
American blacks with guns was not a component of the common sense
through which the black appeared. With the revelation that hegemonic common sense could not make sense of blacks with guns, those truths that such
common sense had secured crumbled. The cinematic appearance of blacks
with guns made visible one of the black's alternative pasts, rendering the

past called forth to support the habituated perception of the black "not neces-sarily true." The appearance of the BPP made visible those aspects of the black's past that constituted a tradition of radical praxis forged in the name of the black against racist American exploitation and oppression. In addition, the Panthers' uniform—leather jackets, berets, guns—was recognizable as that worn by visibly armed anticolonial and anti-imperialist revolutionaries across the globe.[22]

Having previously appeared only according to the dictates of a common sense that accommodated their invisibility in the political arena through an overdetermined visibility in which recognizably black skin secured the nor-mative American citizen subject by providing it with an apparent outside, the Panthers transformed the terms of their appearance by intensifying those aspects of it that threatened State power.[23] They infused the black's imago (through which he is defined) with already legitimated and recognizable reservoirs for affective investment: guns, leather, berets. Calling attention to those natural (i.e., biological, genetic) characteristics through which the black is recognized, most notably his hair, the BPP's appearance (and that of the Black Power Movement more broadly) offered "pride" as the affect that characterized the party's present. By doing so, the BPP's appearance occa-sioned a transformation in the common sense through which the black was recognized. Without such a transformation of their appearance, the Panthers would not have been perceptible. Instead of rupturing the process of imag-ing through which the black appears, the BPP's appearance intensified it, demanding that the recognition of a black be a thinking-through of his nonidentity with the Black, not a habituated reinforcement of his essential inferiority. The BPP's appearance intensified the adversarial valence of the Black, reveling in its necessary status as image.

Revealing the precariousness of the State's claim to represent black peo-ple, the appearance of the Black as Black Panther signaled a profound crisis in the hegemonic construction of reality that secures consensus to State power. In the place of the State's insistence that the post-civil-rights present was the culmination of the Black's teleological progress toward national be-longing, the Panthers made visible a present, irreconcilable with that posited by the State, in which the State consistently oppressed and brutalized blacks. By calling the police "pigs," reciting U.S. laws in support of their actions, and assembling an alternative form of government—complete with their own minister of information, minister of defense, and so on—the Panthers turned the nation's gaze back onto itself as image. While the State asserted its own legitimacy and rationale for existence in the eyes of black people by presenting itself as the source and guarantor of social services and the public's welfare, the Panthers constructed an alternative reality, building schools and health clinics for black people and policing the police in black neighborhoods. The difference between the reality the Panthers constructed and that constructed by the State was rendered "undecideable"—each made a persuasive claim to the legitimacy of the reality they constructed. In addition, the Panthers revealed the State's narrative of the past to be "not necessarily true" by appearing and by simultaneously positing an alternative past of the Black. Criticizing the veracity underpinning the system of judgment through which the State maintained its hegemony, the appearance of the BPP ushered in a set of social, political, and ethical relations associated with "the powers of the false."

As a cinematic image, blacks with guns reveals the powers of the false that Deleuze attributes to the crystalline regime of the time-image. In the movement-image and its organic regime Deleuze identifies "the form of the true." Deleuze differentiates between the two regimes on several points, but his discussion of their differences in terms of narration allows one to understand how the Panthers' appearance threatened to erode the State's organic regime by replacing and superceding it with powers of the false.

The State the Panthers confronted insisted that a chronological time (which is the result of individual and/or collective actions) had culminated in the establishment of the State as the expression of those past actions. For example, the State continued to assert itself as the "representative" of "black people" by narrating the "success" of the civil rights movement and the elevation of the black to American citizen as the outcome of actions that recognized and validated the authority of State power (marching on Washington, boycotting public and private businesses, appealing to federal government requesting that state laws are overturned, etc.). Within this narrative, the black's struggle to achieve his rights, instead of directly revealing the State's inability to function according to its own claims to have been formed as that which upholds the equality of all men, simply reinforces the notion that the State operates according to the consensus of "the people." In the United States, the State's "sovereignty" relies upon its ability to present itself as the true representative of the people's capacity to produce it as sovereign.[24]

The people grant their consent to U.S. sovereignty on the condition that the State's narrative is "true." The State must insist, therefore, on the truthfulness of its narration of its own rise to sovereignty; it must present itself as sovereign because of its "organic" relationship to the people. Consent to U.S. sovereignty relies, at least in part, on the integrity of the State's "organic narration." Organic narration is "a truthful narration in the sense that it claims to be true, even in fiction."[25] Deleuze points out that organic narration belongs to the regime of the movement-image. This is not to say that the organic regime is not complex, only that it relies, in all its complexity, on a principle of chronological time that is dependent on movement. Chronological time posits one true past that has led to one true present that will lead to a true, if indeterminate, future. Its veracity relies upon a perception that operates according to a sensory-motor schema that is intact, calling forth common memory-images in order to recognize a present perception. Organic narration cannot tolerate contradictory presents or alternative pasts. It thus implies a "system of judgment" on which to adjudicate between dichotomous notions: good and bad, true and false, the Black and the White, and so on.[26]

Blacks with guns in the California state-legislature building posed "the simultaneity of incompossible presents" and "the coexistence of not-necessarily true pasts."[27] Blacks with guns thereby revealed that chronological time merely conceals a nonchronological time by presenting time only indirectly. Insofar as the past appears with each present, blacks with guns made visible a past of militant black resistance to American hegemony. Insofar as their appearance involved an assault on the regime that secured the State's version of reality, the Panthers posed a fundamental threat to the U.S. claim to sovereignty based on consensus.[28] In addition, because aspects of their appearance were recognizable as borrowed from the appearance of revolutionary groups in other parts of the world, the BPP challenged common sense to establish a set of correlations between the specific forms of racist exploitation practiced in the United States that had given rise to blacks with guns and the colonialist and imperialist forms of exploitation that occasioned the emergence of other revolutionary groups in different parts of the world.

In order to transform a black common sense that supported only nonviolent reformist demands for national inclusion into one capable of supporting the alternative socioeconomic arrangements that the Panthers strove to enact, the Panthers drew from the political philosophies that animated other struggles in different locales. Not only did they study, interpret, and put into practice the political theories of Fanon (a Martiniquan whose political writings focused on the Algerians' fight to liberate themselves from colonial rule) and Mao Tse-tung, they also adapted the visual iconography (notably, the military berets and rifles) of others struggling against capitalism, colonialism, and imperialism. Aspects of the Panthers' cinematic appearance thus were recognizable to those with access to the memory-images deposited by anticolonial struggles in Algeria, anticapitalist revolutionaries in Cuba, and anti-imperialist fighters in Vietnam, among others. These aspects tied the Panthers' appearance to that of others who similarly appeared to threaten and/or actually destroy aspects of the organic regime that then held colonialism or capitalism in place, and they added to the set of images commonly available to cinematic perception.

The transformation of common sense set in motion by the Panthers' cinematic appearance supported the chartering of party chapters around the world and the emergence of "global emulators of the Black Panther Party."[29] Many of the U.S. chapters ran free-breakfast-for-children programs. Some started schools. Some provided free sickle-cell-anemia screenings. Each of these programs constructed an alternative organization of sociality within working-class and poor black neighborhoods. Noting the success of the free-breakfast program, J. Edgar Hoover claimed that "the BPP is not engaged in the 'Breakfast for Children' program for humanitarian reasons, including their efforts to create an image of civility, assume community control of Negroes, and to fill adolescent children with their insidious poison" and he ordered San Francisco FBI agent Charles Bates to "initiate COINTELPRO actions designed to eradicate the [Panthers'] 'serve the people' programs."[30]

The common sense that supported the Panthers' actions, especially, but not exclusively, their sense of the necessity for caring for folks whose needs the United States had failed to meet, included a withdrawal of consent to the United States's claims to sovereignty. When consensus failed, the United States unleashed COINTELPRO, an extensive, brutally violent, and largely illegal covert operation to "disrupt, discredit, and destroy" the BPP. That the United States had to resort to brutality, murder, and other clandestine operations indicates the extent to which the BPP, and the Black Power Movement of which it was a part, succeeded in eroding black consensus to U.S. sovereignty.

Much of what was innovative, inventive, and therefore terrifying to Hoo-

78

ver about the common sense that maintained the alternative forms of sociality that the Panthers enacted, including its "serve the people" programs,
remains obscured by the Panthers' cinematic appearance as blacks with
guns. In order for the Panthers to be recognizable as black, their appearance
called forth visual markers of blackness: skin color, hair texture, and so on. In
order for them to link their struggle with others globally and appeal to the
"brothers on the block," they used their appearance to reinforce conventional markers of masculinity: guns, military berets, trousers, and leather
jackets, all of which were popularly recognized as masculine accoutrements.
Neither their markers of blackness nor their markers of masculinity challenged common sense to rethink its conception that it takes masculine tactics to effect political change. Nor did they necessitate thinking about liberation as anything other than a masculine or "macho" activity. The cinematic
appearance of the BPP left undisturbed the hegemonic common-sense notion that the struggle for liberation was a decidedly masculine enterprise.

The End of Silence

Historians and eyewitnesses agree that at least one biologically female Pan- 79
ther participated in the protest against the Mulford Bill. During the boom in
membership sparked by that protest, female participation in the BPP also
increased. By 1968, after the "Free Huey" campaign led to another rise in
party membership, females accounted for "approximately sixty percent of
the BPP's membership."[31] While it might be argued that female Panthers ran
the serve-the-people programs (later named the "survival programs") and
that such care-based labor has traditionally been performed by females, such
an argument cannot grasp the extent to which the masculine image of blacks
with guns was one in which the Black Revolutionary Woman recognized
herself.[32]

There are at least two published accounts of the way that the image of
Panthers with guns at the California state capitol led to the political activity of
individual black females.[33] A member of the Panther rank and file who
joined the party in 1968, Regina Jennings recalls that she did so in part
because she "respected their bold image." She briefly describes the context
within which she decided to apply for membership: "In 1968, still in my
teens, I took a late plane from Philadelphia to Oakland, California, to join the
Black Panther Party. As a runaway since the age of fifteen, a witness to vulgar

police brutality, and a victim of racism on my first job, I was ready to become a Panther. Their mystique—the black pants, leather jackets, berets, guns, and their talk—aggressive and direct—attracted me and thousands more across America."[34]

Speaking from a different socioeconomic situation than Jennings, Angela Davis claims that she "needed the appeal of the image of the leather-jacketed, black-bereted warriors standing with guns at the entrance to the California legislature." Davis continues, "That image, which would eventually become so problematic for me, called me home. And it directed me into an organizing frenzy in the streets of South Central Los Angeles."[35]

Both Jennings and Davis refer to the way that the BPP's cinematic appearance appealed to them or attracted them to the party. It is not clear whether Jennings's and Davis's reactions to the image of blacks with guns are representative of those of other black females at that time; it is nevertheless clear that that image had the capacity during the late sixties to attract "females," who expected "full-fledged membership," into the Black Power Movement and/or the Black Panther Party. Yet this same image has become incredibly problematic for feminists, even those who, like Davis, "needed" it as a catalyst for their political activism.

80

Rather than dismissing the image of blacks with guns as politically retrograde because macho or masculine and, therefore, necessarily exclusionary of black women, my argument is that for the Black Revolutionary Woman, the process of self-identification was predicated on the appearance of the Black as blacks with guns. As did Davis, other Black Revolutionary Women recognized themselves in that image and were "called . . . home."[36]

Feminist analyses of the ways that a political praxis based on gendering the Black has informed the struggle for emancipation and liberation have revealed an alternative past for that image recognizable as "black woman." Based on these analyses, I seek to illuminate a way of seeing blacks with guns as inclusive, not dependent on the exclusion of black women in the late sixties. This is so in part because hegemonic conceptualizations of femininity are not visible in the black woman as "natural" attributes; in the black woman femininity appears as either excessive or deficient. This particularity of the black woman's appearance (upon which her identity hinges) continues to inform the ways that she is positioned in the political arena and, especially, in relationship to black males.

As Hazel Carby and other feminist historians (primarily literary historians) have made clear, the slave's struggle for emancipation from slavery necessitated the articulation of the black slave into the category "human" through the extant discourse of gender.[37] Through recourse to the category "woman" and its effects and affects, most notably in regard to the properly emotional bond of "motherhood," female slaves demanded and argued for freedom. Working primarily within the affective registers of a moral argument about the female slave's womanhood, enslaved black females found the discourse of gender differentiation to be an invaluable vehicle through which to gain access to the category "human." For the enslaved black, male or female, arguing for his or her humanity as "man" or as "woman" provided a way of distinguishing between his or her self-articulation as properly human (because "man" or "woman") and the construction of the slave as subhuman (because "ungendered" as chattel).[38]

What quickly becomes apparent in the available historical narratives of the formation of "black woman" as a recognizable image is the extent to which gaining entry into the traditional American or Western discourse governing gender differentiation was simultaneously a historical necessity for emancipation from slavery and a strategy of assimilation into the United States's ethical and social institutions (e.g., "the family") that are charged with reproducing hegemonic relations.

81

The works that have led to these insights are invaluable contributions to our understanding of how "black women" has been consolidated as a category over time. For instance, Hortense Spillers's essay "Mama's Baby, Papa's Maybe" and Angela Davis's pioneering work in the essay "Reflections on the Black Woman's Role in the Community of Slaves" and in the book *Women, Race, and Class* can be understood as interventions into the official commonsense consolidation of "black woman" that accounts (at least partially) for the appearance of the Moynihan Report in the United States' official sociopolitical discourse in 1965. "The Negro Family: The Case for National Action," by Daniel Patrick Moynihan, is an important document for understanding the sociohistorical context in which Black Revolutionary Women became perceptible. Moynihan argues that the "tangle of pathology" leading to the "matriarchal structure" of the black community is a consequence of the particularities of American slavery. He also argues that the black woman is primarily responsible for the "tangle of pathology."[39] Because both Spillers and Davis assume, albeit critically, that accessing a more accurate portrayal and analysis of slavery and slave life will lead to a more satisfactory understanding of the black woman, posited by each as a temporally coherent category, it is important to remain critical of the ways that both Spillers and Davis access and narrate sheets of the past.

As my reframing of Fanon into a cinematic context suggests, the temporality of black identity is such that change is a constitutive element of a black's formation. The black woman, for her part, is certainly no more coherent over time than the Black; as cinematic images, both are vehicles through which invention might be introduced into existence at any-instant-whatever of the image's appearance. The force of Davis's and Spillers's contribution to our understanding of the black woman lies in each writer's endeavor to reshape her in an effort to disrupt her reification within hegemonic common sense.[40]

Seeking an alternative past for the black woman, Davis and Spillers effectively critique the prescription of the Moynihan Report that considers the black woman to be the ground on which to read the black community as pathological.[41] In other words, each works through the official common-sense reification of the-black-woman-as-matriarch-responsible-for-the-Black-community's-pathology by narrating the past according to the powers of the false while undermining hegemonic common sense's organization of both the domestic and the public spheres according to the patronymic. Working to render common-sense understandings of the black woman more critical, Davis and Spillers provide an account of that category's trajectory over time, uncovering several layers of thought about the black woman that existed as invisible sediment in hegemonic common senses prior to the excavations Davis and Spillers conduct.

Spillers uncovers the layer of sedimentation most relevant to my discussion here. In "Mama's Baby, Papa's Maybe" Spillers claims, "We might interpret the whole career of African-Americans, a decisive factor in national political life since the mid-seventeenth century, in light of the intervening, intruding tale, or the tale . . . 'between the lines,' which are already inscribed, as a metaphor of social and cultural management. According to this reading, gender, or sex-role assignation, or the clear differentiation of sexual stuff, sustained elsewhere in the culture, does not emerge for the African-American female in this historic instance, except indirectly."[42] Spillers illuminates the complex (and often contradictory) role that visible corporeal inscriptions of masculinity and femininity play in the production and maintenance of the white racial and masculine supremacy that variously underpins the modern subject according to the shifting demands of material conditions.[43]

In the context of Enlightenment thought, for instance, "masculinity" and "femininity" coalesce in the rhetoric of enlightened democratic citizenship which "worked to deny the gendered specificity that lay within its concept of a universal humanity" even as it posited as its proper arena, a public sphere "devoid of women" and governed by "intellect" and "rationality." Enlightened democratic citizenship rested upon "an underlying masculinist assumption" that was "as definitively raced as it was gendered."[44]

Much has been written about the various ways that, whenever they attempt to claim the rights and privileges accorded the masculine realm of citizenship, black males have been feminized, both discursively and corporeally, most markedly through castration, but also through other modes of violence which intensify the relationship between the black male and his body, thereby reserving the masculine privilege of disembodied subjectivity for white men.[45] While it is certainly important to differentiate between the ascription of femininity onto anatomically male bodies and the "historical framework of the feminine as part and parcel of being born female," it is crucial to realize that black females' entry into the feminine is marked over time by struggles to "reconstruct womanhood" in a way that could accommodate visibly black and female bodies.[46] Whatever social, political, or economic benefits might accrue to the feminine (such as the way that femininity can function as a commodity with which a [usually white] "woman" might negotiate to marry a wealthy man) have not been widely accessible to the majority of black women because such benefits tend to be available to women in the middle to upper classes who do not have to venture outside their homes to work or who only do so by choice, not financial necessity.

Moreover, as my discussion of Fanon shows, the Black is "overdetermined from without," most often appearing only according to the common sense retained by an eye from the black's imago. For the black woman, such a visual overdetermination precludes her access to femininity insofar as it exists only as "private functions of the woman" that ought to be "scrupulously withheld from public view."[47] To the extent that the Black designates an identity always already predicated within public view and that the public view operates according to a cinematic perception that corresponds to a conception of the world that relies upon "black" to collect whatever is evil, bestial, ugly, and irrational, "denigrated femininity" is the only valence of

83

femininity that can accrue to the black body and be made visible under accessible extant versions of common sense.

The sedimentation of notions of femininity into common sense over time, therefore, has tended toward the exclusion of its accrual to black female bodies. It cannot be assumed that "black woman" appears within the dictates of "femininity," even though common sense posits a relationship between the female body and femininity that often is organized through the category "woman."

By the time the BPP appeared, femininity had not accrued in a substantial way to black bodies except in denigrated forms.[48] Within the common sense forming in and informing the Black Power era, the effort to reverse the feminization, both discursive and corporeal, of black males in order to further the argument for their humanity involved a strict repudiation of any connection between femininity and the emergent understanding of blackness. By setting forth a masculine image adequate to the task of making visible and contesting the grounds for the exclusion of the black from the realm of full citizenship, the Black Panthers played a significant role in the common-sense reversal of the denigrating feminization of the black.

84 The Panthers challenged the construction of the normative citizen subject by intensifying those aspects of the black that had been consolidated as that subject's negative or outside in order to secure the propertied white male (later, female) as normative American subject entitled to the rights and protections of the sovereign State. One of the ways the Panthers achieved this was by resignifying blackness as a "masculine" (associated with guns and violence) threat on a par with other efforts toward national liberation, including those undertaken by "the Founding Fathers" who penned the Declaration of Independence of the United States of America.[49] Moreover, in a simple reversal, the Panthers presented femininity as antithetical to Black Liberation, being the province of whites (as in Eldridge Cleaver's *Soul on Ice* and some of Huey Newton's earlier published writing), and/or as an attempt by black women to become "bourgeois" by claiming a form of femininity that, unlike blackness, could and must remain hidden from public view and thereby distancing themselves from "the black people." While the Panthers' praxis effectively revealed and critiqued the complicity of femininity and the forms of sociality that enabled the racist exploitation of black bodies, it did not attend to the destruction of femininity's dichotomous counterpart, masculinity, with the same vigor. Masculinity and its affectations and accoutre-

ments appear as the terms adequate to Black Liberation. Other accessible aspects of the Black, especially his intimate relationship to femininity because of his close association with corporeality, would not have registered as revolutionary or as carrying the potential to liberate a people from the common sense in and against which the Panthers were working. Death, brutalization, and physical violation—acts that previously had inscribed femininity onto the black—were overwritten into heroism and "dying for the people."

The BPP's emphasis on masculinity is understood best within the context of a historical narrative of how the official common sense that was retained from a habituated recognition of a black prior to the mid-1960s had come to carry (to varying degrees depending upon the specific spatiotemporal coordinates within which a black appeared) a "denigrated femininity" that worked in tandem with a shared conception of blackness in order to garner consensus to the formation of a citizenry and an "American" public sphere that was masculine and white (and therefore rational, human, and so on). The BPP's claim to masculinity was part of a claim to the public sphere, to the apparatus of governance, and to the rights accorded to a citizen of the sovereign United States, including the constitutional rights to bear arms, to life, and to liberty. In this respect, even though the Panthers' appearance cannot be separated from that of other anticolonial and anti-imperial organizations globally, the terms within which they were able to appear and the extent to which that appearance was able to unsettle the organic regime of the U.S. State derived from the currency of a specific strand of American common sense that continues to secure consent to the United States's claim to sovereignty—namely, the widely held sense that "all men are created equal."

Relying upon the currency of the United States's insistence that all men are created equal, the appearance of the BPP allowed for the recognition of the black man in the Black. But this need not be understood as precluding black "females" from appearing in blacks with guns, nor does it necessarily indicate an inherent connection between "men" and "males." What is perhaps most innovative about the BPP's cinematic appearance is that it threw into doubt the validity of the common sense that linked "man" with "male" with "masculine," if only for that any-instant-whatever in which one stared in amazement while the Panthers appeared. During that any-instant-whatever, the powers of the false superceded the form of the true that had granted gender its legibility. The powers of the false opened possibilities for alternative socioeconomic arrangements between males and females based on the equality presumed to exist (or that the Panthers argued should exist) between men.

The lyrics to Elaine Brown's song "The End of Silence," published in the BPP newspaper as "A Black Panther Song," indicate that "men" might be understood in the context of BPP rhetoric as a category that includes both males and females. Brown, who later became chairman of the BPP while Newton was in exile in Cuba, recorded "The End of Silence" on an album entitled *Seize the Time*, which was sold as a fundraiser for the party.

> Have you ever stood
> In the darkness of night
> Screaming silently you're a man?
> Have you ever hoped
> that time would come
> When your voice could be heard
> In the noonday sun?
> Have you waited so long
> Till your unheard song
> Has stripped away your very soul?
> Well then believe it my friends
> That the silence will end
> We'll just have to get guns and
> be men.[50]

The addressee(s) of "The End of Silence" need not be male. In addition to the line "screaming silently you're a man," gendered references to the addressee appear later in the song, including

> You know that dignity
> not just equality
> is what makes a man a man

and in the last verse, which states,

> You been burning inside
> for so long a while
> 'Til your old-time grin
> is now a crazed-man's smile.

Each reference to "man" is in the abstract, except in the last stanza, where "old-time grin" and "crazed-man's smile" serve as metaphors that are descriptive of modes of being black. "Old-time grin" connotes a docile Uncle Tom figure and attitude, while "crazed-man's smile" calls for the "bad man" or the "crazy nigger," neither of which are particularly political designations. While it is true that each of these modes of being black can be understood as masculine, the fact that "being a man" needs to be achieved by the song's addressees suggests that they are not already men according to how that term is used in Brown's song. Man in the abstract is the "man" referenced throughout the song. Disembodied man, the citizen-subject, is accorded "dignity / not just equality," and it is he who holds the potential to be heard, ending the silence.[51]

The designation "man," as it is used in "The End of Silence," is associated with masculinity, but it is a future designation that indexes a disembodied citizen-subject, and thus it has not yet been attached to specific bodies. Instead of reading the "we" as self-effacing, necessarily exclusionary of black women, I understand it as an inclusive invitation to a pregendered or "differently gendered" addressee to join Brown—a speaker who could be either male or female in the lyrics, but a voice that is recognizably "female" on the album—in getting guns and being men.[52] Brown's invitation insists on the equality of all Panthers who believe, according to the October 1966 Black Panther Party Platform and Program, that all men are created equal.

For many black feminists, the BPP's focus on revealing masculinity in the black has "become so problematic," to use the phrase Davis employs in reference to the image of blacks with guns that "called her home," because such masculinity reinscribes the sexism connected with the attribution of masculinity to those spheres devoid of women. Yet, for Davis, the masculinity of the Black Power Movement became problematic only in retrospect, as that masculinity became or was revealed to be consistent with, not oppositional to, hegemonic forms of sexism.

When blacks with guns appeared, in many of the hegemonic common senses that perceived it masculinity belonged to neither black male bodies nor black female bodies. Those common senses did not call forth femininity as an accessible or potentially revolutionary characteristic of the black. It has been the work of black feminism since the sixties to provide a critique of the way that black masculinity encourages and incites deleterious effects on the bodies and lives of those who are visibly female or feminine. Such analyses were not widely available at the time of the BPP's appearance, however, so my argument—that black females recognized themselves in the masculine image of blacks with guns even when that image was composed primarily of

87

recognizably black male bodies—is not a contestation of black feminist analysis since the sixties, but a caveat against uncritically deploying its historically specific critiques as though they were true in all times. The black common sense forming in and informing the historical conjuncture referred to as "the sixties" rendered Black Revolutionary Women visible in the masculine image of blacks with guns. In other words, the cinematic appearance of Black Revolutionary Woman was masculine.

The appearance of the Black as blacks with guns, while masculine, was not exclusively male. Indeed, the Panthers' was an increasingly female struggle which led to important attempts to transform "Panther common sense."[53] To claim that the image of blacks with guns was exclusive of females is to uphold the hegemonic notion that masculinity is the form of gender expression proper to males. In addition, any analysis of the cinematic appearance of blacks with guns that reifies the common sense that makes bodies visible as either male or female misses the opportunity to perceive the alternative forms of bodily expression (not reducible to binary conceptualizations of gender) available in that appearance.

The masculine appearance of Black Revolutionary Women provided a highly unstable appearance of black women. Yet it contributed to the appearance (to a cinematic perception operating according to official Western common senses) of a global re-membering of the world according to the powers of the false in ways that, at least initially, confronted hegemonic assignations of gender characteristics according to anatomical characteristics. It challenged common senses to enable cinematic perception to recognize masculinity in the black, the black in the Black Panther, and (for a time, anyway) the Black Revolutionary Woman in the masculine Black Panther.

No less than the organic regime, however, the crystalline regime of the powers of the false, as Deleuze indicates, "throws up its ready-made formulas, its set procedures, its laboured and empty applications, its failures, its conventional and 'second-hand' examples offered to us as masterpieces."[54] In the arena of cinematic appearances, the tendency of every cinematic image is to shrink into cliché, a state of enslavement to the past. An internal threat to the innovations possible in the regime of the time-image, cliché subordinates time to movement, thereby obfuscating the powers of the false and their ability to reveal a new element in a present perception. The appearance of Black Revolutionary Women on television, a medium that remains instrumental in the global re-membering of the world, ensnared that appearance within the contradictory procedures of television's temporality. We can understand television's temporality to be chained to television's insistence on its own "liveness" and to the constraints of a bidirectional pull toward the still and the automatic. Yet it is also (importantly) a temporality that remains open because it is shot through with the operations of "switching."

The Revolution Will (Not) Be Televised

By 1955, the year of the bus boycott in Montgomery, Alabama—a protest that for many historians marks the beginning of the contemporary civil rights movement—more than half of all homes in the United States had installed a television set.[55] The five years preceding the Montgomery bus boycott witnessed the rise of nonviolent direct-action tactics aimed at dismantling color-based segregation in the southern United States. In 1953 blacks in Baton Rouge, Louisiana, also boycotted buses, and blacks in Wichita, Kansas, sat in at lunch counters. The proliferation of television sets directly corresponds to the increase in participation in nonviolent direct-action protests intended to secure civil rights for black American citizens.[56] Sasha Torres, in her astute analysis of the relationship between television and the black civil rights movement, describes a striking historical coincidence: "the simultaneous rise of the southern civil rights movement in the wake of the Montgomery Bus Boycott and of television news as an authoritative force in American public life."[57]

This historical "coincidence" might be considered as further evidence of the significance of another "coincidence," namely, that of the invention of film around the same time as Du Bois's prophetic pronouncement that "the problem of the twentieth century is the problem of the color line," which points to a fundamental convergence between black identity, processes of hegemony, and cinema that coalesces around questions that theorists and critics of black political culture have framed in terms of representation. Cinema's propensity to put into circulation images that dissimulate political proxies not only remains intact with the coming of television, but television claims for itself the capability of providing an instantaneous, "live" image that film cannot offer, thereby intensifying claims to and calls for "accurate representations." Similarly, the black civil rights movement's need to transform national culture so that it might be generative of a national consensus regarding racial equality was imbricated with telejournalism's need to gener-

89

ate a national consensus regarding "the race problem" that would support "television's self-constitution as a properly national form addressing an audience assumed to share certain core ideological assumptions about the privileges of citizenship and the rule of law," so that it might sell that audience to advertisers.[58] The early convergence of the interests of black civil-rights activists with those of telejournalists reveals that an intimate relationship existed between the civil rights movement's reformist politics, which was predicated on a visible, often mediated, deployment of racial difference and black identity calculated to generate a national consensus on the immorality of racist violence and oppression, and television's claims to a privileged relationship to liveness. The relationship between the visibility politics on which the civil rights movement relies and television's claims to liveness hinges on the commonalities between the temporal operations each executes.

Drawing on José Muñoz's insights regarding the extent to which "the story of 'otherness' is one tainted by a mandate to perform for the amusement of a dominant power bloc," a mandate Muñoz characterizes as the "burden of liveness that inflects the experience of postcolonial, queer, and other minoritarian subjects," Torres points out that "it's not enough for television to *be* live: the medium needs to represent 'authentic' persons of color, stockpiling their liveness to be borrowed back in times of political or representational crisis."[59] The civil rights movement, as Torres compellingly argues, took up the "burden of liveness—of producing televisual immediacy via black performances of physical suffering and political demand" and made it a "primary focus of the movement and a crucial key to its success."[60] Though evocative of a different moral register than the silently suffering black bodies battered by fire hoses that characterized the informational liveness of the civil rights movement, the Panthers' spectacular protest of the Mulford Bill also fed into and relied upon television's emergent structural reliance on liveness and, hence, on televisual time, a time Richard Dienst has characterized as "the infinitesimal fissuring of an interminable present."[61]

Dienst proposes that "time moves in two directions on television, toward the still and toward the automatic."[62] These temporal vectors are not the same as those circumscribing film. Yet they are consistent with the workings of the cinematic insofar as they can be understood to be integral to the institutionalization of the deterritorializing possibilities of the time-image, possibilities tenuously contained by and within the electronic time-image. For if "television produces a time-image the moment it has been turned on," as Dienst asserts, then one might understand television to be another "organ for perfecting" cinematic reality, working to assimilate into existing hegemonies the very image regime that film reveals provides a mechanism for thinking differently from the logics that uphold those hegemonies.[63] With television, the possibilities for something different to emerge within a present perception, possibilities that Deleuze locates within film's time-image, become dispersed, "lofted in the world's atmosphere and running circles around earthly existence," but they also tenuously are harnessed and directed to serve "the political and economic concentrations of power that make television possible."[64] Television strives to socialize the time-image.

According to Dienst's analysis, the time-image television makes visible, as cliché or hegemonic common senses, contains socialized time, which is already valorized in advance. Television wrenches the capacity for thinking from the time-image, striving to delimit in advance what "time" appears on television and to limit, according to television's drive toward profit, what can appear as the needs and interests of living beings. Protesting the Mulford Bill while bulbs were flashing all over the place, the Panthers as blacks with guns were caught in a mode of temporality that thrived on a production of a sense of liveness. Caught in the modalities of televisual time, the Panthers' cinematic appearance became a point wherein occurred a transduction of value necessary for the reproduction of capitalist social relations. With the appearance of the BPP on television, the Black is preserved as criminal, militant, dispossessed, violent, and so on, thereby providing one of the formulations necessary to maintain a white supremacy that incorporates a few black faces.

An integral component in the transduction of value effected by the televisual operations that enabled the broad circulation of blacks with guns was the delineation of "gender characteristics" according to the apparent anatomy of one's body and the insistence that there exist only two genders. That one does not see the Black Revolutionary Woman in the image of blacks with guns now does not mean that she did not appear there or that she somehow was not there. Nor does it necessarily mean that her being there was a result of some form of "false consciousness" or self-effacement.[65] What it means is that her cinematic appearance was inconsistent with those recognizable gender markers through which "black woman" habitually is articulated and recognized. Even as the value attributed to blackness changed form and even though "the black family" remained a stubbornly defiant arrangement to assimilate into the American middle-class model of sociality, those hege-

monic gender markers were preserved because they supported the formation of the heterosexual nuclear family. That family is the principle social
arrangement through which capitalist relations were—and are—reproduced.

"My Name Is Peaches"

The appearance of the Black Revolutionary Woman in blacks with guns was
thus a highly unstable appearance of the black woman.[66] While it motivated
black women to join the movement, it also initially provided the grounds for
their limited participation and an alibi for the sexism of Panther men. Today
one receives this image in a different manner than that in which it was
received in 1967. This is so in part because the transduction of the value of
blackness achieved in the late 1960s maintained hegemonic gender relations through which capitalistic sociality was reproduced, but also because of
the pioneering work of "black feminists" who pointed out the extent to which
the masculine appearance of blacks with guns upheld instead of challenged
hegemonic notions of masculinity that enabled the perpetuation of sexism.

In 1967 the presence of women in the masculine space of struggle expressed by the Black Panthers posed a profound challenge to the constitution of the normative citizen-subject insofar as that subject was constructed
through a highly differentiated system of gender inscriptions within which
the feminine accrued to female bodies and the masculine to male. Indeed,
the appearance of Black Revolutionary Women laid the groundwork for the
appearance of a subjectivity capable of challenging forms of sexism, racism,
and homophobia, and one in which gender affectations and distinctions,
such as masculinity and femininity, need not be predicated on a binary opposition between anatomically different bodies, of which there are thought to
be only two varieties: male and female. The appearance of such a subjectivity
would signal a transformation in common sense and cause its further reorganization, either opening itself for new creation or, conversely, unleashing
the violence necessary to maintain the hegemony of gender distinctions.

As the writings by Panther women in *The Black Panther* suggest, black
females and black males did not have equal access to the hegemonic abstrac-
tion "men" even as the "revolutionary" public appearance of both was conditioned by and visible through the masculine. This situation gave rise to a
sustained effort on the part of Panthers to articulate a system of gender
differentiation that would be more consistent with their commonly held

92

sense that masculinity and femininity must coexist. The system they devise is rooted in bourgeois common sense and evinces the violence deployed to pummel Black Revolutionary Women into a form of femininity that functioned according to the strictures of an erotic economy of "black bodies" differentiated according to recognizable anatomical characteristics and accordingly endowed with attributes thought to be proper to those bodies.

As the Panther historian Tracye Matthews explains, the writings by women in *The Black Panther* focus on defining the Black Revolutionary Woman in relationship to the Black Man. Illuminating the extent to which black women were perceived to occupy (at least potentially) the position of man is the fact that, in her "five point inventory" of what a black woman must do to better aid the struggle, the Black Panther Gloria Bartholomew states that the black woman must "stop playing the role of a man, and take [her] place beside [her] man."[67] In an effort to transform the aspects of official common sense evidenced by the Moynihan Report into the means for a more critical way of thinking about black women, Bartholomew's fellow female Panther Linda Greene argues that in addition to being "a worker" and "a mother," the revolutionary woman is "militant, revolutionary, committed, strong, and warm, feminine, loving, and kind." Greene insists that "these qualities are not the antithesis of each other; they must all be her simultaneously."[68]

The force of such efforts is toward the adjudication of what is commonsensically understood as the "public" versus the "private" appearance and function of black women. The Black Revolutionary Woman's appearance as masculine breaks down when it enters the so-called private realm of interpersonal relationships with black men, particularly when the terms of those relationships are calibrated to support the domestic realm created through heterosexual arrangements. Within black common sense, the "masculine Black woman" had been sexualized and presented as a "bulldagger," a pejorative designation for an "unattractive" woman who was sexually unavailable to men and who was to be deplored.[69] The specter of the bulldagger nestled within the Black Revolutionary Woman provides the rationalization for the articulation of the ways in which the Black Revolutionary Woman must be feminine in relation to the Black Man.[70] Such an ascription of femininity is in keeping with its construction as a private function of the woman, a traditionally middle-class hegemonic arrangement of gender difference with roots in the Victorian era.

Ultimately, the refusal of the masculine female or "bulldagger" in the

93

image Black Revolutionary Woman leads to policing black women according to their sexuality, often reducing them to that sexuality or to obsessively demonstrating their heterosexuality. As black cultural feminists, including Michelle Wallace, have argued, black males' claim to manhood via an aggressive masculinity has been won often through the physical and psychic violation of black females, and always with violence leveled at "black women." Joy James notes that "the issue of female abuse and battery by male leaders and the rank and file in the Black Panther Party, led by Newton and Eldridge Cleaver before the split, and its rival organization Us, headed by Maulana (Ron) Karenga, remains somewhat of a taboo among African Americans."[71] Indeed, the violence leveled against women in the BPP coupled with the perception of its inevitability precluded or discouraged the participation of females such as Barbara Smith who later would become part of the Combahee River Collective, a joint effort to articulate and enact a compelling critique of the interrelations between homophobia, sexism, and racism.[72] The masculine appearance of Black Revolutionary Women was, in effect, the appearance of black women presumed to be heterosexual and sexually available to black males, a group whose claim to "manhood" was exclusive of black females.

94

That the violence involved in achieving and maintaining masculinity often is funneled through acts and discourses of sex and sexuality is the primary concern of the next chapter in which I inquire into the consolidation of masculinity and femininity in Pam Grier's early blaxploitation films. The inability of lesbian sexuality to appear in Black Revolutionary Women, despite Black Revolutionary Women's "masculine" appearance, provides both a subtext and a rationale for physical acts of violence against black women in the name of a black liberation that became an alibi for a black masculinity carefully policed according to one's anatomy. Furthermore, the homophobic rejection of the masculine female by the Black Revolutionary Woman sanctions the erasure of the contributions of black women from the popular history of "the movement" as organized by and through the masculine cinematic appearance of the Black as blacks with guns.[73]

Even as it offers a forceful form though which to make a spectacle of the state, helping to usher in the powers of the false and laying the groundwork for a new appearance of the Black, the BPP's unchallenged acceptance of the masculine as the realm within which and the form through which Black Liberation must be won marks a crucial point of consensus with hegemonic common senses.[74]

"A Black Belt in Bar Stool"

Blaxploitation, Surplus, and *The L Word*

The cinematic appearance of Black Revolutionary Women, like all cinematic appearances, was available to become part of the way that value is consolidated by various strains of common sense. In order to be perceptible, an image must be recognizable to some degree according to "official" conceptions of the world. The more a present perception is capable of being recognized according to habit—that is, the greater a present image's ability to conform to preexisting conceptions of the world—the easier it is for that image to become a component involved in the reproduction, dissemination, and maintenance of official common sense. The appearance of Black Revolutionary Women was tenuous because it posed a challenge to the habitual recognition of "black woman." Yet, instead of calling forth a sustainable perception of a black in which hegemonic gender categories do not inhere, it occasioned a violent reterritorialization of black woman according to extant edicts of gender (i.e., a "woman" must appear to be "female" and exhibit "feminine" characteristics, including being sexually available to "men"). Like every cinematic appearance, Black Revolutionary Women could appear only with the active participation of cinematic machines, living and/or technological. Living cinematic machines, the Black Panthers, participated in pummeling the appearance of Black Revolutionary Women into an understanding of black woman that enables the re-production of a properly heterosexual sociality.

The processes particular to television participated in ensuring that the appearance of blacks with guns occasioned not a rupture in or a transvaluation of the official common sense apparent in the Black, but merely a transduction of the value (however "negative" it is judged to be) that the Black must carry in order to help rationalize a society in which white supremacy and bourgeois culture are inseparable. On television, the appearance of blacks with guns was distilled into an imago of the Black that has secured the official perception of blacks today, especially of "black males," as violent and crimi-

5 | *"O-o-h Child"*

nal. Television relies for its legibility on its tenuous ability to put into circulation images of official common sense. With regard to Pam Grier's blaxploitation films and their relationship to her more recent role in the Showtime
series *The L Word*, it is interesting to note the extent to which the invention
of television—a technological cinematic machine that exploits the same perceptual processes that living beings employ in order to interact with other
images—has contributed to sustaining the current situation wherein any
cinematic appearance already is caught up in the processes employed in the
transduction of value indispensable to the maintenance of consent to bourgeois U.S. common sense, that is, "official" common sense.

Images of Value

Retaining from an image's appearance that which serves their interests,
technological cinematic machines function to make common their spectators' sense(s), "producing value and reproducing social relations along the
way."[1] In order to produce value, technological cinematic machines draw on
the affective labor of their spectators. According to Marcia Landy, this form of
labor power, affectivity, is "a form of labor expended in the consumption of
cinematic images, in the enterprise of voluntarily offering up our lives 'as
free contributions to capitalist power.' "[2] I further elaborate Landy's definition, following the direction to which her work points, in order to argue that
blaxploitation, far from being a misnomer or a regrettable diversion from the
progressive history of blacks in American film, signals an intensification
(arising out of a specific sociohistorical political formation) of the exploitation via affectivity (already a function of cinematic machines) of an audience
(market) presumed to consist of "black people." While technological cinematic machines allow for this form of exploitation to become perceptible,
even though in many cases they frame images capable of rapid circulation,
the exploitation to which I refer is inherent in every cinematic appearance,
not only those selected, cut, and framed by technological cinematic machines. In this respect, affectivity has become less a "voluntary" contribution
to capitalist power, as in Landy's more specific formulation of it, than a form
of labor expended in order to reproduce sociality under capitalism. Affectivity is a type of labor that is increasingly necessary to survival; as such, it is a
type of labor that produces and maintains forms of social life—it is, therefore,
biopolitical.

My understanding of biopower and of biopolitical production has been

96

influenced by that of Michael Hardt and Antonio Negri. In their coauthored book, *Empire*, Hardt and Negri develop Foucault's and Deleuze's separate but related insights into the set of transformations in the organization of power characteristic of what they refer to as "a historical, epochal passage in social forms from disciplinary society to the society of control."[3] Hardt and Negri identify biopower, which they define as "a form of power that regulates social life from its interior, following it, interpreting it, absorbing it, and rearticulating it," as that form of power characteristic of the society of control.[4] In my formulation of affectivity I strive to be consistent with an analysis of the dominance of biopolitical production in contemporary societies in the overdeveloped world. I offer this formulation as a way of assessing how the ascent of cinematic processes is part of the consolidation of biopower and, hence, how analyses of cinematic processes and cinematic media might be important components in any assessment of the biopolitics of globalization.[5]

In her discussion of affectivity, Landy points out: "Often dissociated from obvious forms of work identified with and measured in terms of time expended in the factory, the office, and other workplaces, the labor time invested in the consumption of cultural narratives, images, and sounds is a necessary labor in the maintenance of social life under capitalism."[6] Landy's formulation draws attention to the way that a discussion of the cinematic necessitates rethinking the socioeconomic dynamics of the "work day" in overdeveloped countries. Calling attention to the way that affectivity is a "necessary labor" that is at the same time productive for capital, Landy's formulation points to the growing obsolescence (in the context of the contemporary situation in overdeveloped countries) of traditional conceptions of "labor" and "work time."

In the overdeveloped world, the work day Karl Marx described, in which a worker toils a portion of the day in order to reproduce himself as worker (necessary labor) and the rest of the day in order to realize surplus value for the capitalist (surplus labor), has been extended through various means, including the circulation of images through cinematic processes, so that "non-work time becomes subject to the same kinds of antagonisms that cut across labor time."[7] Capital thus succeeds in continuing to realize surplus value by increasing the productive capacity of "living labor," expanding the realm of "work" to include so-called leisure activities, thereby minimizing the degree of difference between necessary labor and surplus labor while failing to abolish the limits that necessary labor poses to the expansion of capital.[8] The circulation of money, labor, and commodities, including films, via processes of exchange gives rise to forms of socially necessary labor, a category that designates labor expended in the reproduction of social life under capitalism. As a type of socially necessary labor, affective labor is involved in the production and reproduction of social reality according to local and/or official common sense(s). It participates in the untidy processes of consensus that enable existing modes of domination and exploitation. While circulation itself does not produce surplus value, it nevertheless enables capital to produce it via socially necessary labor at any instant whatever in capital's circulation. The production of surplus value is thus co-extensive with the value produced via socially necessary labor.

As "a form of labor expended in the consumption of cinematic images in the enterprise of . . . offering up our lives as free contributions to capitalist power," affectivity is perceptible only within a context of global circulation because it indicates a level of social capital possible only through such broad circulation. At any point whatever in the circulation process, surplus value can be produced. Affectivity constitutes one productive point in the circulation process of cinematic images; what it produces most often (when it reacts to images according to a habituated sensory-motor apparatus) are images of value in process, that is, hegemonic or official common senses. Yet even official common sense is multivalent and responsive to challenges posed to it and innovations arising from within it. It is not a mode of unilateral command, but the outcome of local negotiations between groups struggling for hegemony.

Under these conditions, socially necessary labor such as affectivity opens at once onto at least three dimensions of valorization, each of which carries as its condition of possibility the exploitative relationship that gives rise to capital. In one dimension, affectivity entails the (re)production of sociocultural value as one of the forms of surplus value necessary to support capital's drive to amass wealth; it therefore can enable capital's drive toward self-valorization to continue its movement in circulation by producing surplus sociocultural value. This is clear in the context of the reception of Hollywood images. When employed by a Hollywood film, though affectivity often (re)produces cultural value via investments in social forms and ideas that serve to solidify and sustain the categories and institutions that today enable and support the reproduction of capitalism, such as race, family, religion, heterosexuality, and the law, it is capable as well of undermining the logic that supports such institutions.[9]

The first dimension of valorization based on affectivity therefore always carries a second which constantly threatens to explode the first process from within. At any instant whatever in the production of sociocultural value for the valorization of capital, capital's ability to direct affectivity into the maintenance of the already existing categories of socioeconomic relations might be overwhelmed by the impact of a present perception on a living image (affect). Having discussed this possibility in terms of a present perception's ability to jam the sensory-motor apparatus's capacity to recognize it according to habit, I now consider this dimension of valorization under a rubric adapted from Roderick A. Ferguson—"the multiplications of surplus."[10]

On the third plane of valorization onto which affectivity might open, affectivity produces images of the antagonistic relations characteristic of the production of value itself. In this case, what appears remains an image of value in process, but it is an image of value that has been diverted from the process of its own constitution to the extent that it yields something of the conditions of its production as an image of value. The appearance of blacks with guns marks one such instant in the production of the Black as an image of official common sense. When that image appears, the organic regime that consolidated the Black according to an official common sense crumbles under the affectivity required to make sense of that image, revealing that the Black appears according to the powers of the false and that the insistence upon recognizing the Black according to the form of the true entails violently constricting affectivity's capacities to excavate what official common sense conspires to hide in a present perception or to punch holes in what such common sense insists upon.[11] Images that solicit an affectivity that breaks out of the constrictions imposed upon it by the regime of the true circulate more slowly because their production as images of value requires more affective labor time.

Like all productive labor, affectivity can be considered in temporal terms. The chronological, measurable time upon which movement insists imposes itself upon affectivity by establishing connections between the sensory and the motor mechanisms of the affected living image. The rapid circulation of cinematic images seeks to keep this temporal schema intact so as to reduce affective labor time, thereby increasing surplus labor time and, hence, surplus value. Yet squeezing affective labor time eventually leads to diminishing returns, and something different must be introduced in order to reaccelerate the rate at which the production of cultural values supports the generation of

99

profit, even if that means an initial increase in affective labor time (i.e., the recognition of something different or the appearance of something previously hidden in the image that must occur in order to continue movement is forced to take place within "the hidden ground of time," the nonchronological time that has become visible in the image).

This cycle is what occurred with the appearance of Black Revolutionary Women as blacks with guns. In order to be elaborated into forms capable of sustaining organizations of sociality different from those that continue the movements necessary to life under capitalism, the nonchronological time revealed in the appearance of Black Revolutionary Women required for its sustenance an immeasurable labor time, far more, or different, than what the Panthers were able to wrest away from the capitalists in power. The state-sanctioned violence and FBI-orchestrated internal divisions unleashed by COINTELPRO, coupled with the official installation into Panther common sense of expedient hegemonic conceptualizations of "man," "woman," "masculinity," and "femininity," ensured that the affective labor time required to produce new or, at least, different values concerning gender relations that would be antagonistic to capitalism and white supremacy was not available.

100

That affectivity might produce unpredictable sociocultural values when "consuming" a present perception does not mean that the relationship of exploitation fundamental to the production of value is nullified or lessened, but it does point to the creative capacity of affectivity and to affectivity's ability to reroute value toward the consolidation of a different (capitalist) project requiring a different structure of (capitalist) command. Yet, because it is not only an activity engaged in the pursuit of pleasure and entertainment (as when watching a film or television show) but also a form of labor that helps to ensure one's survival when confronted with a present image (such as a car turning its lights off before speeding up in front of your house), affectivity remains vulnerable to processes of habituation, adopted in the name of survival, that require it to function in the interests of the current hegemony.

Blaxploitation and Common-Sense Black Nationalism

Extracting surplus sociocultural value from affectivity, blaxploitation merely intensifies the process of exploitation inherent in every cinematic appearance. The blaxploitation phenomenon was made possible during the late

1960s by the Hollywood film industry's need to adjust to a changing global socioeconomic terrain and by the innovations set in motion by Black Power. Blaxploitation films emerged at a time when the American film industry was undergoing a fundamental reorganization that had precipitated a financial crisis and when the sociopolitical, economic, and cultural terrain of the United States was in the midst of one of its most chaotic reformations.[12] These films worked to keep the film industry afloat during its financial crisis and to enable the socioeconomic reformation of American political culture to proceed more smoothly, even though they certainly did not achieve either of these feats alone.

A term coined by the entertainment-industry trade journal *Variety*, "blaxploitation" refers to "exploitation films" made between 1970 and 1975 that belong to the "Black Action Film" genre.[13] Most accounts of the emergence of blaxploitation films note that the black sociopolitical movements of "the 1960s" played a role in demanding more and better representations of black people in Hollywood films. The specificity of the social terrain out of which blaxploitation appeared continues to affect the circulation and popularity of such films. Indeed, "blaxploitation" now is linked so closely to "Black Power" that aspects of its iconography often stand in for the less widely circulated conceptions of the world that contended for hegemony under the rubric of "Black Power." Blaxploitation played a profoundly important role in adjudicating between a range of political positions vying for recognition as Black Power during the late 1960s and early 1970s and in presenting their resolution in the form of common-sense black nationalism. Insofar as Black Power arose as a political movement within which a critical and coherent conception of the world elaborated from the viable nuggets of what Gramsci referred to as "good sense" within black nationalism might have been worked out, blaxploitation is one way of mediating that process. By encouraging the articulation of Black Power to proceed according to those strictures of common-sense black nationalism which lent consent to U.S. white bourgeois sociality, blaxploitation forestalled the elaboration of the kernel of good sense in common-sense black nationalism.

Framed in this way, blaxploitation can be understood as a generic reformation of common-sense black nationalism that seeks to cut, select, and circulate images of value-in-process capable of a broad circulation. Melvin Van Peebles's *Sweet Sweetback's Baadasssss Song* (1970) is credited with having established that there is a large, black teenage audience for films that feature a "macho black hero."[14] *Sweet Sweetback* generally is recognized as the film that proved the strength of the black box office to Hollywood, thereby ushering in a roughly five-year period of cheaply made feature films with predominately black casts. *Sweet Sweetback* itself was shot in less than three weeks and cost $500,000 to make. By the end of 1970, the film had grossed $10 million dollars nationwide. Based on the success of *Sweet Sweetback*, the distribution strategies for many blaxploitation films limited the films' releases to urban theaters selected for their accessibility to this young, urban, black audience.[15]

Gordon Parks's 1971 film *Shaft* and Gordon Parks Jr.'s 1972 *Super Fly* are widely recognized as having set the blaxploitation genre's narrative and aesthetic formula for financial success and the "horizon for audience expectations" of blaxploitation films: an individualistic, macho, black action hero fights against injustice (and/or "the white man") in an urban milieu outside of the legal mechanisms ostensibly in place to fight injustice.[16] The mise-en-scène features urban spaces (often shown in long tracking shots of city streets) populated predominately by blacks and traversed by big fancy cars, well-dressed (according to emergent fashion trends of the day) male outlaws such as drug dealers, pimps, and other hustlers, black militants who often are discredited in the film's narrative, and naked women who, when clothed, might be one of the male characters' girlfriends or "lesbians." (Such females might be lesbians while naked as well.)

One of the innovations of the blaxploitation genre that quickly became perhaps its most distinctive characteristic was its use of contemporary music. Indeed, the soundtracks to some of the more popular blaxploitation films, such as *Shaft* and *Super Fly*, proved very successful financially (and might be seen as progenitors to the multilevel product-saturation strategies employed to advertise the blockbuster films of the New Hollywood). For instance, Curtis Mayfield's soundtrack to *Super Fly* sold over a million units in 1972.[17] Isaac Hayes's soundtrack for *Shaft* earned $2 million dollars within weeks of the film's release.[18]

As commodity tie-ins to blaxploitation movies, each musical soundtrack provides additional opportunities for the audience's affectivity to be exploited at the same time as they increase the possibility that a film's affection will overwhelm its capacity to secure a certain "meaning." By putting sound-images into circulation, the soundtracks also open onto other realms of valorization corresponding to the spatiotemporal particularities of sound-images. For instance, floating through the airwaves as pure sound-images being projected from an eight-track cassette playing in a passing car, Mayfield's innovative soundtrack to *Super Fly* might open a direct image of time in which a "black experience" of poverty gives rise to a struggle against racist domination and exploitation that takes the form of a struggle against drug addiction. Narrating drug addiction to the rhythm of the circulation of black culture as commodity, Mayfield's *Super Fly* soundtrack provides the critique of capitalist exploitation that the film fails to make.[19] "Little Child Runnin' Wild," the first song on that soundtrack, narrates poverty and drug addiction in a way that illuminates how racism and capitalism conspire to create a social milieu that operates according to a sense of being outside of the norms of justice, fairness, and personal safety upheld by U.S. bourgeois society, yet inside of that society's dominant common-sense assertions of what life is supposed to be like. Mayfield sets his listeners (a subset of which is the film's audience) affectivity to work on a critique of the sociopolitical and economic contexts in which drug trafficking and drug addiction are part of the maintenance of existing conditions of racialized poverty as lived in U.S. ghettos.[20] Blaxploitation movies' soundtracks, however, provide a set of cinematic sound-images that are related to, but relatively autonomous from, those put into circulation by the films themselves. The soundtracks expand the domain for the production of values occasioned by the film in unpredictable ways and into unexpected places.[21]

Theories of blaxploitation's conditions of possibility that posit the preexistence of a young, urban, black audience whose black nationalist sentiment is ripe for exploitation obscure the extent to which that audience itself is called into being by blaxploitation (meaning the films themselves, the critical theories and narratives crafted to consider them generically, and other discourses that inform the category) as a population that might be isolated as an audience that is in excess of the audience Hollywood assumes exists for its mainstream feature films. The move in the mid-1970s from the low-budget, niche-marketing strategies of blaxploitation to the big-budget, mass audience strategies of blockbuster films reflects the extent to which blaxploitation's audience was isolated by virtue of its particular demographics (young, urban, black) and cut away from the "mainstream" American audience, but then relatively quickly returned to the mainstream as blaxploitation films became exhausted. At the end of the blaxploitation cycle, Hollywood found it could "capture the lucrative black audience and at the same time attract whites," as Guerrero explains, citing surveys that "showed that as much as

35 percent of the audience for the megahits *The Godfather* (1972) and *The Exorcist* (1973) was black."[22]

Under such circumstances, the young, black urban audience drawn out by blaxploitation's marketing and distribution strategies can be considered to be both part of the mass audience that patronized mainstream Hollywood films and a potentially identifiable "surplus population" available to be consolidated as an "audience" in order to provide a boost to the rate at which Hollywood generates profits. In other words, the audience for blaxploitation films —the young, urban black audience—operates as part of the American industry's industrial reserve army of value-producing consumers of blaxploitation.

My understanding of surplus populations is informed by Roderick A. Ferguson's important work in the introduction to his *Aberrations in Black: Towards a Queer of Color Critique*. Ferguson points out, "Capital, without pressures from the state or citizenry, will assemble labor without regard for normative prescriptions of race and gender."[23] If one can understand watching films and television shows as a form of affective labor that has become necessary under capital, then we are in a position to understand that assembling blaxploitation's young, urban, black audiences is one of the ways that the film industry seeks to valorize itself via that audience's affective labor. Ferguson's creative and astute reading of Marx draws out the implications of capital's ravenous drive to find cheaper and cheaper labor to exploit, a drive that enables "social formations marked by intersecting particularities of race, gender, class, and sexuality" by encouraging the migrations of and nonnormative familial and communal relations between members of racialized ethnic minority groups.[24] These populations (on which capital relies to produce surplus value) are racialized in such a way that gender and sexual transgressions are constitutive components of that racialization.

Simultaneous to the constitution of these nonheteronormative racialized social formations is the proliferation of racialized discourses of gender and sexuality and attempts by the state to produce and regulate heteronormativity as a universal category of citizenship.[25] Drawing on Ferguson's insights, one can understand the young, urban, black audience to be a latent surplus population, appearing *as such* only when the film industry's accumulation of capital slows or when other products emerge that engage that population's productive capacities in a way that threatens to diminish the film industry's reserve army.

I emphasize *as such* in order to point out that blaxploitation's target audience is identifiable as young, urban, and black when it is targeted by films that themselves actively solicit those characteristics and that this targeting makes that audience perceptible as a surplus population. Insofar as "young, urban, and black" demarcates a set of shared knowledges and styles of expression, including a common structure of feeling, it indexes a potentially productive reservoir on which blaxploitation films might capitalize. When young, urban, and black ceased to be as productive for blaxploitation or, as Guerrero would have it, "when Hollywood no longer needed its cheap, black product line for its economic survival," that population simply was reabsorbed into the mass audience. There, the productive capacities gained by the characteristics young, urban, and black become redundant, or, from the point of view one must inhabit to produce analyses of cultural products, one might say that they simply retain a latent potential to disturb normative analyses of a blockbuster film's meaning.

My point is not to privilege an analysis about the film industry's profit motive at the expense of one about the film industry's racism. It is simply to insist that processes of racialization and, hence, the logics of racism inform both of the operations that generally are discussed with respect to "the black audience": that in which such an audience is ignored and that in which it is targeted. From the film industry's perspective, the black audience in general is simply a surplus population held in reserve to be consolidated *as such* in times of crisis. While ignoring the black audience (assuming such an audience exists as a potential within the mass audience) by providing stereotypical, or at least limited, representations of blackness is clearly a racist practice, calling the black audience out of reserve and setting them to work on black-themed films, even "positive" ones, is a racist operation as well, assuming that racism involves practices of selective discrimination, abuse, or exploitation rationalized via the constitution of one "race" as a desirable universal (i.e., "the citizen" or "the human" or "the mainstream audience") in contradistinction to another race that is constituted as particular and subordinate (i.e., the non- or not-yet-citizen or "the young, urban, black audience" of blaxploitation).

The process of extracting surplus sociocultural value from an audience's affective labor on a film is not neat, tidy, or clean. It is perverse, messy, and complicated, because an audience's interactions with a film inevitably shake loose forms of surplus sociocultural value that might not be directed immediately back into recognizable and normative forms of cultural value.

105

They appear to be refuse, garbage, waste, or, simply good examples of bad taste.[26]

Pam Grier's Blaxploitation Films

If, in general, blaxploitation harnesses and redirects the affectivity that had begun working to articulate a viable Black Power movement, those blaxploitation films starring Pam Grier and Tamara Dobson strive to assimilate the affectivity unleashed by the appearance of Black Revolutionary Women, but they do so via the multiplications of surplus. The perverse forms of surplus value shaken loose via an interaction with those films are what generate but also escape the genre's framing by such interested parties as the Coalition against Blaxploitation (CAB)—a group formed in Los Angeles that comprised various black civil rights and community groups such as the National Association for the Advancement of Colored People, the Congress of Racial Equality, and the Southern Christian Leadership Conference—critics and theorists of black film, and even, often, blaxploitation's defenders.[27] Once shaken loose, such perverse surplus, valorized by that segment of Hollywood's reserve army that can be described as young, urban, and black, remains available and already has provided some of the start-up required for such projects as Quentin Tarantino's films *Pulp Fiction* and *Jackie Brown*, Snoop Doggy Dogg's star image, and Darius James's book *That's Blaxploitation! Roots of the Baadasssss 'Tude (Rated X by an All-Whyte Jury)* in which blaxploitation is pinpointed as providing the "roots of the baadasssss 'tude.' "[28]

Having set to work on blaxploitation, one quickly realizes that the erotics generated via blaxploitation may or may not be procreative or reproductive of existing organizations of sexual relations; working on blaxploitation generates its own excesses, those aspects of the analysis, interpretation, or expression that remain unnamable, unlocatable, and unknowable according to the terms of the analysis, interpretation, or expression itself.

In keeping with the masculine overtones that have been attributed to blaxploitation, one might say that much of the surplus value generated by working on these films are like "wasted seed," nonreproductive, nonheterosexual, and nonheteronormative, queer, stuff. Might such surplus be invested in order to craft another project? Perhaps that of the black lesbian who inheres in Pam Grier or the valorization of the black lesbian that Jennifer Brody identifies as lurking in another of blaxploitation's heroines, Tamara

Dobson's character Cleopatra Jones, even after those lesbians supposedly have been expunged from the blaxploitation heroines' images and rendered commonly imperceptible as such?

In examining Pam Grier's blaxploitation films, one engages in a process that is consistent with that Ferguson attributes to capital: one is participating in the multiplications of surplus. One engages with and through the racialized discourses of gender and sexuality that blaxploitation makes available and labors affectively on a set of commodities, collectively known as blaxploitation. I use Ferguson's phrase "the multiplications of surplus" to mark something more than, but inclusive of, what has been described as "a queer reading" of blaxploitation films. The multiplications of surplus is a byproduct of capital's requirements for its own valorization, and it describes the context out of which nonheteronormative racial formations emerge. If one can understand mass-cultural forms such as blaxploitation and serial dramas on cable-television channels to be part of the way that capital valorizes itself, then one's participation and engagement with those mass-cultural products, one's affective labor on them, must be understood to be part of capital's processes of valorization as well. Reframed in this way, blaxploitation films, which were produced during a period of economic crisis for the film industry and that solicited the formation of surplus film-going populations recognizable as young, urban, and black, can be understood as both the site of the material production of nonheteronormative racial formations and a discursive locus of anxiety about that very production.

In other words, blaxploitation films are "queer," if we can understand "queer" to mark an antinormative positioning with regard to sexuality. Relying upon the affective labor of a young, urban, and black audience to valorize its depictions of pimps, prostitutes, drug dealers, and the like, blaxploitation films disrupt gender ideals and sexual norms while simultaneously staging and seeking to quell some of the anxieties that attend such disruptions. For instance, in Pam Grier's _Foxy Brown_, as in several of her other blaxploitation films, the image of a "stud broad," "butch," or "masculine female" that threatens to result when one who is recognizably female claims masculinity (for example, by taking on what had become the masculine role of blaxploitation hero) brings a number of internal tensions to the surface of the common-sense black nationalisms the films participate in forging.[29] The violent feminization of Grier's characters is one way that the films strive to keep these tensions from becoming visible. The other way that her charac-

107

ters' relationship to female masculinity is obscured in these films is via the policing of their sexuality. Heterosexuality seeks to delimit the sole context of her characters' sexual circulation. This formula was in place in Grier's image (as constructed through her blaxploitation films) as early as *White Mama, Black Mama* (1972), the film that landed her the leading role in *Coffy* (1973).

In *White Mama, Black Mama*, a B-film gem, Pam Grier stars as a woman who is jailed for prostitution. In jail she must refuse the lecherous advances of the white female warden who takes a sexual interest in her. Eventually, Grier's character is handcuffed to her adversary, a white female revolutionary (who, incidentally, did not refuse the warden's advances). They escape from jail, but remain handcuffed to one another for the remainder of the film. Like many of Grier's subsequent blaxploitation films, *White Mama, Black Mama* relies upon the mainstream erotic appeal of a potential or an implied lesbian sexuality. In fact, Grier's first starring role was as Grear, a jailhouse "bull-dagger," in the 1971 film *The Big Doll House*. Given this debut, one can understand the later condition for Grier's circulation as blaxploitation heroine to have hinged on the expulsion of "Grear" from Grier's star text, as each of her blaxploitation characters had to visibly and consistently demonstrate her heterosexuality, even as her insertion into the traditionally masculine role of blaxploitation hero threatened to disturb the common-sense articulation wherein a female body must be feminine and sexually available to men. Invariably, the drive to enforce heterosexuality as the context for Grier's character's sexual circulation as constructed by the films' narratives is dramatized by her character's violent confrontation with an image recognizable as a "butch lesbian." In both *Coffy* and *Foxy Brown*, made in 1973 and 1974, respectively, Grier's characters emerge from these violent confrontations victorious, feminine, and heterosexual. Grier's films, even more than those of Tamara Dobson, are generative of surplus that has proven productive for contemporary transvaluations of femininity and sexuality, such as in the recent cable-television show, *The L Word*, a series in which Grier has a starring role.

The Butch Problem

One confrontation with a butch lesbian occurs in *Foxy Brown* when Foxy rescues another prostitute, Claudia, from the pimps and drug dealers for whom they both are working. (Foxy, trying to infiltrate a drug ring, is under cover as a prostitute.) With an authoritative air, Foxy tells a hysterical Claudia to pull herself together: "This is no time to fall apart. . . . Claudia, listen now, listen to me! Now, I'm gonna take you to a place where you can wait for me. . . . I've got everything all worked out. . . . You just do what I tell you, okay?" Claudia chooses instead to go to the neighborhood lesbian bar, where Foxy finds her being hit on by a white butch lesbian named Bobby. Foxy strolls in and asks Claudia what she is doing there. Bobby tells Foxy to "go find one of [her] own" and warns that she's got a "black belt in karate." Foxy picks up a bar stool and hits Bobby with it, knocking her to the floor. The camera angle is from Bobby's point of view as Foxy stands over her and retorts, "And I've got my black belt in bar stool." Foxy and Claudia beat up several lesbians before running out of the bar together, leaving the remaining lesbians to fight one another.

Foxy's attempt to liberate and then control the prostitute (feminine body) leads to a confrontation with a butch lesbian who stakes a similar claim to the feminine prostitute. Through this confrontation, the butch lesbian is expelled from Foxy's characterization as Foxy beats her up (though a "lesbian reading" of Foxy remains accessible in that image).[30] Foxy's heterosexuality (thrown into doubt when she liberates the prostitute and seeks to control her) is reinforced in the film's narrative shortly thereafter when Foxy's true identity as the girlfriend of a man killed by the drug dealers (and thus her motivation for undermining the drug dealers and freeing Claudia in the process) is discovered. As punishment for her transgressions, Foxy is sent to "the ranch" where she is drugged and raped by "the boys," in a violent sequence that functions to "feminize" Foxy.

In _Coffy_ dramatizing the purgation of the butch lesbian from Grier's character is not such a tidy operation. On a fact-finding mission as part of her vendetta against the drug dealers in her community, Coffy visits Priscilla, a white junkie who used to work for King George, a pimp and drug dealer. The walls of the small apartment in which Coffy finds Priscilla are adorned with colorful paintings and posters of half-naked black women, one of whom bears a strong resemblance to Pam Grier. When Coffy's questioning becomes intense, Priscilla warns her, "My old man is coming back any minute and if she catches you here, she's gonna kick your ass." Foxy explains that she just wants to ask Priscilla a few questions about King George. Priscilla asks Coffy playfully whether she wants to "get in the life."[31] The conversation eventually becomes a fight. Coffy straddles Priscilla as she is lying on her

109

back on the bed and threatens to cut her face with a broken bottle if she does not provide the information Coffy needs. Fearfully, Priscilla tells Coffy what she wanted to know, and Coffy throws the broken bottle onto the floor, but remains on top of Priscilla.

Harriet, a black butch whose heavy boots and crisply creased pant legs the camera follows as she walks up the stairway to the apartment, sees Coffy on top of Priscilla. Framed by the doorway that she authoritatively fills, legs apart, Harriet asks in a deep voice, "What the hell is going on here?" As Coffy dismounts Priscilla and prepares to defend herself, Priscilla exclaims that Coffy "busted in here trying to make me." Harriet throws a chair at Coffy and aggressively pursues her around the room, but Coffy escapes by pushing over a table to stop Harriet's advance. Harriet chases Coffy out the door, and Coffy sprints down the steps. When Harriet turns to go back inside, she is once again seen from inside the apartment in a medium shot using a wide-angle lens. As before, she occupies most of the doorway and stands with her legs apart and her hands on her hips as she hollers at Priscilla, "I go away for half an hour for you to turn a trick. When I come back I find you balling some nigger bitch, you lousy white tramp."

A quick cut to Coffy's amused smile as she listens to Harriet's tirade from the bottom of the steps before walking away untouched seeks to reinforce Coffy's distance from the lover's violent quarrel (and thus her heterosexuality) at the same time as it registers that Harriet is insecure in her masculinity. Nonetheless, the erotic (and/or lesbian) reading available in the scene into which Harriet walks—Coffy straddling the white woman on the bed—is retained by Harriet's accusation, the end of which carries over onto the visual image of Coffy smiling.

Unlike *Foxy Brown*'s dramatization of Grier's character's ability to beat the butch and remain heterosexual, in *Coffy* Grier does not beat the butch physically, but she does better her by revealing the extent to which Harriet is insecure in her masculinity; by refusing to correct the charge that Coffy was "trying to make" Priscilla, Coffy allows Harriet to believe that Harriet, a pimp, is unable to control Priscilla, her prostitute. In *Foxy Brown* the differences between Foxy and Bobby are registered on a visual level in terms of skin color and mannerisms in a way that implies that a feminine black woman easily could defeat even a white butch claiming to have a black belt in karate. In *Coffy* the differences between Coffy and Harriet are more nuanced and complex. Harriet is darker skinned than Coffy (whose name itself im-

110

plies a lighter skin tone) and physically bigger.[32] Coffy's hair is worn "natural" in an Afro, while Harriet's is permed (or perhaps she wears a wig).

These physical differences are important within the context of the film's repackaging, according to common-sense black nationalism, of the embryonic sentiments and philosophies of Black Power, especially its resignification of black as "beautiful." One of the ways that the project of "reclaiming" black male's masculinity was achieved in some of the black nationalist thinking that contended for dominance as Black Power was through the effeminization of whiteness.[33] As this rhetorical strategy became accepted as a strand of black common sense, it led to two related consequences that are relevant here. On one hand, white men were presented by and large as "fags" (i.e., effeminate), while male homosexuality was excluded from the domain of blackness.[34] On the other hand, white women's currency (as anatomically female and as feminine because white) meant that having sex with them was the most efficient way to become a man.[35]

From the point of view of common-sense black nationalism, masculinity accrues to Harriet not simply because she controls sexual access to the white feminine body (Priscilla) but also because she is dark-skinned. Her processed hair and her heavy body type and men's clothing juxtaposed with her shoulder-length hair and long fingernails (read as feminine markers), however, preclude a reading of her beautiful or alluring, especially in comparison to Coffy, whose physical beauty is reinforced by the fact that it is replicated in the paintings on the wall in the apartment. Significantly, from the perspective of common-sense black nationalism, Coffy's light skin shade and women's clothing militate against her being read as masculine (according to her physical characteristics), while her Afro testifies to her blackness and thus accounts for her "beauty." Harriet's fake (i.e., not "naturally black") hair works against her blackness even as her dark skin tone works to ascribe to her the masculinity that Black Power rhetoric attributes to blackness. According to the film's dialogue and the fact that violence ensues between Harriet and Priscilla as Coffy walks away, Harriet's masculinity (here achieved through ownership of a feminine body) is thrown into question by Coffy's actions.

The film is unable to expunge the lesbian completely from Coffy's appearance. The scene with Harriet and Priscilla discredits the black butch lesbian, feminizes Coffy, and forecloses the possibility of a sexual encounter between Coffy and Priscilla. Yet something different might appear in Coffy when she mounts Priscilla. A "queer reading" of this scene might here recognize Coffy as potentially a "femme lesbian."[36] The black femme lesbian perceptible here is a figure who escapes and defies the common-sense categories constructed to rationalize the differentiation of bodies into masculine and feminine according to their anatomical characteristics and to match those bodies to their "proper" sexual object choices, that is, masculine male with feminine female.

Blaxploitation films are cultural commodities produced at and productive of a rupture within normative formations of race, class, gender, and sexuality. As commodities, the films exist as part of capital's attempts to valorize itself. As cultural texts, they participate in the multiplications of discourses about social life that attend capital's attempts at self-valorization. One might understand these two drives within the cultural commodity to be at odds with one another, or, at the very least, one could say that the tensions between them always threaten to appear. Moreover, one could schematize, at least provisionally, the apprehensive relationship between blaxploitation's narrative system and its stylistic system by characterizing the film's narrative systems as heteronormative attempts to reign in and regulate the nonheteronormative ruptures made available in the film's excessive combinations of images and sounds.

Significantly, *Foxy Brown* and *Coffy* attempt to conform the formal excesses they unleash to the dictates of normative understandings of gender and sexuality, but they are unable to account for the extent to which the social milieu they valorize—a racialized world of drug dealers, pimps, and prostitutes—itself is nonheteronormative.

"Someday We'll . . ."

The common-sense black nationalist project of securing black masculinity that informs these films proceeds to a large extent via physical violence and procedures of violent feminization directed at living images who can be recognized as anatomically female.[37] In recording this violence, I have sought to account further for the instability of Black Revolutionary Woman's cinematic appearance as blacks with guns. The violent processes whereby the appearance of Black Revolutionary Women was pummeled into a common-sense black nationalist understanding of "gender differentiation" also were leveled against many Panther women.

Although a few black feminists have called for critical explorations and investigations of "the issue of female abuse and battery by male leaders and the rank and file in the Black Panther Party," there have been few sustained efforts to account for the mode of thinking that supports such violence within "revolutionary" groups or that continues to inform the silence (in the name of black solidarity) with which those accusations are met.[38] While I am not suggesting that abuse of female Panthers was rampant nor that all Panthers were complicit in the abuse of some, it is with an eye toward articulating the way that common-sense black nationalism rationalizes violence against women that I have undertaken my consideration of Pam Grier's blaxploitation films. I have sought to examine, following Wahneema Lubiano's lead, the ways that common-sense black nationalism provides consent to official notions of gender and sexuality and the fundamental role that constructing and policing notions of masculinity and femininity play in securing this consent. The violent process of purging the butch lesbian from the cinematic appearance of Black Revolutionary Women is fundamental to the engendering and policing of sexuality that continues to accompany the appearance of black woman.[39]

Hammered into the common-sense black-nationalist framework that making sense of the films requires and (re)constructs, Black Revolutionary Women are part of the social milieu the films produce. They do not fit neatly within this framework, however, even after considerable force. The violent effort to conjoin Black Revolutionary Woman and black nationalism, an effort that (re)constructs both categories for circulation as common sense, proceeds by feminizing Black Revolutionary Woman and disciplining the butch lesbian that threatens to appear with her.

Although I suggest that this effort (as evident in Grier's blaxploitation films) has a corollary in the way that some female Black Panthers were battered, raped, and otherwise abused, I am not arguing that the experience of these Panthers is somehow represented in Grier's films. I have sought to differentiate between "the real world" and "the film's world" not in terms of representation, but in terms of speed, circulation, degree of commodification, and the manner in which the medium (in this case, film) through which images are received strives to restrict and direct the range of possible meanings according to each film's specific formal properties.

In order to make sense of the films and to enjoy them, viewers work with them (via affectivity) to construct the sociopolitical order on which making

113

sense of the films relies. The commercial project of securing the conventions of the blaxploitation genre, in place by the time Grier became a blaxploitation star, guide the viewers' efforts. Making (common) sense of the cinematic appearances of Black Revolutionary Women is labor intensive as well. The labor that activity requires is performed as an act of survival, part of the labor required to live in the world without slipping into madness. Yet, working on blaxploitation according to the multiplications of surplus, affectivity inevitably shakes loose forms of surplus value that exceed normative strategies to contain them. If the black butch and/or femme lesbian appears at any moment whatever of the appearance of Black Revolutionary Woman as blaxploitation star, it is because the multiplication of surplus on which the films rely for their own valorization make available to affectivity the possibility of participating in a different project. That project corresponds to another organization of social reality, one pioneered by black butch and femme lesbians, one that coexists in an antagonistic relationship with the reality upheld by official common sense.

Postscript on Pam Grier and *The L Word*

Because blaxploitation participates, by virtue of its own formal excesses, in the processes described by Ferguson in terms of the multiplications of surplus, the surplus value shaken loose by interactions with blaxploitation might support unpredictable coalitions.[40] For instance, there is a long-standing affiliation between the images valorized by that portion of the mainstream audience available to be consolidated as "lesbians" and those valorized by adolescent and adult heterosexual males, even though it is not at all clear that those populations valorize those images in the same way.

The Queen of Blaxploitation's most recent appearance in Showtime's hit series *The L Word* might be understood as a conduit through which to assemble such an unpredictable coalition to valorize the first lesbian-themed serial drama on television. As Eve Sedgwick points out in her review of *The L Word* in the *Chronicle of Higher Education*, "In the demographic calculus that lay behind the decision to underwrite the series, Gary Levine, Showtime's vice president for original programming, told the *New York Daily News* its potential appeal to nonlesbian viewers rested on the understanding that 'lesbian sex, girl-on-girl, is a whole cottage industry for heterosexual men.' "[41] The series certainly exploits this connection between what it presents as lesbian sex and male heterosexuality by frequently staging that version of lesbian sex for a male or presumably heterosexual gaze within its narrative, a tactic that raises complicated questions about the possibilities for the production of a feminine female sexuality that cannot be recuperated into heteronormative dictates of female sexuality. Without a butch masculinity or some other alternative to normative femininity present to complicate normative assumptions about gender, sexuality, and bodily expression, the depictions of "lesbian sex" in which *The L Word* traffics, coupled with the series' reliance upon recognizable television genre conventions, raise serious questions about *The L Word*'s ability to achieve anything other than the conservative goal of mainstreaming forms of lesbian sociality that do little to unsettle existing hierarchies of race, gender, class, and even of sexuality.

The preceding consideration of blaxploitation might assist an assessment of recent efforts to elicit and address a lesbian and gay audience, efforts such as *Queer as Folk*, *Will and Grace*, and *The L Word*. These efforts are perhaps most remarkable for the way they seek to detach lesbian and gay social formations from their historical imbrications within and among working-class communities of color and make them visible as simply the unintentional off-shoots of heteronormativity, that is, these men and women could be your (white) sons or daughters, your (white) brothers or sisters, your (white) fathers or mothers, and so on. If Pam Grier is a locus of desire for both heterosexual males and, as Darius James points out, for lesbians such as the Lesbian Avengers' lesbian partygoers, then her presence on *The L Word* is another way the series seeks to bring these populations together in a shared project of value production.

The surplus that might be produced via this diverse audience's encounter with *The L Word*, however, remains difficult to detect because the series currently is at such pains to regulate that surplus by relying upon familiar televisual conventions, by presenting a middle-class, primarily white milieu of straight-appearing lesbians or, as they often say in reference to themselves, of "gay women," and by degrading and distancing its gay women from those lesbian social formations, such as butch-femme, which might not be as easily regulated or mainstreamed in the present moment.

Pam Grier's appearance in *The L Word* complicates this assimilationist project, because she reveals where, in its efforts to satisfy its own requirements for self-valorization, *The L Word* attempts to draw on Grier's prior accumulation of value as sexy blaxploitation heroine while remaining inattentive to the ways that value relies upon a nonheteronormativity that was simultaneously racialized, sexualized, and gendered. Pam Grier's presence in *The L Word* might introject into the series some of blaxploitation's surplus value and its surplus populations (and with them the potential for a critique of normative ideals of race, gender, class, and sexuality).

In her first appearance in the series, Grier's character, Kit Porter, is associated with the street and with street life.[42] Introduced by a police car's siren that situates Kit in an adversarial relationship to one of the most overtly disciplinary mechanisms of the State, Pam Grier's debut scene on *The L Word* stands in sharp contrast to that of her half-white sister, Bette (played by Jennifer Beals), and Bette's white lover, Tina—wherein Tina expresses white, middle-class concerns about finding a sperm donor and making a baby—and it invokes Grier's status as the queen of the blaxploitation genre. On the way to her first paying gig as a singer in over a year, Kit rides in a 1970s-style car with a license that has been revoked and flirts with the police officer who pulls her over. Associations with the street, its excesses, and the unpredictable (queer) coalitions it might foster enter *The L Word* through Kit Porter.

116 In a scene from episode 9 of *The L Word*, the series' effort to assemble viewers across differences is dramatized when Snoop Doggy Dogg's character, Slim Daddy, who incessantly asserts his heterosexuality by ogling the gay women and making references to how hot they would look together, produces a video that features Kit. Operating under the assumption that Kit is a lesbian like her half-sister Bette, Slim Daddy puts Kit in leather and surrounds her with other leather-clad feminine women, thereby illustrating how lesbian sexuality might be produced to serve heterosexual male erotic fantasy and desire.

Rap artist Snoop Doggy Dogg's star text also relies upon an investment of some of the surplus made available via working on blaxploitation. Although in the scene under consideration Kit remarks on her own distance from the types of characters Pam Grier played in blaxploitation films by saying, "I ain't twenty. I ain't nobody's hoochie," those twenty-something blaxploitation characters remain an integral part of Grier's star image because they have become legendary (in part through the work of a new generation of references to and depictions of black pimps, hustlers, and gangstas such as those produced by Snoop). Slim Daddy's insistence that "without Kit Porter none of us would be here" explicitly links Snoop Dogg's presence and that of the young, urban, black communities on which his own star text relies for its valorization to that of Pam Grier, implying that without her presence in *The L Word*, the racialized nonheteronormative working- and under-class forms of sociality their star texts index would not appear in the series. As *The L Word* seeks to assemble an audience of heterosexuals and lesbians capable of valorizing it, by drawing on the value accrued by the Queen of Blaxploitation herself and by that accrued by a well-known gangsta rapper whose own star text relies in part on the returns on an investment of blaxploitation's surplus, the series makes perceptible a rupture within its efforts to finesse the production of a normative lesbian sociality. In other words, Kit Porter currently is the receptacle for the excesses unleashed in *The L Word*'s effort to reproduce itself as cultural value. Because of this, she holds *The L Word* open for unpredictable innovations within normative understandings of race, gender, class, and lesbian sexuality and within the forms of sociality they might engender. Kit forces one to engage in an urgent conversation about such things as queer liberalism and the production of normative lesbian sexualities and normative forms of lesbian sociality.[43]

Playing the only heterosexual recurring female character on the show, Grier's presence in *The L Word* is what might make the series available to a critique of normative notions of gender, sexuality, femininity, class, and race, because it is her character and the surplus value that affectivity's interactions with Grier generates that threaten to rupture the series' efforts to regulate nonnormative engagements with it. Linked to a similar nonheteronormative, racialized milieu of the street and of street life valorized in and through blaxploitation, Kit Porter troubles *The L Word*'s insistence on its gay women characters' transgressive sexualities by threatening to open them up to a critique that draws on the excesses of the street with its pimps, pushers, studs and fishes, and prostitutes. For all the talk about lesbian representations on *The L Word*, perhaps it is the show's only heterosexual female character that might offer something of value to those who remain interested in working to create and sustain queer forms of social life that still might not be accommodated by hegemonic hierarchies of race, class, gender, and sexuality.

"What's Up with That? She Don't Talk?"

Set It Off's Black Lesbian Butch-Femme

The blaxploitation film cycle put into broad circulation some of the images of common-sense black nationalism that were most capable of continuing the movement of capital. Inviting its audiences to participate in the production of a common-sense black nationalism that directed, responded, and conceded to the broader socioeconomic and cultural changes that attended the transduction of value that Blackness was undergoing at the time, blaxploitation disseminated a set of images loosely associated with the political

6 | *"Ghetto Heaven"*

sentiments of Black Power. To the extent that Black Power was an inconsistent attempt to unify diverse and contradictory expressions of black nationalism into a conception of the world that might be capable of supporting a broad-based movement toward Black Liberation, elements of the revolutionary nationalism of the Black Panther Party, the cultural nationalism of the Black Arts Movement, and the assimilationist black American nationalism of the upwardly mobile beneficiaries of the civil rights movement are recognizable in the images of value blaxploitation offered. Making a set of contradictory and fragmentary images of Black Power commonly available for further transductions of value, Blaxploitation films reveal the versions of gender and sexuality that animate the production and consumption of those images.

The convergence between gender and sexuality that undergirds blaxploitation's common-sense black nationalism proceeds by both violently expelling "the butch" from any perceptibly female body that makes a claim to the mechanisms that secure masculinity and by tenuously foreclosing the possibility that "the femme" might appear in that body upon the butch's expulsion. Both operations are incomplete, however, and the butch and the femme remain possibilities offered by blaxploitation films, particularly those whose stars are perceptibly female. Among the viewers to whom butch and femme are perceptible are those for whom butch and femme exist as viable alternatives to heterosexuality. The set of images that blaxploitation makes commonly available includes the butch and the femme as latent strands of common-sense black nationalism's conceptions of masculinity and femininity.

F. Gary Gray's 1996 ghetto action film *Set It Off* announces its relationship to blaxploitation during its title sequence.[1] After a violent opening scene in which the audience is introduced to Frankie, played by Vivica A. Fox, the words "Set It Off" are legible onscreen while Parliament's funkadelic song "Flash Light" plays loudly at the 1970s costume party that Stony, played by Jada Pinkett, is throwing for her brother's graduation from high school. Introducing its audience to three of the film's four main protagonists while each of them is dressed in the fashions of the 1970s, *Set It Off* announces visually that its filmic forefathers are the blaxploitation films of the early 1970s.

Starring four "females," *Set It Off* funnels the butch who threatens to erupt from the insertion of a perceptibly female body into a traditionally masculine diegetic space, genre, or narrative into the character Cleo, played by the rap artist Queen Latifah.[2] Where the figure recognizable as the black femme is perceptible in the blaxploitation heroines, particularly Pam Grier's and Tamara Dobson's, only via what generally is called a queer reading, or what I refer to as a "queer common sense," the black femme of the lesbian butch-femme paradigm in *Set It Off* is perceptible to hegemonic common sense(s), including common-sense black nationalism. She functions as part of the effort to rationalize the existence of the butch by making Cleo visible according to the terms of a conception of the world that is understood best as "ghettocentric." The black femme's femininity is made visible insofar as she serves as the currency that secures Cleo's masculinity.

Black Butch Masculinity and Ghettocentric Common Sense

In the context of a discussion of black film Ed Guerrero uses the term *ghettocentric* in order to describe the preoccupations of what he calls "the new Black movie boom."[3] Taking his cue from Guerrero, S. Craig Watkins uses *ghettocentric* to refer to the same body of films as Guerrero, relying upon the term to describe the films' setting and thematic concerns.[4] Insofar as I invoke ghettocentrism in reference to a film (*Set It Off*) that is set in "the ghetto" and preoccupied with the issues that setting currently raises, my own use of the term is akin to Guerrero's and Watkins'. But, my use of *ghettocentric* is more nuanced and narrow than theirs. Taking my cue from Robin D. G. Kelley, I use the term to refer to an innovation within common-sense black nationalism. That innovation is a conception of the world consolidated by and circulating in gangsta rap and its related products and practices. I understand ghettocentrism to be a historically specific reaction to and articulation of a cinematic social reality (the postindustrial city's ghetto) produced at the juncture between globalizing capitalism and contemporary U.S. racism. The reproduction of this reality serves the interests of bourgeois American nationalism and its State.

Kelley explains that he uses the term *ghettocentric* in order to locate the way that

> the criminalization, surveillance, incarceration, and immiseration of black youth in the postindustrial city have been the central theme in gangsta rap, and at the same time, sadly, constitute the primary experiences from which their identities are constructed. Whereas Afrocentric rappers build an imagined community by invoking images of ancient African civilizations, gangsta rappers are more prone to follow Eric B. and Rakim's dictum, "It ain't where you're from, its where you're at." . . . The construction of the "ghetto" as a living nightmare and "gangstas" as products of that nightmare has given rise to what I call a new "Ghettocentric" identity in which the specific class, race, and gendered experiences in late capitalist urban centers coalesce to create a new identity—"Nigga."[5]

I embrace Kelley's use of *ghettocentric* because of its specificity; it describes a new social reality. Kelley offers the term in contradistinction to the "Afrocentric" conceptions of the world that continue to function within the common-sense black nationalism that was refined in the sixties and seventies. In the context of an analysis of *Set It Off*, my embrace of ghettocentricity is meant to signal a shift in the consolidation of common-sense black nationalism. The shift to ghettocentrism for some of those who operate according to common-sense black nationalism hinges on a recognition of a new reality—the postindustrial city's ghettos—that sets it apart from the experiences of ghetto life that precede it. The concern with ghetto life that pervades blaxploitation films provide a set of shared memory-images on which ghettocentrism often draws in order to recognize the new reality. Recognizable from the blaxploitation cycles, yet significantly different, the ghettocentrism of mass-cultural commodities marketed to "blacks" and "youth" in the United States since the early 1990s marks the (re)emergence of a diffuse

120

national preoccupation with urban life. Within black common sense, the most recent roots of a collective preoccupation and fascination with urban life are perceptible in the revolutionary nationalism of the Black Panther Party and its emphasis on the lumpenproletariat as a "revolutionary" force and, more generally, in Black Power's formulation of the ghetto as the seat of the black community.[6] Significantly, however, as Kelley points out, the conditions particular to the postindustrial city constitute "a fundamentally different reality" of the black working class from the urban realities that existed prior to 1970. Recognizing the specificity of the situation that shapes ghettocentrism, I use the adjective *ghettocentric* to refer to cultural products that consolidate and enable the circulation of narratives about the postindustrial city's ghettos, which are populated predominately by blacks and immigrants of color, primarily those from Asian, Central American, and South American countries.[7]

The significance of the widespread popularity of gangsta rap to the cycle of ghetto action films released during the early 1990s has been noted by others.[8] Beginning with Mario Van Peebles's choice to cast gangsta rap artist Ice T in the commercially successful film *New Jack City* (1991) and John Singleton's casting of Ice Cube, formerly part of the pioneering gangsta rap group NWA (Niggaz with Attitude), in the role of Dough Boy in the influential film *Boyz N the Hood* (1991), ghetto action films established cross-marketing links to the themes, beats, rhythms, and worldviews promulgated by gangsta rap.

Unlike the blaxploitation films of the early 1970s to which the ghetto action films inevitably invite comparisons, the success of the latter was predicated not on the films' ability to capitalize on the innovations of a fledgling sociopolitical movement as much as on the popularity and profitability of other commodities, existing forms of mass-produced entertainment (rap music and music video) to which the films were linked via marketing strategies (such as casting rap stars in lead roles and featuring musical soundtracks containing the work of well-known rap artists), thematic concerns (most notably, a central focus on ghetto life), and stylistic innovations. Of course, rap music itself might be understood as a highly commodified and commodifiable artistic articulation of a particular conception of the world that has enabled a sociocultural movement. In this regard, the ghetto action films that rely upon the profit-making potential of rap music, insofar as they continue that sociocultural movement, can be understood as vehicles for the circulation of gangsta rap's ghettocentric common sense—much like a two-hour version of a music video.

121

In the case of *Set It Off* the comparison to music video is provocative, not least because of Gray's background as a director of hip-hop music videos. *Set It Off*, like other ghettocentric films such as *Boyz N the Hood*, draws heavily upon the affectivity provided by a target market whose cinematic perception was being habituated according to the ghettocentric common sense forming in and informing gangsta rap. Yet the comparison between ghetto action films and hip-hop videos threatens to obfuscate some of the most remarkable aspects of *Set It Off*. Operating as a technological cinematic machine that seeks to make senses common, *Set It Off* serves as a vehicle whereby ghetto-centric common sense might become hegemonic within various common-sense consolidations of blackness, including that which predominately consolidates blacks: common sense black nationalism.

The gangsta-rap market is not *Set It Off*'s sole market, even given the film's generic affiliation with the ghetto action films released prior to it. Within a "black film" historical narrative based on generic cycles, *Set It Off* would be situated between two related but competing cycles in black popular film: the ghetto-action-film cycle and a more recent cycle of films, such as *Waiting to Exhale* (1995), *Love Jones* (1997), *Eve's Bayou* (1997), and *Soul Food* (1997), that targets those elements of common-sense black nationalism that consolidate a "black middle class" market. In their determinations of the generic horizon of expectations that one might bring to *Set It Off*, reviewers of the film most often compared it to *Waiting to Exhale*, the 1995 adaptation of Terry McMillan's best-selling novel. Most reviewers received the film as a blaxploitation-style, "Girlz N the Hood Exhaling" type of movie. The difficulty that reviewers had in situating *Set It Off* into their existing generic categories and their reluctance to understand it according to the available categories of ghettocentrism familiar from previous films points to the second remarkable aspect of the film—the way that it functions as a vehicle for innovations within, transformations of, and challenges to some of ghettocentrism's organizing principles, most notably, the prevalence of sexism and homophobia in the practices forming in and informing gangsta rap.

The sexism and homophobia endemic to the ghettocentrism that has pervaded mass culture in various ways since the early 1990s undermines not only ghettocentrism's own ability to articulate a conception of the world that enables a social movement that is radically different from those that currently are perceptible, but also the potential for ghettocentrism's salient critique of postindustrial urban reality to be seen and heard by official common sense and its burgeoning categories of political correctness. Instead of perceiving social reality through the lens offered by ghettocentric narratives in a way that would force it to recognize its own role in perpetuating the violent conditions holding that reality together, official common sense is calibrated to recognize mainly gangsta rap's derogatory and violent references to "bitches," "hoes," and "faggots." Official common sense uses the glaring sexism and homophobia of these references and their "political incorrectness" as locations into which it siphons off the pernicious homophobia and sexism that maintain its intelligibility.[9]

Set It Off removes much of ghettocentrism's blatant sexism and homophobia from view by putting issues affecting "black women" at the center of the film's framing of ghettocentric reality and revealing something new in the cinematic image of ghettocentrism—"female bank robbers." Released a couple of years after the ghetto-action-film cycle seemed to have run its course and in the midst of a burst of films consolidating and targeting black women, *Set It Off* introduces a different image of ghettocentrism in order to extract surplus value from an already well-habituated affectivity. Framing something different within ghettocentrism, *Set It Off* capitalized on the labor expended to make sense of female bank robbers according to ghettocentricity's categories.

Of the four bank robbers in *Set It Off*, Cleo's characterization is tied most closely to hip-hop culture and, more specifically, to gangsta rap. Obviously, casting the rap artist Queen Latifah as Cleo brings Latifah's hip-hop roots to bear on her portrayal, but the film establishes an affiliation between Cleo and gangsta-ism via other means as well. For instance, when stealing cars to use as escape vehicles after robbing banks, Cleo sorts through each of the compact discs in the car, rejecting as "bullshit" and throwing out those that are not consistent with the rhythms, beats, and sentiments of rap music, the type of music that she "rides to." When the four friends go to see Black Sam (played by gangsta-rap artist Dr. Dre, formerly of the rap group NWA) in order to buy guns, Cleo references her prior relationship with him (she used to steal cars for him) and otherwise indicates her knowledgeability about and familiarity with the protocols of gangsta-ism. Later, during a conversation with Stony on the steps of the office building that they clean at night as employees of Luther's Janitorial Service, Cleo admits, "The hood is where I belong." Cleo claims that being "nothin' but a hood rat" is alright with her. She asks, laughing, "I mean what am I gonna do in Hollywood or Thousand

123

Oaks or some shit?" By her own admission, Cleo cannot see herself in a life outside of the one she lives in the postindustrial city that defines and restrains her. Cleo's self-identification as "belonging" in the hood, in addition to other elements of her characterization, allows her to be recognized as a representative of the ghettocentric worldview expressed in gangsta rap.[10]

Into Cleo's character, *Set It Off* funnels much of the black masculinity that is, in addition to a focus on narratives describing the violence and unpredictability of ghetto life, one of ghettocentricity's fundamental mechanisms for rationalizing and reproducing ghettocentric social reality. A receptacle for the embattled, outlawed, and virulently heterosexual articulations of black masculinity that undergird ghettocentrism, Cleo carries the weight of black masculinity so that the film's other perceptibly female characters, Stony, Frankie, and Tisean, can be recognized as "ladies." Seeking to appeal to the broadest market possible, *Set It Off* allows for the "female masculinity" perceptible in Cleo to be rationalized in terms consistent with hegemonic common senses, including the ghettocentric common sense that consolidates the film's target market.[11] Cleo thus is caught in the sights of the sensory-motor schemas of living beings; she is in the process of becoming part of the way that value is (re)produced via the affective labor expended to make sense of her. Cinematic perception calls forth a hegemonic version of femininity, and recognizes Cleo's lover, Ursula, according to it in order to rationalize Cleo's existence.

Early in the film, when Cleo and Ursula kiss in front of Frankie, Tisean, and Stony, Cleo becomes visible as a "thug" or as a "butch." Prior to that kiss, Cleo appears to be one of the girls. Associated with gangsta rap, Cleo is harder or more "masculine" than the rest, and, of course, queer common sense might funnel her into the category "lesbian" even before she kisses Ursula, but she does not necessarily appear to hegemonic common sense(s) —which already habitually call forth versions of masculinity in order to recognize "black woman"—to be a "female" who has sex with "females." Without a pretty girlfriend, Cleo's apparent female masculinity alone is not enough to confirm that her version of black masculinity is consistent with the virulent (hetero)sexuality of ghettocentricity's valorized thug. In order to establish and rationalize Cleo's female masculinity, cinematic perception calls forth a black femme, Ursula; after all, as Ja Rule put it, "Every thug needs a lady."

Establishing Cleo's masculinity, markers recognizable to hegemonic common senses as feminine are perceptible in Ursula. Throughout the film, the characters make reference to Ursula's attractiveness. On Ursula's first appearance onscreen (after she kisses Cleo), Frankie comments that she thinks Ursula's outfit is "cute." Luther refers to Ursula as Cleo's "little girlfriend," and Cleo explains why she hasn't shown up to work by showing Ursula off: "Look at what I got here. I bought my baby some new things. Check 'em out." (Cleo shows off the lingerie Ursula is wearing). The film asks ghettocentric common sense: what thug after robbing a bank would not have done the same for Ursula? Sexy and alluring, Ursula's relationship to Cleo calls forth a ghettocentric common-sense version of masculinity and makes Cleo's female masculinity recognizable according to ghettocentric masculinity's contours. Like gangsta rap's thug, Cleo possesses a fine lady.

Ursula secures Cleo's masculinity and in that way justifies Cleo's decision to rob banks. The film goes to great lengths to provide reasons why each of its protagonists becomes a bank robber, except in Cleo's case. In *Set It Off* each of Cleo's friends suffers some social injustice that results from her economic situation. Stony loses her brother to police brutality because he was in the wrong place (Acorn Projects) with the wrong hairstyle at the wrong time. Tisean loses her son to the foster-care system because she cannot afford to pay for childcare while she works. Frankie is fired from her job as a bank teller because she is accused wrongly of helping some men she happened to know because they lived in the same projects with her to rob the bank where she worked. While the three other primary characters in the film have some rationale for getting revenge or making money by robbing a bank, Cleo's masculinity seems to be enough justification for her to resort to crime.[12]

The logic here regarding Cleo's turn to crime is familiar from blaxploitation, gangsta rap, and from the slew of ghetto action films of the early 1990s. It goes something like: men (or in the case of Cleo, masculine women) rob banks or become criminals because they are the ones who are supposed to make the money, and when legal means fail, they find other means; women, on the other hand, find men to support them financially, and thus they do not rob banks without a very good reason. The impoverishment of the postindustrial ghetto leaves black masculinity with few options for survival and women with few financially stable black masculine partners. Like her gangsta-rapping counterparts, Cleo directs attention to the lack of legal means of employment for ghetto dwellers. While the four buddies are sitting on a roof smoking marijuana across the street from an abandoned factory, Cleo points

125

to the factory and recalls, "Before they started laying people off, they was paying folks fifteen dollars an hour at that place. . . . Man, for fifteen dollars an hour, I would be an old . . . 'what-I-gotta-do-sir Muthafucker.' . . . They'd have to pull me off that damn machine. Overtime be like twenty-two fifty an hour!" Part of the film's effort to rationalize their decision to rob banks, Cleo's observations about the abandoned factory provide a context for the soon-to-be-criminals' lack of options.

The film offers several images that describe the violence and devastation that propel Stony, Frankie, and Tisean into crime. These images of "injustice" impact the viewer's sensory-motor schema, where the images can be absorbed by a center of indetermination. In that center, affection surges, laboring to express (via tears, anger, compassion, resentment, etc.) the quality of the injustice it has absorbed. If affection is able to express a quality as a result of its efforts, that expression will be "value," a contentless and simple element necessary to the continued survival of cinematic reality. Affective value thus takes the form of laughter, tears, and the like. Such expressions indicate that movement has been continued by affection. Insofar as it is an internal movement, a motor tendency on a sensitive nerve, affect carves out or flows through connections between one's sensory facets and one's motor mechanisms. The production of affective value can occur when habituated sensory-motor connections break, when something has become too strong in the image and a purely sensory situation occurs. In such a time, affection carves out new connections between one's sensory and one's motor mechanisms, thereby creating new pathways for the production of value. The (re)production of affective value can occur once these pathways have been carved out, when the processes of sensory-motor habituation are in place.

An understanding of how the viewer's sensory-motor schema has been calibrated or habituated to react according to the common sense that glues together the different social groupings with which the viewer feels a sense of belonging can provide a way of predicting how the images of injustice offered by *Set It Off* might be received by the viewer; however, there remains a significant degree of indeterminacy that influences whether or not a quality will be expressed and what form that expression will take. Yet the quality expressed is itself the pay-off that the film promises for the viewer's material investment (of time and money) in the film.

For the viewer's money, *Set It Off* allows for tears, laughter, anger, a critique of "the system" and postindustrial poverty, and a sense of empathy

126

with Stony, Frankie, and Tisean based on what can be recognized clearly as injustices committed against them. In order to generate value from Cleo's characterization, *Set It Off* relies upon sentiment that is already accessible in ghettocentric common sense concerning the difficulties heaped upon black masculinity. Cleo's car, her ghettocentric masculinity, and her lady provide all the justification Cleo needs to "set it off."[13] Cleo's death scene is the violent affective pay-off that is characteristic of ghettocentric narratives, the senseless death of the black masculine body.

Cleo's Spectacular Death

Relying upon the reservoir of value generated by affectivity in order to (re)consolidate and redeploy the ghettocentricity that circulates in gangsta rap and in previous ghetto action films, *Set It Off* must contend with its ghettocentric viewers' possible negative reactions to Cleo's recognizably female body. Within the context of the film's valorization of ghettocentric black masculinity via the character Cleo, Cleo's homosexuality is simply a by-product of her female masculinity. Introducing Ursula in order to legitimate Cleo as the film's representative of ghettocentric black masculinity also has the effect of making visible the butch, who threatens to erupt from a cinematic appearance of an image that is recognizable as a masculine black female. But the butch is derided within ghettocentrism, even though heterosexual black masculinity is valorized. In order to extract value from the ghettocentric viewer's interactions with Cleo, *Set It Off* subjects that viewer to the spectacle of Cleo's violent, heroic death.

Cleo dies in a barrage of bullets fired by police officers waiting for her car to emerge from the tunnel into which it was chased. Before emerging in her newly souped-up ride from the tunnel to confront the waiting helicopters and cop cars, Cleo instructs Stony and Frankie (Tisean has died already) to get out of the car with the money and run. After assessing the situation from her car, Cleo makes up her mind to go down fighting the uniformed representatives of the system. Cleo is shot at multiple times, first while in her car and then when she emerges from the car with her own guns blasting. During this extended and highly stylized sequence, the film's soundtrack emphasizes a slow ballad narrating the futility of Cleo's efforts to better her life and the muffled sounds of Cleo dying. Portions of the chase scene and Cleo's death itself are shown as framed within the television sets that Keith, Black

127

Sam, and Ursula watch. On the soundtrack, the emotionally evocative ballad to which Cleo dies fades as the banal pronouncement of the news anchor is emphasized aurally: "We've just had a horrible moment here. This is our greatest fear for what were to happen. This is the most tragic culmination of the day's events."

Black Sam and the other perceptibly black male images who, forty-ounce bottles of beer in hand, watch the live broadcast of Cleo's death on television also serve to legitimate Cleo's masculinity and thus to authorize an expression of its value within ghettocentric terms. As with Ursula, Black Sam's relationship to Cleo makes Cleo's masculinity translatable into the heterosexist terms of ghettocentrism. This is clear when Cleo approaches Black Sam to buy guns and as part of their negotiation he asks her to hook him up with her "girl," Frankie. Cleo rejects his offer, saying that she will pay him back "with interest, Black Sam, and that's it." By approaching Cleo about including Frankie as part of their deal, Black Sam recognizes Cleo's masculinity within the terms of common-sense black nationalism consolidated by blaxploitation films. Via Black Sam, Cleo is included in the circulations and exchanges through which masculinity is consolidated. Not only does Cleo possess a pretty "little girlfriend," but she also is perceived as controlling access to Frankie.

When Black Sam sees how many helicopters and police cars are chasing Cleo, Frankie, and Stony, he comments, "Man, they're through. They got helicopters and shit. Ain't no escaping that shit." When Cleo dies, Black Sam mutters, "Damn," covering his eyes with his hand and lowering his head as if to mark his distance from the patronizing voice of the news anchor disingenuously sputtering the official apologia for the brutality of the State and the violence necessary to maintain American bourgeois hegemony and its laws. An outlaw like Cleo, Black Sam expresses grief. His expression of grief is an indication of Cleo's entry into the realm of value generated by an affectivity operating according to ghettocentric common sense. Cleo's public execution thus functions on one level as yet another instance of the senseless waste of black masculine life at the hands of the State. Black Sam and the other males watching the execution on television offer a point of identification for those of the film's viewers who have been habituated to perceive images according to ghettocentric common sense.

Cleo's death is spectacular not only because it is broadcast live on television but also because, like the spectacle Guy Debord describes, Cleo's death scene is the stark and bloody aestheticized appearance of bourgeois State power.[14] Unlike that of Frankie and Tisean who occupy spaces of value, however precarious, even before their deaths, Cleo's death itself is the vehicle whereby her existence is valorized. This is clear not only because her death takes its place and time according to television's spatiotemporal mandate that each televisual image is an image of value in process, but also because it conforms Cleo to ghettocentrism's own mandate that each manifestation of black masculinity is a tendency toward death, an outlaw on the path toward a ghetto heaven.[15] Consistent with the way that ritualized deaths such as public executions have served to continue hegemonic organizations of life, Cleo's death generates Stony's "freedom," a middle-class lifestyle toward which Stony was heading at the beginning of the film when she thought she would be sending her brother to college. Cleo chooses death deliberately, knowing that her death will be more valuable than her life.

"What's Up with That? She Don't Talk?" The Black Femme Function

While Black Sam's reaction to Cleo's death assists in shaping a ghettocentric common-sense recognition of Cleo's outlaw masculinity, thereby enabling affectivity to produce value and reproduce ghettocentric social reality, Ursula's reaction, included as a part of the film's sequence portraying Cleo's death, opens onto an alternative possibility, one that arrests the ghettocentric sensory-motor schema's movement toward the simple reproduction of ghettocentric sociality by forcing it to rethink some of its assumptions in order to make sense of Ursula.

Because they can perceive Ursula to be "attractive," hegemonic common senses can find themselves invested in the life of a black butch without fundamentally challenging their existing assumptions concerning sexuality, the currency of femininity in erotic economies, or what constitutes an acceptable model for the organization of social life. Ursula renders Cleo's masculinity perceptible as a version of ghettocentric black masculinity and thus justifies Cleo's decision to rob banks. In this way, Ursula works to make Cleo's character reproductive of value by continuing already commercially viable ghettocentric movements. This is the invisible, affective labor Ursula performs to make the film comprehensible according to ghettocentric common sense.

The affective labor Ursula does in the film coincides with the affectivity of the film's audience, a form of labor that produces social networks and forms of community. Ursula aids the audience in consolidating a ghettocentric black community glued together by, among other sentiments and realities, the shared sense that what it recognizes as black masculinity is, to invoke the cliché, an "endangered species." Both Ursula and the film's audience thereby provide the affective labor necessary to continue the movement of capital by enabling the film's primary representative of black masculinity, Cleo, to be reproductive of value. Ushering a version of female masculinity into the realm of value, albeit via her death, *Set It Off* cuts alternative pathways into sensory-motor apparatuses habituated according to ghettocentrism, thereby preparing the way for further transductions of the value of black masculine death scenes.

Set It Off itself unleashes a considerable amount of violence in its attempt to direct Ursula's affective labor away from the production and valorization of butch-femme and into the valorization of ghettocentric black masculinity. The violence the film unleashes limits Ursula's role in *Set It Off* to that of an erotic object via which black masculinity is consolidated and valorized. It also silences her. (Ursula does not speak in the film.) Confronted with Ursula's tears for a bulldagger whose butchness Ursula's femmeness helped to create and sustain and vice versa, the audience's ghettocentric affectivity can reconsolidate hegemonic heterosexual sociality only by violently conforming butch and femme to heterosexual sociality's categories. While Cleo does not survive the violence necessary to make her reproductive of the value of black masculinity, Ursula does.

The violence the film deploys has a correlate in the physical violence that sometimes occurs when living images are confronted with a present perception, like "the black butch" or "the black femme," that arrests the movements via which those living images make sense of the world. The epistemic violence whereby the versions of masculinity and femininity that emerge in the process of consolidating the black lesbian butch-femme are pummeled into those produced in and through traditional gender roles is another correlate to the violence the film unleashes to forestall Ursula's ability to direct affectivity into an alternative movement, one not yet capable of serving the film's interests.

Ursula herself, the image who works to make the film's masculine female a viable character, does not make sense to the very same common sense in whose interests she labors. The common sense whose assumptions Ursula initially secures cannot accommodate the fact that Ursula labors to meet the erotic and emotional needs of a bulldagger who, at the beginning of the film, cleans white people's offices for a living and drives an old jalopy. In addition,

130

as Jewelle Gomez and others point out, hegemonic common senses generally posit femininity as proper to white women, and therefore they have
difficulty conceiving of a feminine black woman, much less recognizing one
within a cinematic appearance, and even more difficulty with a feminine
black lesbian.[16] Had Ursula not appeared as Cleo's girlfriend, the image I am
recognizing here as "the black lesbian femme" could not have appeared to
ghettocentric common sense at all. Ursula would have appeared to be like
Frankie, an attractive black woman assumed to be heterosexual.

An attractive black female will become perceptible as a lesbian to hegemonic common senses only when she explicitly announces herself as such.
At the beginning of the film, Ursula kisses Cleo, a gesture for which the
film's commitment to ghettocentric black masculinity calls, but one that also
delineates the limits of ghettocentric common sense's current ability to accommodate the forms of sociality engineered by black butches and femmes
as viable alternatives to existing organizations of social life, most notably
compulsory heterosexuality. Kissing Cleo, Ursula reproduces value insofar
as she is a sexy and alluring erotic object, but she is inconceivable except in
those terms. Unable to use Ursula herself to continue the movement of
ghettocentricity or of other types of hegemonic common sense, *Set It Off*
leaves her as an anomaly that is incapable of speaking or of existing except in
relationship to Cleo. Ursula's silence throughout the film is so conspicuous
that Frankie comments on it, asking Tisean about Ursula, "What the fuck is
up with that? She don't talk?" The very thing hegemonic common senses
need to be able to preserve their assumptions while transducing images
of black masculine death, the black femme—in this case, Ursula—is also
what might force them to rethink those assumptions according to a new
perception of the intersection of sexuality, femininity, lesbianism, and black
woman. In other words, the black femme's cinematic appearance might
force hegemonic common senses to make space and time for something
new. In her silence, Ursula directs hegemonic common senses, including
ghettocentrism, toward a recognition that there exist within them alternative
organizations of cinematic reality.

"Prove It On Me": Black Lesbian Butch-Femme

The "butch" and the "femme" I have been formulating throughout this book
comprise the "lesbian" "butch-femme" paradigm, a socioeconomic arrangement pioneered by working-class "lesbians."[17] Like all identity categories,

"butch" and "femme" locate a set of "problems" or "projects" or "things thrown forward" as "projections" or "substitutes" for something(s) inaccessible or unrepresentable. My interest in "butch" and "femme" is not rooted in questions of "identity," but in what an exploration of the constitution of those categories within common sense can reveal about the way that cinematic social reality is produced and about the possibilities for alternatives to that reality to emerge from within the processes of its production. My interest therefore has less to do with the status of "butch" and "femme" as identities than with the extent to which they are available as recognizable figures that have served a vital function (according to certain historical narratives of the twentieth century in the United States) in the formation and sustenance of organizations of "black lesbian" sociality from within a society that actively and violently threatened their very survival.

The term *lesbian* here is merely descriptive. I employ it to indicate that both the butch and the femme are recognizable as anatomically female and that the relationship between them is erotic and physical. Though I use the term *lesbian* in reference to even those whose invisibility within that category secures its very legibility to official common sense, I am not suggesting that *lesbian* necessarily provides a coherent or desirable project for those who simultaneously consider themselves to be "female," feel that they are "black," and develop erotic relationships with other "females."[18] (My reliance on the term *female* is simply a way of marking it as a foundational assumption concerning "gender" within hegemonic common senses.)

Butch-femme has been given a history by "lesbian historiography."[19] In the early twentieth century, most noticeably during World War II, when women in the United States were getting jobs and thus gaining a degree of independence from men, butch-femme lesbian social arrangements enabled the formation of relatively autonomous working-class lesbian communities.[20] During this time, butch-femme surfaces as a set of aesthetic codes through which lesbians could be visible to each other (and, often, to others) and as a set of behavioral codes that allowed for a certain degree of erotic tension and fulfillment and social stability through which what are now recognized as lesbian communities could survive in a violently oppressive world. Butch-femme becomes a vehicle that enables the survival of lesbian forms of sociality.

In the 1970s, when the nascent lesbian and gay liberation movement was achieving some cohesion and visibility as a national presence, lesbian feminists, primarily white, argued strenuously against butch-femme, seeing it as a replica of oppressive gender roles in heterosexual relationships and championing the "woman-identified woman" to the exclusion of other expressions of "same-sex" erotic attachment. As a result of the transformed sociopolitical and economic environment some lesbians enjoyed and of the success of the feminist arguments against it, butch-femme became less common, except in working-class black communities and other working-class communities of color.[21] The dismissal of butch-femme by white middle-class lesbians was enabled further by the fact that butch-femme was no longer particularly useful for those lesbians for whom the women's and lesbian and gay movements had achieved some degree of visibility and safety. (White) butches and femmes quietly left the "lesbian feminist" movement then in formation.[22] While lesbian feminists created the woman-identified woman, many who recognized themselves as butches and femmes, particularly those in black communities and other places that remained invisible to lesbian feminism, simply continued to sustain their own forms of community according to the butch-femme sensibilities they had been carving out for themselves.

It can be argued that in those communities where butch-femme persists, the oppression and exploitation that butch-femme provided a means of surviving had not lessened to the degree that it had for middle-class white lesbians, so butch-femme continued to enable the survival of a community. In addition to this possibility, it is important to recognize the extent to which butch-femme has sedimented stubbornly into black lesbian (and other versions of lesbian) common sense, where to some extent it continues to rationalize existing organizations of lesbian sociality, particularly in those communities where its logic is still useful for the survival of such sociality.

Whatever the reason for the prevalence of butch-femme in communities of color, even in the face of derision and debate, two things are apparent from the discussions that continue to surround butch-femme and from its continued existence as a recognizable practice among black lesbians. First, butch-femme still meets certain needs, whether erotic, economic, or something else, for certain living beings. As an element of black lesbian common sense, butch-femme contains nodes of consent to dominant hegemonies, and it often enforces a rather rigid behavioral and aesthetic code that may have outlived its usefulness for some. At the same time, however, butch-femme also is a malleable form of sociality that still functions as a vehicle for the survival of forms of black lesbian community and as an expression and organization of erotic desire.

Second, having been useful for survival, butch-femme has sedimented

133

into a range of black lesbian common-sense conceptions of lesbianism, becoming a habituated mechanism for recognizing black lesbians and for organizing black lesbian sociality. The elements of butch-femme that proved useful to those who sought to achieve a degree of visibility as butches and femmes and to others has sedimented into various configurations of common sense. A version of lesbian butch-femme that confirms sexist heterosexual gender roles has come to exist also in heterosexist and homophobic common senses. Such hegemonic common senses generally recognize "lesbian" by ordering her appearance into a form of butch-femme. (Hence, the frequency of questions based on heterosexual gender roles, such as "Which one is the man?" and "Who does the cooking?")

Ursula and the Out-of-Field

When Cleo and Ursula kiss at the beginning of the film, Frankie, Stony, and Tisean turn their heads away, a habituated response to the butch-femme eroticism that the kiss makes visible. They react similarly when they walk in on Ursula dancing over Cleo, who is reclining on top of her newly detailed ride. Both reactions emit the violence necessary to (re)consolidate hegemonic forms of sociality, particularly the binary gender assumptions that support existing organizations of heterosexuality, in the presence of a butch-femme eroticism that Cleo's and Ursula's interactions with each other make visible and that is productive of butch-femme sociality.

Because she is productive of ghettocentric masculinity and of butch-femme sociality simultaneously, Ursula's existence troubles the film throughout, but nowhere so strongly as when she reacts to Cleo's death. Immediately after Cleo is barraged by bullets on television, the film's viewer is confronted with Ursula staring at the television screen, her lips trembling as she tries to hold back tears, which flow despite her effort. The anchorman's voice is privileged on the film's soundtrack. It seeks to provide a spatial continuity between three discontinuous spaces, one that includes Ursula, one that is the scene of Cleo's death, and one that includes Black Sam, who serves as a normalizing force that conforms Cleo's death to the contours of ghettocentric masculinity. The visual image of Ursula in the frame alone responding to her lover's televised death scene is overlayed by the sound image of the anchorman's standardized pronouncement of regret over the death of an outlaw, of the black masculine image.

Offered as a way of conjoining three spaces, the televisual voice is disjunctive with the visual images of those spaces. The official pronouncement that Cleo's life held value is undermined by the image of the aftermath of her death: the red lights of police cars, the buzz and whirl of helicopters, and the swarm of living representatives of State power with "police" boldly written on their backs all confirm that Cleo's death itself is the official pronouncement on her life. Ursula's reaction to Cleo's death insists that there are things about Cleo that the official common sense visible on the television screen cannot know or will not recognize about Cleo's life.

Sitting alone in one of the any-space-whatevers characteristic of the post-industrial city's ghettoes while the anchorman spews officially true lies, Ursula sheds tears in reaction to the death of her lover. This is the last image of Ursula the film is able to offer. Ursula's raw expression of grief indicates her capacity to continue the butch-femme movements that *Set It Off* previously held tenuously at bay. Unable to reconcile the official lamentation of Cleo's death with the State violence unleashed to kill her with Ursula's own lamentation in a way that makes each commensurate with the others, the ghettocentric sensory-motor apparatus jams. When it jams, its movements, reproductive of ghettocentric sociality and reality, are arrested.

Perceiving Ursula in the frame alone for the first time as she cries watching Cleo die is a unique challenge to cinematic perception, particularly to those operating according to hegemonic notions of masculinity, femininity, gender, and sexuality. Such sensory-motor schemas cannot recognize a feminine black woman whose erotic energy is directed toward another image that is recognizable as female without fundamentally altering the movements those schemas enable. For the ghettocentric viewer, Ursula reveals that another organization of sociality exists in the ghetto, an organization of social life that makes visible a different past—one in which femininity and masculinity are deployed creatively in order to sustain forms of "butch-femme community." Ursula's expression of grief over her lover's death makes it clear that ghettocentricity operates according to the powers of the false.[23] In other words, Ursula's tears reveal that in its claim to be an expression of reality, the ghettocentric organization of life, particularly its notions of femininity and masculinity, is not necessarily true, because it is exclusive of competing realities that coexist with it.

Ursula's reaction to Cleo's death exposes the fact that Ursula loved Cleo and that Ursula's efforts in *Set It Off* were not aimed simply at continuing the

135

existing movement of ghettocentric black masculinity but also at enabling butch-femme sociality to survive by clearing pathways for its movement. Ursula's emotional reaction to Cleo's death reveals that the narrative I have been formulating by privileging ghettocentricity is not necessarily true, because Cleo and Ursula also have been laboring toward the valorization of an alternative to ghettocentric masculinity, that is, butch-femme sociality, an organization of life that undermines the hegemonic notions of black masculinity within common-sense black nationalism.

Ursula's tears indicate Cleo's value as generated by an affectivity that participates in the production and valorization of an organization of sociality according to an alternative conception of the world that I will refer to as "butch-femme common sense." Along with Ursula, such common sense recognizes Cleo as a butch whose death is heroic not simply because she died protecting her "people" (Frankie and Stony) but also because she died fighting for a better life for herself and her femme. Ursula's existence in the film and the quality of her sorrow over Cleo's death is an indication of the success of butches' and femmes' past efforts to create an alternative organization of sociality.

Ursula's existence in the film thus constantly calls attention to the film's "out-of-field," to off-screen space, and to "what is neither seen nor understood, but . . . nevertheless perfectly present."[24] Deleuze points out that "all framing determines an out-of-field," and he differentiates between "two very different aspects of the out-of-field, each of which refers to a mode of framing."[25] In *Set It Off* Ursula directs attention to both aspects of the out-of-field. One, the relative aspect, is apparent when Ursula first enters the film's frame from off-screen space. While Cleo, Stony, Frankie, and Tisean are talking and laughing in and on Cleo's car, Cleo calls "Ursula, come here, Ursula" into off-screen space just as Ursula walks into the frame, where she and Cleo kiss. Later in that same scene, Cleo instructs Ursula, "Girl, next time I page you, you better be calling me back"—a spatial reference to a set of images which is not seen but which nonetheless exists elsewhere in the film's ghettocentric reality. Presumably, something in the space from which Ursula entered the film's frame kept her from returning Cleo's page. Ursula's silence in response to the question, like her "failure" to return Cleo's page, testifies that Ursula's presence in the frame always carries a reference to another space wherein Ursula has a life and, apparently, a reason not to call Cleo back.

Ursula's whereabouts and actions prior to entering the frame remain unknown, like her existence when she is not with Cleo. When she is not with Cleo, Ursula exists in the film's out-of-field. By virtue of her limited role in the film, her presence in the frame carries a reference to another place that remains unseen. This is true at the end of the film as well. Ursula's reaction to Cleo's death opens onto another set in which butch-femme reality might be framed. Ursula's tears, evidence of past affective labor expended to consolidate butch-femme sociality, render her incapable of advancing the film's interests. In that shot, the only shot in the film in which Ursula occupies the frame alone, her presence in the frame itself "testifies to a more disturbing presence, one which cannot even be said to exist, but rather to 'insist' or 'subsist,' a more radical Elsewhere, outside homogenous space and time."[26] The final shot of Ursula rips her from the order of the visible, from the realm of the common sense she had labored until then to secure. Crying for her butch lover, she is incomprehensible to ghettocentricity's categories.

After that shot, Ursula is left suspended in the film's out-of-field. While all of the film's other characters die or, like Keith, Black Sam, and the cops, return to foreseeable, relatively predictable lives, Ursula disappears from the film after Cleo's death. But the viewers are given no sense of to where or to when Ursula disappears. There and then, she insists on the presence of a more radical Elsewhere that even butch-femme cannot define. In the out-of-field, Ursula remains a disturbing, potentially self-valorizing image, an insistence that keeps the film's ghettocentric reality from being perfectly sealed or closed.

I refer to these aspects of Ursula's role in *Set It Off* as "the black femme function." The black femme function points to a radical Elsewhere that is "outside homogenous space and time" and that "does not belong to the order of the visible."[27] It is a capability of affectivity; it is affectivity's creative, self-valorizing capacity. Because it can be harnessed to reproduce cinematic reality, the black femme function is internal to the cinematic, never outside of it. It represents affectivity's capacity to disturb the reproduction of social life by insisting on the existence of alternatives to existing organizations of social life, even if those alternatives are deemed irrational within hegemonic common senses, an insistence that upsets common sense's operative categories. The black femme function is affectivity's potential for self-valorization that rips the cinematic open from the inside.

137

Reflections on the Black Femme's Role in the (Re)production of Cinematic Reality

The Case of *Eve's Bayou*

The black butch and femme are caught in the processes of transvaluation constitutive of common senses and thus in the processes involved in the consolidation of power and consensus through which the cinematic produces and reproduces a social reality that serves the interests of globalizing capital. Haile Gerima's film *Sankofa* forecloses the possibilities within the slaves' survival and thus ignores what alternatives might reside in the common sense of the film's "seeing slaves." Expunging the genital

7 | *"On and On"*

from the Black, *Sankofa* banishes the black femme to invisibility while violently seeking to close the set of what appears as African. In the Black Revolutionary Woman, one can sense the black femme's presence right after the butch is purged from the image blacks with guns and right before the Black Revolutionary Woman takes her place beside her man. One first caught a glimpse of the black femme in Pam Grier's blaxploitation films, wherein she threatened to disrupt the economy of masculine and feminine bodies that were intrinsic to blaxploitation's consolidation of common-sense black nationalism. Finally, in *Set It Off* the black femme becomes visible, recognizable in Ursula, the sexy lover of Cleo, the film's butch.

Ursula, like the seer-slaves in *Sankofa*, survives. While common-sense black nationalism valorizes death, presenting "dying for the people" as a more noble form of resistance than surviving enslavement and violence, it devalues the tactics used by those who forged ways of sustaining life and communities in the face of violence, exploitation, and oppression, even if that survival meant reproducing the conditions of enslavement until the particular forms of danger passed. In this chapter, we catch up with the witch whose flight we have been following. What impossible possibility might we glimpse once we arrest the flight of the black femme?

Kasi Lemmon's 1997 film *Eve's Bayou* returns us to questions of the past, memory, gender, and liberation's present (im)possibilities, throwing forward another set of problems, no less haunted, that dissimulate agents of power different from those Mona-Shola serves at the end of *Sankofa*. *Eve's Bayou* opens with a tale of the survival of slaves. At the beginning of the film, the narrator—the adult Eve, who tells the story through the eyes of the child Eve—retells local folklore about how the town Eve's Bayou came to be: "The town we lived in was named after a slave. It is said that when General Jean Paul Batiste was stricken with cholera, his life was saved by the powerful medicine of an African slave woman called Eve. In return for his life, he freed her and gave her this piece of land by the bayou. Perhaps in gratitude, she bore him sixteen children. We are the descendants of Eve and Jean Paul Batiste. I was named for her."

The Batistes' myth of origin is rooted in slavery. Their conception, however, is not predicated on a life-or-death struggle for recognition by the Other, but, rather, on a series of exchanges between master and slave. Eve, a slave, saves the life of Jean Paul, a master, with her medicine, and he, in turn, frees her and gives her the land that becomes the town of Eve's Bayou. But the exchange continues because "perhaps in gratitude" Eve gives birth to sixteen of Jean Paul's children. The qualifier *perhaps*, which precedes the qualitative description of the final exchanges between Eve and Jean Paul, highlights three things at once: (1) the story's status as "folklore" (as opposed to "official history" with its claim to "accuracy") or as an element of the common sense that glues the residents of Eve's Bayou together as a "community"; (2) the affective (and, hence, subjective) character of the procreative exchange between Eve and Jean Paul; and (3) the indeterminacy that must be accorded to any attempt to measure the value of that exchange apart from the quantity of its expressions ("sixteen children"). That is, the phrase "perhaps in gratitude" draws attention to the legend's inability to provide an evaluation of the bond that existed between Eve and Jean Paul. Marriage and slavery, the two primary institutions that officially sanction procreative sexual relations between white men and black women, are not mentioned in the narrative as possible evaluations of Eve and Jean Paul's union. Instead, a quality, gratitude, is offered as a possible evaluation (one that likely remains contentious among those for whom the story helps to rationalize the survival of their community) of the bond that produced the Batiste "family," the "we" to which the narrator belongs.

The "we" that is consolidated through the tale's narration thus traces its lineage to a series of exchanges between Eve and Jean Paul Batiste. Even though they are between a master and a slave, these exchanges are not readily assimilated to the master-slave dialectic that informs the existence of Frantz Fanon's "negre" and that habitually is called forth in order to recognize the Black. Where Fanon argues that in the original traumatic experience of slavery and colonization, the Black's inferiority comes into existence permanently through the Other, thereby creating a colonized and civilized society that is stuck in a type of "prehistory" of "the human," *Eve's Bayou* presents a group of living beings, the Batistes, who came into existence as expressions of an exchange between "master" and "slave," the quality of which is measured by the Batiste's financial success. The black that emerges from Fanon's analysis of the (im)possibility of ontology in a colonized and civilized society is a conception of the Black that informs both official common sense and the common-sense black nationalisms that have become hegemonic within black common sense.

The differences between Fanon's black and the "we" who are the descendents of Eve and Jean Paul Batiste are significant because they highlight the extent to which what appears in *Eve's Bayou* calls forth a past different from that habitually relied upon to recognize the Black. Through the myth of the origin of the community it frames, *Eve's Bayou* innovatively redirects the habituated mechanisms whereby the Black commonly is recognized away from a traumatic past of slavery and into a still-present past wherein slavery and freedom are indiscernible; the difference between the powerful medicine woman Eve's status as slave and her status as free resides in the adjudication of the phrase "perhaps in gratitude" and in the monetary value of her newly acquired property, "this . . . land by the bayou." The films' spectators are given no system of judgment with which to decide whether Eve chose to give birth to sixteen of Jean Paul's children out of gratitude or whether the terms of her slavery simply were transferred into serving as Jean Paul's mistress and baby machine. *Eve's Bayou*—both the story the film tells and the land called Eve's Bayou, on which the story takes place—is predicated on the common sense of a slave woman for whom the nonevent of emancipation opens another form of enslavement in which gratitude might dissimulate the nonchoice of survival. At the beginning of the film, the "we" who indexes the exchange between master and slave is ensconced in the social networks productive of the heterosexual bourgeois family, a formation one might recognize as one of the exploitative mechanisms that supports the hegemony of contract labor and the state's demand for heteronormativity.

The first Batistes who the audience sees are Mozelle and Roz, elegantly dressed at a party, each with a champagne glass in her hand. Roz's husband, Louis Batiste, is "the best colored doctor in Louisiana." The descendants of Eve and Jean Paul are well-to-do, steeped in the trappings of bourgeois respectability; they wear glamorous clothes, live in fancy houses, throw formal parties, and speak French Creole. Significantly, the myth of the origin of the Batistes, predicated on an exchange the value of which the Batistes themselves are the expression, supports the continuation of bourgeois American sociality and its affiliation with "whiteness." Bearing a white French general's surname and staking a claim to the land on which they live, the Batistes appear at first to be simply a vehicle for the perpetuation of American bourgeois sociality.

For the remainder of this film, however, the networks via which the Batiste's bourgeois sociality is reinforced and sustained—the exclusive sexual connection between "husband" and "wife" that is productive of "family," the economic ("professional") relationships that generate "wealth," and the commonly held conceptions of the world that currently rationalize hegemonic relations—crumble.[1] Sexual networks that are not productive of normative notions of family (such as Louis's various affairs with other women), work that is not paid labor (such as Louis's sexual labor, the "work" that keeps him out all night and on Sundays ostensibly tending to his patients, or the domestic labor Roz performs to keep her children safe and comfortable, or the caring labor Roz's and Louis's daughter Cisely does for her father to keep him from "divorcing" his family), and conceptions of the world that confound conventional rationality (such as the epistemological orders of voodoo, fortune-telling, and the spirit world), slowly appear, filling the film's frame, while the rationality and viability of the bourgeois family quickly disintegrates. Orchestrating the disintegration of the primary institution of bourgeois sociality and the innovation of an alternative to it, the film's narrator, Eve, the character with whom the film's spectators are most closely allied, frames images from her childhood.

As I point out in chapter 6, Deleuze asserts that "all framing determines an out-of-field," and he distinguishes between what he refers to as "two very different aspects of the out-of-field": a relative aspect and an absolute aspect.[2] Deleuze uses the terminology of "the frame" or "framing" to refer to "the parts of all kinds which become part of a set," and this set is "everything which is present in the image." According to Deleuze's formulation of cinema, the set is a closed system, but it is relatively or artificially closed. This

141

set, what is in the frame, is only relatively and artificially closed, because, by the very fact of its formation, it determines that which is not framed, that which is not seen, the out-of-field.

Deleuze's relative aspect of the out-of-field is that which, were it to be framed, could be seen according to the terms of the system: "When a set is framed, therefore seen, there is always a larger set, or another set with which the first forms a larger one and which can in turn be seen, on condition that it gives rise to a new out-of-field."[3] The absolute aspect of the out-of-field, on the other hand, is qualitatively different from the relative. Deleuze explains that it is the absolute aspect of the out-of-field that enables each closed system to open onto a "duration which is immanent to the whole universe, which is no longer a set and does not belong to the order of the visible."[4] While the relative aspect of the out-of-field functions to add space to space, the absolute aspect introduces "the transspatial and the spiritual into the system which is never perfectly closed."[5]

In *Set It Off* Ursula enters the frame from the out-of-field, a spatial designation that exists within the film's ghettocentric milieu and that potentially could be seen. Due to her limited role in the film, even when she enters the frame Ursula carries a reference to the relative aspect of the out-of-field, off-screen space, and she functions to add space to the space the film framed prior to her entry into it. In the last shot of Ursula, however, the film's off-screen space is obliterated by affectivity's effort to rationalize that space according to the terms of ghettocentricity when confronted by something those terms render impossible—a black femme.

Crying at her butch lover's violent death, Ursula excavates an outside to ghettocentric reality, rendering that reality "problematic." But because the outside she excavates is "butch-femme sociality," the reality toward which she directs affectivity is still within cinematic reality, and, hence, it, no less than ghettocentric reality, operates according to cinematic processes. When recognized as a black femme, Ursula makes ghettocentric reality (which valorizes a virulently heterosexual masculinity) visible as a "problem" insofar as that reality purports to include her, yet is unable to rationalize her existence within it. But the outside to ghettocentric reality that is excavated when Ursula is framed at the end of the film—butch-femme reality—is no less problematic, because it, like ghettocentric reality, is consolidated by cinematic processes whose business is the projection of problems. Thus, even my attention to the black femme is inherently problematic and quite possibly will be subject to debate about the choices I have made in my own framing of her.[6]

Nonetheless, in my formulation of her, the black femme both provides the affective labor necessary to reproduce hegemonic sociality and, along with the black butch, simultaneously does immaterial labor to produce alternative social networks. She is a figure who currently exists on the edge-line between what commonly can be "seen" and understood (common sense) and what is neither seen nor understood (the Open or, when she makes visible a problem, the outside). With one foot in an aporia and one foot in the set of what appears, the black femme currently is a reminder that the set of what appears is never perfectly closed and that something different might appear therein at any-instant-whatever. Like all sets, the set of what appears determines an out-of-field to which the black femme currently points (except when what appears is black butch-femme common sense, an appearance that creates another out-of-field). If the entire set of what appears can be understood as cinematic reality, then it is clear that the black femme, while a product of that reality, also might be a portal to a reality that does not operate according to the dictates of the visible and the epistemological, ethical, and political logics of visibility. Eve and her Aunt Mozelle allow one to think this possibility within cinematic reality.

The black femme haunts previous black lesbian and other feminist and womanist projects insofar as these have been predicated on the construction of a collective that is or might become recognizable according to particular characteristics assumed to be common to the collective. Challenging affectivity to recognize the Black in the black femme, the appearance of the black femme makes visible that the set of what appears as black is problematic. Similarly, wherever and whenever she is visible, the black femme reveals that the set of what commonly appears then and there as "woman" and the set of what commonly appears as "lesbian" are problematic. Moreover, operating according to "the method of AND," she imposes a difference in potential between at least three images.[7] The black femme is "black" (recognizable as such by skin color) AND "woman" (recognizable as such by anatomical characteristics) AND "lesbian" (recognizable as such by her erotic desire for another who also is or might be revealed as visibly "woman"). And she is each of these in such a way that each category's claim to be an expression of her identity is exploded by the effort required to maintain the validity of that claim. In each case, the black femme urges the project expressed by the category to recognize an alternative potential within it. Today, the unity and coherence of the collectives thought to have been represented by the production over time of the identity categories "black," "woman," and "lesbian" are shattered with the appearance of "a black femme," an image that is only the most recent in a history of projects that have rendered the entire concept of identity problematic.[8] The black femme here appears as a continuation of the project "woman-of-color feminism." She, too, is problematic and produced within the very structures she might challenge. She, too, points to alternative organizations of life that are immanent to present conditions of capitalist exploitation.

I used the phrase "the black femme function" in order to mark a potential for creativity and self-valorization within affectivity that also is useful to the reproduction of cinematic reality. While it is the case that "the black femme" indexes an existing set of embodied experiences, it is also the case that expressions of those experiences currently are not amenable to furthering existing hegemonic socioeconomic arrangements. While it might be argued that this is valid for any number of representations, especially for ones that are not commonly visible, the sets of images that the black femme might rip open have been my concern because in order to recognize a black femme in a present perception, the official and hegemonic constructions of race, sexuality, and gender must be called into question in ways that might dislodge the racist, sexist, and homophobic conceptions of the world for which those constructions currently work to maintain consent.

Many common-sense considerations of the existence of black lesbian butch-femme are forced to admit that several of the categories on which those common senses rely to rationalize the reality they (re)produce are open and fluid, not static and closed. In order to maintain themselves when confronted with the possibility that "black femme" might describe a present perception, black common senses—in which varieties of common-sense black nationalism, including ghettocentricity, are hegemonic—must readjust their notions of masculinity, femininity, gender, and sexuality. In addition, many of the operative categories in most lesbian feminist common senses, Freudian-Lacanian common senses, and Marxist common senses are unsettled when confronted with a present perception that could be a black femme. For this reason, the black femme is not visible as such to most living images.

The black femme is invisible within these common senses because the things that distinguish her as a black femme are not visible to those common senses until she is placed in relationship to the butch. The logic of her identification is not immediately specular in the same way as it is for the black, the woman, the white male, and so on. As a black lesbian who is feminine, she defies the specular logic that generally organizes "lesbian," as well as that which organizes "black" and "woman." For example, she does not appear to most hegemonic common senses to be a lesbian until her appearance is altered via references to her erotic desires. In the case of the black femme I have been formulating, her erotic desires are directed toward the butch in a way that mitigates against the nomination *femme* being merely descriptive of physical characteristics. Within the butch-femme paradigm out of which I have gleaned the black femme, those desires stipulate that the identity of the black femme corresponds to a way of being (that is also a way of "being against" heteronormativity). For her, becoming visible to official and other hegemonic common senses is a dangerous task because to do so she confronts them with the tenuousness of their own versions of reality, thereby threatening the stability of the regime of truth on which their hegemony relies.

My point in attempting to make the black femme visible to certain of the common senses that (in)form black studies, lesbian and gay studies, women's studies, and film studies is not to inaugurate another identity-based project or movement, but to interrogate the common senses that animate each of those areas of specialization.[9] By drawing attention to a figure who is constructed according to cinematic processes of specular identification, but who defies the specular logics that congeal existing categories, I have been posing questions concerning what interests and movements are furthered by the habituated recognition of the black, the woman, and the lesbian. I insist that each of those categories, when exploded or made problematic, might harbor alternatives based on what within that category remains unassimilated into hegemonic common senses and thus into the racist, sexist, and homophobic forms of sociality those common senses rationalize. Some of those alternatives still might be excavated within cinematic reality. Pointing to an outside beyond each set of what appears as black, as woman, and as lesbian, and even beyond cinematic reality itself, the black femme might restore a critical belief in the world by revealing that alternatives persist within it.[10]

The black femme carries an erotic sexual valence, and she sustains and/ or redirects social networks, most noticeably those constitutive of butch-femme sociality. The black femme function refers to the affectivity that disentangles itself from the project of reproducing capitalist relations (but does not [yet] break with that project) in order to participate in an enterprise that is more consistent with sustaining the conditions such affectivity perceives to be necessary to its own survival. The aspect of affectivity I isolate here as the black femme function has been identified in the service of a prior project articulated to address a different historical conjuncture than our own—that of the "African slave woman," which Angela Davis put into circulation in 1971. It is an affectivity of slaves.

The Cinematic Community of "Slaves"

Written in the Marin County Jail in San Rafael, California, Davis's seminal essay "Reflections on the Black Woman's Role in the Community of Slaves" set out to refute the Moynihan Report's "consecration" of the "myth" of "the matriarchal Black woman." To do so, Davis reached into the fecundity of pasts in order to retrieve an image she called "the African slave woman" and to offer that image as a prototype of "the Black woman" she was formulating in opposition to Moynihan's "Black matriarch." Davis argued that the African slave woman in the United States, by virtue of her oppression as a woman, an oppression that added domestic labor to her workload, performed "the only labor of the slave community which could not be directly and immediately claimed by the oppressor," doing so "in the infinite anguish of ministering to the needs of the men and children around her (who were not necessarily members of her immediate family)."[11]

Today, one would understand the labor that Davis's African slave woman performed in the slaves' living quarters to be "immaterial labor," affective labor, "labor in the bodily mode" (which is generally associated with contact between living beings) whose "products are intangible, a feeling of ease, well-being, satisfaction, excitement, or passion."[12] By "ministering to the needs" of other slaves who were not necessarily family, Davis's African slave woman worked to establish and sustain forms of community among slaves.[13]

Davis later revised her argument by including a reference to the labor (such as hunting and gardening, which produce tangible products) that her African slave man performed for the sustenance of the slave community.[14] Davis's initial suggestion, however, that the domestic labor of enslaved African women could be relatively autonomous from the slave master's command opened up an understanding of the revolutionary potential in the slave's condition. Precisely by providing labor necessary to reproduce the slave, to ensure the slave's survival by "ministering to his needs," the African slave woman occupied a central position in weaving what Davis called "the theme of resistance" into the fabric of the slave's daily existence. Davis's African slave woman, in other words, was in the position to infuse the common sense that enabled the survival of the slave community with the theme of resistance. The labor performed by Davis's African slave woman could be understood as the immaterial labor of molding common sense and the affective labor of creating social networks and forms of community. As Davis explained, "If resistance was an organic ingredient of slave life, it had to be directly nurtured by the social organization which the slaves themselves improvised."[15] Survival and resistance were, in this sense, inseparable —the (re)production of the slave was a form of resistance, which highlights the continuing relevance of Fred Moten's insights about the fact that "objects can and do resist."[16]

For her part, Davis presented the position of black women in the "black community" of her essay's present as part of a revolutionary inheritance available to "black people" as a whole, not as a pathology to be overcome in the name of equality, as Moynihan recommended. Out of the common sense that formulates the black woman as pathological, Davis fashioned an image of a black woman who continued to enable the survival of black community and made her available for circulation as a common concept. Davis did this by creating a historical narrative for the black woman's emergence that built on the narrative provided by official common sense (as elaborated by the Moynihan Report).[17] Davis presented the black woman as revolutionary, or at least as potentially so, by providing an alternative historical context for the crucial function that the black woman continued to fulfill in the (re)production of social reality.

The "community of slaves" in Davis's title is best understood as referring to a social order created by enslaved Africans in the United States. As such, it corresponds to a particular set of spatiotemporal coordinates. Herein lies one of the primary differences between the role fulfilled by Davis's enslaved African woman and that which I characterize as the black femme function in the cinematic. Clearly, slavery, the ownership of one living being by another, still exists, so it remains important not to dilute the word *slave* by wrenching it from its particular denotation. In addition, it is important to maintain the

147

coherence of those pasts characterized by the enslavement of Africans in the Americas, leaving them available to further innovative excavations, even while insisting on a critical awareness of the way "slavery" often functions to posit an originary production of black subjectivity that is presumed retrospectively to cohere over time.[18] I therefore retain the specificity of the enslavement of Africans in the Americas as a particular form of exploitation corresponding to specific spatiotemporal coordinates, the consequences of which are still being lived out all over the planet. At the same time, I seek to make available to a sustained analysis of contemporary processes of extracting labor power the specific insights gleaned from a critical interrogation into the enslavement of Africans.

Processes of globalization extract labor power through forms of affectivity and construct subjectivities necessary to the continuation of their projects. Insofar as affectivity increasingly characterizes efforts to make sense of the world, it locates the (non)choice of survival in cinematic reality: through affectivity, one offers up one's life as a contribution to capitalist power to the extent that one consents to remain alive. The present constitution of power resembles the system of slavery because it depends on types of labor, forms of affectivity, that might be placed in the category of "inorganic condition of production," forms of labor posed as "natural conditions of the producer's existence."[19] In the cinematic, labor power, through affectivity and other immaterial forms of labor, is immediately available for the consolidation of an alien and oppressive power, much like slave labor during slavery, a tyrannical system still in existence.

Yet, just as slaves were forced to "improvise" forms of community and sociality that fulfilled some of their needs, black women "in the life" forged a black butch-femme paradigm, a working-class economic and social arrangement that emerged as one of the ways of accommodating their needs and erotic interests. Ministering to the needs of black femmes and black butches by providing the caring labor necessary to reproduce them, and helping to establish and sustain forms of community by working to make black lesbian butch-femme visible, if only to others who long for such community, the labor of black femmes and of black butches, like that of Davis's enslaved African women, can be understood as immaterial, affective labor.

Black butch-femme thus fulfills the function Davis assigns to the black woman in the community of slaves. Davis's enslaved African woman and my black butch-femme are each primarily responsible for the (re)production of the social reality of a particular collective ("slaves" and "Black lesbian butch-femmes," respectively) and the common sense that characterizes and enables the survival of their fragile communities. This function was, according to Davis's analysis, fundamentally productive and supportive of insurgency because it created and sustained forms of community wherein resistance to the oppressive power of the slave system could be nurtured. Creating and reproducing the slaves' social reality in a way that made sense to the slaves, the enslaved African woman ensured the survival of black people in the Americas, but in doing so, she also ensured the endurance of an exploitable population. Laboring in the domestic sphere, the one place that might be deemed relatively autonomous from the slave master's command, Davis's enslaved African woman actively infused the common sense negotiated for the blacks' survival with a recognition of the urgent need for insurgency. She thereby unleashed the potential for the production of insurgent subjectivities and alternative social realities.

Today, this potential might be grasped under the rubric of the black femme function in order to highlight the current existence of a figure hidden within the histories and logics generated by U.S.-based struggles against racism, sexism, and homophobia, a figure whose invisible, affective labor ensures the survival of forms of sociality that were never meant to survive. Though named for a particular figure, the black femme function is available via affectivity in general. As long as it can be said that cinematic reality exists, the Black femme function can be said to persist within it, threatening to rip open the set of what appears in any-instant-whatever and to reveal the alternate organizations of life hidden therein.

Eve's Bayou

Eve's Bayou engages affectivity's black femme function in order to consolidate a common sense that might support the film's own survival as a profitable commodity. Unlike *Sankofa*, Pam Grier's blaxploitation films, and *Set It Off*, *Eve's Bayou* was not made for a single, existing, identifiable demographic. Even though it was thought to be a film "for African American women," its success eventually rested upon its ability to find a market in addition to African American women and/or to create a market that valorized the film. The first feature film by an African American woman to have a theatrical release, *Eve's Bayou* was "the top grossing 1997 picture made by a company not affiliated with a studio."[20] Commenting on the difficulty of producing *Eve's Bayou*, Ray Price, the senior vice-president of theatrical marketing at Trimark Pictures, said, "We couldn't say 'This is like such-and-such' because there were no correlations."[21] Made for four million dollars, the film was marketed primarily to critics as an "upmarket" art film, and it grossed roughly fifteen million dollars.[22] According to Price's assessment of *Eve's Bayou*'s financial success, the film had to be recognizable as an art film in order to be profitable.

In order to be recognizable as an art film, *Eve's Bayou* avoids "the clichés of recent African American cinema," which presumably include a ghetto-centric setting, images of "senseless violence," and a script that directs attention to the dismal or heroic or dismally heroic quality of black American existence.[23] At the time of its theatrical release, *Eve's Bayou* was distinguished from the two preceding financially successful films that also targeted and consolidated "African American women," *Waiting to Exhale* and *Soul Food*, by its ability to be perceived as an art film. Like Julie Dash's film *Daughters of the Dust* (1991), *Eve's Bayou* creates a conjunction between film critics and black women that defies the hegemonic common senses that (in)form each category. Price makes reference to this similarity between *Eve's Bayou* and *Daughters of the Dust*, but he does so in order to mark Dash's film as imposing a limitation on *Eve's Bayou*'s ability to circulate rapidly and be profitable: "We could have said, 'This is like *Daughters of the Dust*,' but you can't make a $4 million film based on a picture that made only $1 million."[24] As the top-grossing nonstudio film of 1997, *Eve's Bayou* is not only quantitatively different from *Daughters of the Dust*, it also is qualitatively different because it relies upon formal conventions that are more familiar than the latter's. Where Dash's film creates an aesthetic considered to be adequate to habituate a common sense that might organize an antihegemonic expression of the black woman, *Eve's Bayou* relies upon more widely circulated formal techniques that have been proven effective in extracting surplus value from affectivity.[25] For instance, *Eve's Bayou* draws on the value amassed by certain black film stars—the cast of Lemmons's film includes "stars" such as Samuel Jackson, Lynn Whitfield, Diahann Carroll, and Debbi Morgan—and it presents a linear narrative by offering a young girl, Eve, as the spectator's point of identification.

Yet the stylistic and narrative innovations that *Eve's Bayou* does execute within a "conventional" film form are components of the film's effort to carve out a sensory-motor schema that would valorize the film. Two of these innovations—the sequences that frame Eve's and Mozelle's visions and the sheets of past accessed in order to explain the Batiste family's existence—help delineate the way that the financial success of *Eve's Bayou* depends on its ability to direct its spectators' affectivity toward not only the reproduction of value but also, increasingly, toward a valorization of the spectacle of the disintegration of the bourgeois family, a fundamental form of bourgeois sociality, and the creation of alternative social networks and relations.

Eve's Bayou must create alternative social networks in order to extract value from its spectators' affectivity because the images that the film works to valorize are inimical to bourgeois sociality. They are the images frequently called forth to provide bourgeois sociality with an irrational "other," thereby enabling bourgeois sociality to appear rational through comparison. In order to valorize itself, *Eve's Bayou* has to carve new sensory-motor pathways through which its images might circulate and produce value. One of the ways that it attempts this feat is by distinguishing itself from the spate of ghetto action films that immediately preceded it.

In contradistinction to ghettocentric films, *Eve's Bayou* is set in the bayous of Louisiana in the summer of 1960. The film focuses on the well-to-do Batiste family, the descendants of Eve and Jean Paul Batiste. The opening sequence calls attention to the fact that the film is framed though the perceptual schema of a young girl as that perception has been remembered by an adult Eve. One of the shots in the opening montage is of a man and a woman in a passionate embrace, an image framed in a young girl's iris (the viewer later finds out that the eye is Eve's and that the man and the woman are Louis, Eve's father, and Matty Meraux, Louis's friend's wife). The voice-over that follows the opening montage situates what is to come as the narrator's memory of "the summer [she] killed her father." That summer, Eve tells the audience, she was ten years old. Framing Eve's memory of that summer on a black screen, *Eve's Bayou* provides the how and the why of Eve's assertion that she "killed" her father.

Eve discovers her father's affair with Matty Meraux at the dinner party with which the film opens. What Eve sees of their encounter is what was framed in black-and-white, slow-motion, close-up shots in the film's title sequence. When the film's spectators are given access to one of Eve's visions, in which Eve "sees" her uncle's death, the spectators are capable of recognizing that the film's opening sequence frames a "vision" much like those available to Eve and her Aunt Mozelle.

Both Eve and Mozelle have "the gift of sight": by holding someone's hand

151

in theirs, they can see that person's past, present, and future in images. When *Eve's Bayou* displays these visions, it generally does so in black-and-white sequences of apparently disconnected visual images that relink over autonomous sound-images. Each vision sequence inevitably produces an "any-space-whatever" wherein viewers (and Eve and Mozelle) see what Deleuze has identified as cinematic time, a present that passes and a past which is preserved.

A clear example of this occurs in the sequence that shows Mozelle advising her clients, residents of Eve's Bayou who come to Mozelle for "psychic counseling." One client's son is missing, and when she touches Mozelle's hands, the any-space-whatever that contains him sitting on a toilet giving himself an overdose injection of drugs becomes visible. Mozelle is able to relink the disconnected spaces and times available to her as visions into a narrative that is comprehensible to her client, telling her that she will find her son in Detroit at St. Michael's Hospital the following Tuesday. The irrational cuts that characterize Mozelle's visions render the film's viewer incapable of making sense of the images; there is no way for the viewer to glean the spatiotemporal coordinates of the vision's images: "Detroit," "St. Michael's Hospital," "next Tuesday." During each of the vision sequences, what was the out-of-field is obliterated because it is what occupies the frame. Mozelle's clients ask for knowledge about events that have occurred, that will occur, or that are occurring in the film's off-screen space, and *Eve's Bayou*, via Mozelle, a seer, makes that space and time visible.

When the film's out-of-field itself is framed, not only is its relative aspect obliterated, but its absolute aspect is destroyed as well. There is no longer an out-of-field, because the set of what appears has become the Open; undecidable, unlocatable, nonchronological pasts, presents, and futures are framed as visions. A time-image appears that jams the spectator's sensory-motor schema, rendering her a seer. Confronted with these visions, the film's spectator works, largely to no avail, to recognize the present perception. While the film's viewer becomes a seer, like Mozelle, she becomes one who must rely on Mozelle, an image, framed by the film, whose sensory-motor schema is habituated to make sense of the incomprehensible visions in order to communicate (and thus make common) what she sees. Operating according to a sensory-motor schema for which the irrational, the absolute out-of-field, or a more radical Elsewhere can continue movement, Mozelle provides the labor necessary to communicate the image's "meaning" to her clients (and thus to the film's viewers). Such communication, however, reestablishes for the viewer an out-of-field and imposes an order that fills the space opened by its temporary dissolution.

Mozelle gets paid for communicating, or making common, what appears to be irrational. She thus assists in valorizing a subterranean epistemology that rationalizes a set of subaltern customs, behaviors, relationships, and beliefs, such as voodoo and fortune-telling, that challenge official and hegemonic common sense, such as the medical knowledge upheld by Louis. For instance, when Madame Renard comes to see Mozelle and finds out that her own niece spent all of her money, she asks Mozelle for help. Mozelle tells Madame Renard to get a small bag, put a piece of lodestone and some other materials into it, and tie it with a "devil shoestring." Mozelle instructs her further to "sprinkle five drops of holy water" into her right hand and to "keep the bag next to [her] skin." Later, when Louis pays a house call to Madame Renard, he notes that her condition is getting better, and he attributes the improvement to the medicine he prescribed. Madame Renard agrees that "everything will be just fine now," and she indicates (to the viewer, but not to Louis) that she believes her improved condition is due to the pouch that Mozelle gave her. Like Madame Renard, many of the residents of Eve's Bayou share a conception of the world in which certain things that official common sense deems irrational—voodoo, magic, communicating with spirits, seeing nonchronological time—operate to make the world appear reasonable and amenable to their survival.

Mozelle's ability is referred to as a gift, the "gift of sight," but it causes Louis, Mozelle's brother, to perceive Mozelle to be "crazy." Louis says as much after Mozelle sees a vision that she communicates as a child being hit by a bus. Based on the images Mozelle accessed as visions, Roz decides to keep her children indoors until Mozelle says it is safe for them to go outdoors again. Louis finds both Mozelle's visions and the fact that Roz trusts them to be incomprehensible. He reminds his wife, "Roz, you know I love my sister, but she is not unfamiliar with the insides of a mental hospital." When Cisely agrees that "Aunt Mozelle is crazy," Eve objects, explaining that Aunt Mozelle "knows things. People trust her." Louis makes Eve aware of the official assessment of Aunt Mozelle's "gift": "Sweetheart, your Aunt Mozelle is a little eccentric. That fortune-telling is just something we let her do to keep her out of trouble." Having spent time in mental hospitals because she "knows things" that official and hegemonic common senses deem to be

153

unknowable, Mozelle puts the unthought into thought and thereby elicits from people an affective response.[26] As Eve explains in defense of Mozelle against the claim that Mozelle is crazy, "People trust her."

Eve's Bayou puts the viewer into the image in much the same way as Mozelle and Eve become part of the images to which they have access. In this way, the viewer's ability to continue the movements productive of bourgeois rationality is arrested while the irrational becomes visible and the out-of-field shatters the frame, thereby making the viewer into a seer who either must harness her affectivity's creativity and direct it toward an alternative to bourgeois rationality or violently finesse a habituated movement through that which bourgeois common sense currently constitutes as irrational. In *Eve's Bayou* the irrational not only defines the composition of Mozelle's and Eve's visions—that is, the way that their images are cut into or over other images rendering them all unrecognizable and unlocatable any-space-whatevers to the viewer—but it also provides the impetus for the formation of social networks and complicates, sometimes even frustrates, the viewer's attempt to "interpret" the film's narrative.

The frustration that many viewers experience at the end of the film is evidence of the fact that *Eve's Bayou* requires nothing less of its viewers' affectivity than for it to prepare the sensory-motor pathways through which a social reality corresponding to the seers' (Mozelle's and Eve's) common sense might be created.[27] As the film's narrative is revealed, the Batiste family becomes more disjointed. Louis, Eve's father, is absent from the home more and more often, and Eve, her sister, Cisely, and her brother, Poe, watch their mother, Roz, absorb more and more pain from their father's actions. When, at the end of the film, Eve and Cisely push their father's handwritten version of what happened the night of the storm into the engulfing, mysterious waters of the swamp, it is clear that the old order of the Batistes, rationalized by the father's written word, has been overthrown in favor of the enigmatic, undecidable, irrational visions available to the viewer and to Eve. Faced with two versions of the same event—Cisely's oral version of the kiss between herself and her father, and Louis' handwritten version of it—Eve relies upon her gift of sight in order to adjudicate between the competing stories. When Eve takes Cisely's hand in hers, the kiss between Cisely and Louis fills the frame. But that image does not provide a commonly held system by which to judge what happened and which of the available competing versions is "the truth." As a spectator, one knows only that something happened in the past and that whatever happened continues to shape the contours of the present. Just as Mozelle does for her clients, Eve labors as the film's narrator to make common the visions to which the film provides its spectators access. In order to communicate via the images it puts into circulation, *Eve's Bayou* puts the unthought—voodoo, fortune-telling, nonchronological time, a kiss between father and daughter—into thought and obliterates the out-of-field, making its spectators into seers without a system of judgment by which to adjudicate what they see, but equipped with a sense that something happened that upset Cisely and made Eve want to kill her father.

In order to consolidate a market that would operate in its interests, *Eve's Bayou* carves out sensory-motor pathways capable of valorizing Cisely, Eve, and Mozelle, descendants of Eve, a powerful medicine woman who saved a man's life and, perhaps out of gratitude to her master, set into motion a vital community. The descendant named after her—the film's narrator, Eve, a seer—orchestrated her own father's death in exchange for her sister's life.[28] Gifted with "sight," Eve frames the disintegration of the form of sociality set in motion by her ancestors Eve and Jean Paul and creates the sensory-motor pathways that support a form of sociality in which she, her sister, her Aunt Mozelle, and her mother Roz might survive. Orchestrating her father's death and rejecting the written Law of the Father in favor of the wisdom of sensuous visions, Eve at the end of the film seems to have made possible a new community, one in which seers, though still fettered to the mechanisms whereby cinematic reality and its hellish cycles are reproduced, are capable nonetheless of acting and surviving. As Eve holds hands with Cisely and faces the bayou, her capacity for self-valorization and the reality it might create remain suspended in a direct image of cinematic nonchronological time containing the seeds of a new movement. Finally, however, *Eve's Bayou* is unable to put into motion the new organization of life whose corresponding sensory-motor pathways it forges.

The narrator closes the film by ruminating, "Like others before me, I have the gift of sight. But the truth changes color depending on the light and tomorrow can be clearer than yesterday. Memory is the selection of images. Some elusive, others printed indelibly on the brain. Each image is like a thread. Each thread, woven together to make a tapestry of intricate texture and the tapestry tells a story and the story is our past."

Emboldened by the narrator's admission that what *Eve's Bayou* makes visible is that "the truth changes color depending on the light," official and hegemonic common senses normalize the failure of the Batiste family, presenting the pain caused by that failure as one of the costs of being human and thus of forming bourgeois families. This is evident in statements made in reviews of the film, including quotations attributed to members of the film's cast. For instance, Diahann Carroll claims that working on the *Eve's Bayou* "felt so refreshing because this was a story unlike anything we've seen before. . . . Even though all the characters are Black, that's not what the movie is about. This is not a story about the 'hood, about the problems and challenges that face a certain group of people. This is about the things that happen in the lives of a family, about sexuality and fear and love and things that anybody can understand and relate to."[29]

More insistent about funneling *Eve's Bayou*'s images into the hegemonic categories that valorize the bourgeois family, Trimark's marketing executive relies upon clichéd appeals to "the universal" and "the human" in order to explain the film's financial success: "This is one of the few times that a film was made with an all-Black cast about the African American experience outside urban issues and crime issues. It was about human issues, the kind of thing you get from Tennessee Williams—timeless, universal stories absent politics."[30]

While it is not my specific aim to untangle the deplorably racist common sense that siphons "the propertied white male" into the "universal category" of "the human" by funneling "urban issues" and "crime issues" into the domain of the Black and then expunging the latter three from the human on the basis that they are "particular" experiences of no interest to the propertied white male (the human), it is important to mark that this is the common sense that regularly rationalizes the financial success of *Eve's Bayou*: that is, *Eve's Bayou* was financially successful because it wasn't "black," but "human."

My argument about *Eve's Bayou* is substantially different from Price's and Carroll's. I claim that by framing nonchronological time and other "irrational" images and by valorizing living images that are capable of making those irrational images common, *Eve's Bayou* introduces into the project of "the human" elements of cinematic reality that exist outside of that project. The film thereby provides the opportunity for affectivity to be directed into a project that is inconsistent with that of the human. The film does this in order to ensure its own survival as a profitable commodity. Another way of describing *Eve's Bayou*'s success is to say that the only way a film made by a black woman and valorizing black women and girls can get made and be financially successful is if it recreates the very categories within which it will be received. Such a film either must open the human to include the black woman, or it must explode the human by excavating an outside within cinematic reality and laboring to make that outside common. *Eve's Bayou* attempts the latter.

If *Eve's Bayou* works to make common an outside to the human, are the common senses of film studies, women's studies, or black studies presently adequate to retrieve *Eve's Bayou* from those who would have it be a projection of a universalized notion of the human? The Black, which continues to (re)appear and on which many of us rely in order to continue the movements necessary to our survival, is a projection with intimate ties to the human. *Eve's Bayou* offers an opportunity for a different projection, one that corresponds to a sensory-motor schema that makes common that which appears to be irrational, incomprehensible, and unthought, stuff habitually assigned to the realm of the feminine and/or the Black. Such a sensory-motor schema corresponds to an alternative cinematic reality, one in which what has been purged from the human in order to rationalize the racism, sexism, and homophobia intrinsic to capitalist relations might be valorized. Pointing toward such an alternative, *Eve's Bayou* unleashes the black femme function.

Of course, the risk inherent in every deployment of the black femme function is that it will produce simply another market whose affectivity will function to reproduce value and further the movements of globalizing capital. For Trimark's marketing executive, the possibility that *Eve's Bayou* might consolidate a new exploitable market is a sign of progress. He proclaims that "the good news is that now maybe there are five producers out there saying, 'I have something just like *Eve's Bayou*.' "[31] Yet *Eve's Bayou* was able to confound the common sense or the conventional wisdom that motivates decisions about which images are selected, cut, framed and asked to survive as profitable commodities. That common sense perceived *Eve's Bayou* to be a "picture for African American women" and was surprised to discover that the film "was able to cross demographic boundaries. Fifty percent of the people who came to see it were white."[32] Drawing on the affectivity of film critics and other "connoisseurs" of "sophisticated films," *Eve's Bayou* consolidates a collectivity that does not conform to the reigning "racial" logic thought to differentiate "the American film market"; it proved to be a "crossover" film with an "all-Black cast."

157

What is perhaps most relevant to the present discussion about *Eve's Bayou*'s financial success, however, is the extent to which watching the disintegration of the bourgeois family can be a pleasurable experience that invites the consensual participation of even those whose interests are served by the reproduction of bourgeois sociality. Nonetheless, *Eve's Bayou*, even though it seeks to valorize the common sense of slaves and points the way toward another register of rationality, is not capable of setting into motion another form of sociality. Like Mozelle, who listens to Louis's voice and decides to let herself drown and marry a fourth husband despite Elzora's warning that she is cursed, the narrator's conclusion marks the film's failure to stop and allow space and time for the new that is becoming visible while Eve and Cisely hold hands by the bayou.[33] The narrator's mundane musings at the end of the film about how truth is relative and the past is a "tapestry" of images, a narration jazzed up by the music that elevates it to the level of poetry, continues the movements necessary for the film to make (common) sense, but it fails to capitalize on the fresh grooves cut into the viewer's sensory-motor apparatus. To the common sense that *Eve's Bayou* secures with its perfunctory voice-over ending, those grooves remain irrational and ignored—invisible. In spite of the narrator's attempt at closure, the black femme function persists in *Eve's Bayou*, insisting on the existence of a radical Elsewhere.

158

Introduction

1 Deleuze, *Cinema 1*, 8.

2 For Deleuze, there are two regimes of the cinematic image: the movement-image and the time-image. Dienst provides a list of those who "discovered" the movement-image in nonfilm realms: "Einstein and his Special Theory, Cezanne and the early avant-gardes, John Dos Passos, almost-forgotten experimenters in aesthetic cognition, George Harriman, Coco Chanel, Henry Ford, LeCorbusier, and so on." Dienst adds, "With all of these figures and many more besides, one of two reciprocal movements takes place. Variable elements are brought to bear on a single image that expresses them, or else a single image is varied, multiplied, and distributed throughout the world" (*Still Life in Real Time*, 153).

3 This raises the issue of the relationship between the VHS or DVD versions and the celluloid versions of a film, an issue that hinges upon an examination of the varying ways in which they structure "our" time. In a book that heavily influenced *The Witch's Flight*, Amy Villarejo considers how lesbian pulp fiction enters into and influences the temporal structures of modernity (*Lesbian Rule*, 159–61).

4 As Deleuze puts it, "Money is the obverse of all the images that the cinema shows and sets in place" (*Cinema 2*, 77).

Notes

5 Deleuze would perhaps have characterized *The Witch's Flight* as "monstrous." Describing his own relationship to the history of philosophy, Deleuze states that he saw "the history of philosophy as a type of buggery or (it comes to the same thing) immaculate conception. I saw myself as taking an author from behind and giving him a child that would be his own offspring, yet monstrous. It was really important for it to be his own child, because the author had to actually say all I had him saying. But the child was bound to be monstrous too, because it resulted from all sorts of shifting, slipping, dislocations, and hidden emission that I really enjoyed" (*Negotiations*, 6).

6 Because those chapters elaborate the theoretical underpinnings of *The Witch's Flight*, they are, in effect, two takes with the same soundtrack. Each chapter reveals something different in the same song.

7 In a book about the life of Tupac Shakur (about whom I have written elsewhere), Armond White notes that in June 1971 Tupac was born and "Smiling Faces (Sometimes)" was released. About the song and its place in the historical trajectory of black pop music, White writes, "No longer joyful, this Black protest admits a new element of pop paranoia that would lay in wait until rap. The pop world of 1971 didn't know what it was getting in 'Smiling Faces (Sometimes)'—bass notes and lowering tempos, with stark interjections piercing the strong male lead as the trio strains not to lose the murky melody. It's sinister sound mixed with Tupac's birth cries" (*Rebel for the Hell of It*, 23).

8 See Moten, *In the Break*, 26, 41–52.

9 Marx, *Economic and Philosophic Manuscripts of 1844*, 141.

10 Douglass, *My Bondage and My Freedom*.

11 Du Bois, *The Souls of Black Folk*, 188.

12 Ferguson, *Aberrations in Black*, 11–18.

13 Du Bois, *The Souls of Black Folk*, 184. Simone's version of "O-o-h Child" emphasizes its relationship to "the sorrow songs," especially those dimensions of them that Du Bois identifies when he writes, "Through all the sorrow of the Sorrow Songs there breathes a hope—a faith in the ultimate justice of things. The minor cadences of despair change often to triumph and calm confidence. Sometimes it is faith in life, sometimes a faith in death, sometimes assurance of boundless justice in some fair world beyond. But whichever it is, the meaning is always clear: that sometime, somewhere, men will judge men by their souls and not by their skins. Is such a hope justified? Do the Sorrow Songs sing true?" (ibid., 186).

1 The Image of Common Sense

The Undisputed Truth, "Smiling Faces Sometimes," *The Undisputed Truth* (Gordy Records, 1971).

1 In their discussion of "biopolitical production," Michael Hardt and Antonio Negri first claim that neither Michel Foucault nor Deleuze and Felix Guattari can grasp the "real dynamics of production in a biopolitical society" (i.e., neither attend to "the dense complex of experience," but work instead through ideal forms in which enabling notions of "agency," "ontology," and "creativity" cannot be located), then discuss "communication" as "the immaterial nexuses of the production of language, communication, and the symbolic that are developed by the communications industries." For Hardt and Negri, "communication not only expresses but also organizes the movement of globalization." Hardt and Negri, *Empire*, 27–34.

2 This is a formulation from which I will quickly distance myself. I invoke Walter Benjamin's well-known formulation of "mechanical reproduction" in order to situate my concerns in relation to a body of thought (based in many cases on a reading of Benjamin) that assumes that the relationship between film and reality is one that concerns matter ("reality") and its degraded and empty reproduction ("image")—a widely held assumption that I hold in question. See Benjamin, "The Work of Art."

3 I leave for a later project a sustained consideration of the extent to which the advent, at the close of the twentieth century, of what has been called "the digital age" signals a transformation in or an intensification of those cinematic processes with which I am concerned in *The Witch's Flight*.

4 Bergson, *Matter and Memory*, 56.

5 As Deleuze explains, "We ask ourselves what maintains a set in this world without totality or linkage. The answer is simple: what forms the set are clichés, and

160

nothing else. Nothing but clichés, clichés everywhere. . . . Now what consolidates all this, are the current clichés of an epoch or a moment, sound and visual slogans. . . . [T]hey are these floating images, these anonymous clichés, which circulate in the external world, but which also penetrate each one of us and constitute his internal world, so that everyone possesses only psychic clichés by which he thinks and feels, is thought and felt, being himself a cliché among the others in the world which surrounds him" (*Cinema 1*, 208–9).

6 Deleuze, *Cinema 2*, 54.

7 Deleuze explains that, after World War II, "daily life allows only weak sensory-motor connections to survive, and replaces the action-image by pure optical and sound images." In addition, "even metaphors are sensory-motor evasions and furnish us with something to say when we no longer know what to do: they are specific schemata of an affective nature. Now this is what a cliché is. A cliché is a sensory-motor image of the thing" (*Cinema 2*, 20).

8 Ibid.

9 My reading of Walter Benjamin's essay "The Work of Art in the Age of Mechanical Reproduction" has benefited from discussions that took place in Paul A. Bovè's graduate seminar on Walter Benjamin held during the spring of 1998 at the University of Pittsburgh. My reading has benefited also from those of Susan Buck-Morss, Miriam Bratu Hansen, and Vivian Sobchack, among others. See Buck-Morss, "The Dream World of Mass Culture"; Hansen, "Benjamin and Cinema"; and Hansen, "The Mass Production of the Senses." 161

10 Benjamin writes, "The violation of the masses, whom Fascism, with its *Führer* cult, forces to their knees, has its counterpart in the violation of an apparatus which is pressed into the production of ritual values" ("The Work of Art," 241).

11 Marx, *Economic and Philosophic Manuscripts*, 143. Marx's invocation of "a sensuous consciousness" belies the Hegelianism of his thinking about the role of industry in the teleology of the proletariat's subjectivity.

12 Deleuze, *Cinema 2*, 77.

13 See Deleuze, *Cinema 1*, 210.

14 Benjamin, "The Work of Art," 250.

15 Ibid., 240.

16 Ibid., 250.

17 Ibid., 241. The increasing formation of "the masses" marks, for Benjamin, the emergence of a collective sense and, therefore, the potential for a collective reaction on the part of the masses against the forces seeking to constitute it as such. For both historical and political reasons, Benjamin's engagement with cinema is limited to a consideration of those images Deleuze discusses under the rubric of "the movement-image."

18 Deleuze, *Cinema 2*, 21.

19 Ibid., 77.

20 Debord, *The Society of the Spectacle*, 32. Jonathan Beller uses a version of this Debord quotation as the epigram to his essay "Dziga Vertov and the Film of

Money." Beller claims that "cinema is the becoming self-conscious of social relations, literally, the relations of production." I disagree with Beller's formulation of
consciousness, but I concur with his assertion that cinema can render the relations of production visible in its images. See Beller, "Dziga Vertov," 154. For
another reading of Deleuze's movement-image in relation to DeBord's spectacle,
see Dienst, *Still Life in Real Time*, 158. There Dienst writes, "As industrial product and mechanized optic in one, the movement-image fulfills DeBord's definition of the image as the highest stage of commodity reification." My reading of
Deleuze on this point is consistent with Dienst's, except I would add that the
time-image does not escape this internalized relationship with money, a point of
which Dienst is well aware.

21 Deleuze, *Cinema 2*, 21.

22 Ibid.

23 Deleuze, *Cinema 1*, xiv.

24 Throughout this chapter, I have been delineating the processes of motor habituation with an eye toward its economic interests. For, in the context of discussing
the ways that the existence of private property estranges "man" from his senses,
leaving only the sense of "having," Karl Marx makes the often quoted claim that
"the *forming* of the five senses is a labor of the entire history of the world down to
the present." Marx's discussion of the need for an "emancipation of the senses"
resonates with Deleuze's insistence on the time-image's capacity to reveal "a pure
optical and sound situation." Marx, however, is contending with the implications
of his idealist understanding of subjectivity wherein man comes to be for himself
through his interactions with external objects. Marx's argument is that "man
himself" has to become "the object" before his senses can be emancipated:
"Thus, the objectification of the human essence, both in its theoretical and practical aspects, is required to make man's *sense human*, as well as to create the *human
sense* corresponding to the entire wealth of human and natural substance." Marx
recognizes that the "antithesis" between "subjectivism and objectivism, spiritual-
ism and materialism, activity and suffering" must be resolved in practice: "Their
resolution is therefore by no means merely a problem of understanding, but a *real*
problem of life, which *philosophy* could not solve precisely because it conceived
this problem as *merely* a theoretical one." See Marx, *Economic and Philosophic
Manuscripts*, 141–42.

    It might be argued that with Bergson and, later, with Benjamin, this "prob-
lem" is no longer merely theoretical, but dangerously "real" and that, for Benjamin, cinema (film) stands as one of the "necessary" technological innovations
that prepares "human emancipation." But, in arguing this, I already am beginning a narrative of technological progress that an antiracist praxis such as the one
I am attempting here cannot afford and that Benjamin himself throws into serious doubt with his claim that "the destructiveness of war furnishes proof that
society has not been mature enough to incorporate technology as its organ, that
technology has not been sufficiently developed to cope with the elemental forces

of society" ("The Work of Art," 242). (Marx's discussion of "species being" has been considered at great length by others. I will point out here merely that I am cautious about the vague understanding he provides in *Economic and Philosophic Manuscripts* concerning what might constitute properly "human" senses.)

25 In this regard, I attribute a greater range of possibilities to the study of common sense than does Deleuze. While Deleuze does align common sense with the process of recognition, as I have done here, his explorations of how common sense might be exploded, or of thinking "as involving encounters which escape all recognition," do not attend to the historical construction of common sense as a category that might contain within it possibilities for thinking that had been foreclosed during past struggles for hegemony but that might be glimpsed under present conditions. For Deleuze's formulation of common sense, see, for instance, his *Difference and Repetition*, especially pp. xv–xvii and 191–96. For an argument against philosophical methods that proceed according to recognition, see Deleuze and Guattari, *What Is Philosophy?* For an exegesis of Deleuze's theories of cinema that attends to his understanding of common sense, see Gregory Flaxman's introduction to *The Brain Is the Screen: Deleuze and the Philosophy of Cinema*.

26 Bergson defines common sense as "the continuous experience of the real" and invokes it as a way of demonstrating the validity of his arguments. According to Bergson's definition, common sense provides a degree of "sense certainty," a type of knowledge that he believes is more reliable than other, less concretely produced forms. In *Phenomenology of Spirit*, for instance, G. W. F. Hegel posits "sense-certainty" as the first moment in the teleology of Spirit. For Hegel, however, sense-certainty provides the "instance" wherein "pure being" splits into "This" and "I," object and subject. By positing common sense as the continuous experience of the real, Bergson rejects the notion of the instance wherein one's sense-certainty is mediated by an object. But his subsequent reliance on common sense as a methodology gives too much credence to "experience" as an unmediated form of knowledge. For Bergson, common sense is a protean form of reason whose validity is unquestioned because it derives from experience of the real. My usage of the term must be differentiated from Bergson's on the grounds that experience is a category of common sense and, hence, does not provide unmediated knowledge of reality. My usage of *common sense* must be further differentiated from his in terms of common sense's relationship to forms of rationality. See Hegel, *Phenomenology of Spirit*, 59. For Bergson's definition of common sense, see his *Creative Evolution*, 213.

27 Gramsci, *Selections from the Prison Notebooks*, 9. Like much of my work in this study, my reading of Gramsci has been informed by those of Marcia Landy.

28 Gramsci, *Selections from the Prison Notebooks*, 9.

29 Ibid. Gramsci's thinking about common sense draws on the formulations of those who preceded him, including Bergson (through Georges Sorel's work) and Giambattista Vico. According to José Nun, Vico "situated common sense outside the sphere of rational thought, at the level of creativity and imagination, indispensable for the attainment of all that is useful" ("Elements for a Theory of Democracy," 201). Admittedly, in his argument that Gramsci's conceptualization of common sense ultimately falls prey to a "rationalist cast" inherited from Marxism, Nun assumes a coherence to Gramsci's thinking about the imbrication of culture and politics that is precluded by the fragmented form of much of his writing on common sense while in prison.

30 Nun and others have argued that Gramsci's political commitment to a form of Marxist politics that sees a unified and transparent proletariat as the agent of radical revolution caused Gramsci to embrace a teleological narrative of the development of revolutionary subjectivity from which his thinking about common sense and hegemony cannot be divorced. These arguments, however, have often been advanced at the expense of the richness and nuance in Gramsci's conceptualization of common sense and with the assumption that Gramsci's prison writings can be taken as an internally consistent body of work. While Gramsci does rely on the language of rationalism to advance his understanding about the possibilities for a subaltern hegemony, he also thinks that subaltern common sense contains the seeds from which a new, widely acceptable conception of the world might be elaborated.

31 Gramsci, *Selections from the Prison Notebooks*, 12.

32 Landy, *Film, Politics, and Gramsci*, 78.

33 For a reminder that the consolidation of hegemony always involves a struggle and, hence, concessions and negotiations, see Lipsitz, "The Struggle for Hegemony."

34 Lowe and Lloyd, introduction to *The Politics of Culture in the Shadow of Capital*.

35 Gramsci, *Selections from the Prison Notebooks*, 325–26. I have chosen the alternative translation for "un divenire storico"—"historical becoming"—because it registers that common sense locates a becoming, an ongoing struggle, not a finished historical process.

36 Ibid., 324.

37 Ibid.

38 Deleuze, *Cinema 2*, 20.

39 Landy, *Film, Politics, and Gramsci*, 80.

40 Ibid.

41 Deleuze, *Cinema 2*, 79.

42 Ibid., 81.

43 Ibid., 78.

44 It is clear that the cinematic designates a reality that has been worked over by a mode of production wherein time is money.

45 Deleuze, *Cinema 2*, 78. Of course, I cannot speculate about what will take money's place or into what money will transform, just as I cannot see beyond my own common sense. The best I can do is to hold open the possibility of the impossible and point out that the temporality that might shatter the infernal cycles that continue to reproduce colonial reality converges with what becomes perceptible when something becomes too strong in the image.

46 Landy, *The Folklore of Consensus*, xii.

47 Ibid. Dallas Smythe's arguments regarding the labor of the television audience also provide an important earlier articulation of the work that audiences do to serve money's interests. It should be clear, however, that my claim reaches beyond Smythe's. See Smythe, *Dependency Road*, 22–51.

48 Landy, *The Folklore of Consensus*, 297.

49 Deleuze, *Cinema 1*, 65.

50 Here, I am recalling Karl Marx's description of slavery in order to draw a parallel between the exploitation of labor power that accompanies affectivity and slavery, an existing practice of buying and selling another living being's entire productive capacity. See Marx, *Grundrisse*, 489. I am setting up a further claim, namely, that the slave labor of Africans in the so-called New World offers an analog to the affectivity expended in the (re)production of cinematic reality.

2 In the Interval

The Undisputed Truth, "Smiling Faces Sometimes," *The Undisputed Truth* (Gordy Records, 1971).

1 At the beginning of the first chapter of *The Souls of Black Folk*, Du Bois writes, "Between me and the other world there is ever an unasked question: unasked by some through feelings of delicacy; by others through the difficulty of rightly framing it. All, nevertheless, flutter round it. They approach me in a half-hesitant sort of way, eye me curiously or compassionately, and then, instead of saying directly, How does it feel to be a problem? They say, I know an excellent colored man in my town" (3).

2 See, for instance, Morrison, *Playing in the Dark*, and Dyer, *White*.

3 See the *Oxford English Dictionary*'s entry for problem.

4 Derrida, *Aporias*, 11. A careful and directed consideration of Derrida's discussion of the tension between "problem" and "the aporia" reveals that the structure of identification that gives rise to the Black and the White, like all structures of identity, relies on a conception of the aporia as its condition of possibility.

5 Within the epistemological framework that Du Bois characterizes, he himself, a "colored," is a representative of all other coloreds, so that the statement "I know an excellent colored man in my town" is offered according to the perception that Du Bois in some way substitutes for that "excellent man." It is framed by the speaker's sense that Du Bois is a projection of the colored man in the speaker's town. The statement itself is a remark on the underlying situation, that is, Du Bois's status as a "problem," specifically as one of "the Negro problem." See Du Bois, *The Souls of Black Folk*, 3–4.

6 See Keeling, " 'In the Interval.' "

7 Bergson, *Matter and Memory*, 9.

165

8 Deleuze, *Cinema 1*, xiv.

9 Fanon, *Black Skin, White Masks*, 192. In this chapter subsequent citations to Fanon's book will appear in parentheses.

10 Ronald A.T. Judy's description of "Fanon's elaboration of identification according to his reading of Lacan's mirror stage" informs my discussion here. Judy explains that "very much like the Lacanian infant, the Antillean experiences an event (its body) and although having perception of it does not have the conceptual framework for understanding. Nonetheless, there is a 'perceptual memory' that later, when the understanding of the European culture has been achieved, is recalled. But, because the Antillean's self identity is in terms of the white, what is now remembered is intolerable. So when the scene of corporeal schema gets recalled by something in life . . . the self is constructed in such a way as to prevent the actual perception from coming to mind. Instead the self experiences the affect that it would have felt at the time of the original event if it had been the self it is now. We could say that the original event at the time of its happening is what will have been the trauma of recognizing oneself as a *nègre*." Judy, "Fanon's Body of Black Experience," 69. My reading of Fanon has been informed by Judy's.

11 Except for the final line "Y A Bon Banania," the translation of this passage is taken from the text cited. Lewis R. Gordon cites the French reference, " 'Y a bon banania," explaining that he keeps this reference in his translation because "it refers both to the fruit and to the popular French breakfast food Banania. . . . Fanon no doubt chose that product both because of its advertisement, which has a smiling Senegalese, whose face eventually became so caricatured by the late 1980s that it resembled a chimpanzee, and because of the associations of blacks with apes and apes with bananas" ("The Black and the Body Politic," 83n5). I have kept Gordon's reference here in order to allude to the importance of commercial visual imagery (for which Fanon is "responsible" "above all else") in Fanon's account of "the lived experience of the black."

12 Bergson, *Matter and Memory*, 78. Subsequent citations to this text will appear in parentheses.

13 Bergson continues, "It is the whole of memory . . . that passes over into each of these circuits, since memory is always present; but that memory, capable, by reason of its elasticity, of expanding more and more, reflects upon the object a growing number of suggested images. . . . [I]t will be seen that the progress of attention results in creating anew not only the object perceived, but also the ever widening systems with which it may be bound up; so that in the measure in which the circles B, C, D represent a higher expansion of memory, their reflection attains in B', C', and D' deeper strata of reality" (*Matter and Memory*, 104–5).

14 In addition to my essay "In the Interval," see also chapter 3 herein.

15 As of today, the victories over colonial rule, the successful movement for black civil rights in the United States, and struggles for "Black Power" have made available to the black different qualities of affect, most notably "pride." But the temporality of the colonial mode of representation continues to bind the black to colonial (and neocolonial) pasts.

16 Marriott, *On Black Men*, 81. I am grateful to Aziz Jeng for bringing Marriott's book to my attention.

17 Ibid., 81–82.

18 Kawash, "Terrorists and Vampires," 238.

19 Ibid., 239–40.

20 Deleuze states, "In perception . . . , there is never anything else or anything more than there is in the thing: on the contrary, there is 'less.' We perceive the thing, minus that which does not interest us as a function of our needs" (*Cinema 1*, 63). See also Deleuze, *Cinema 2*, 21.

21 Whether we refer to the current configuration of domination and exploitation as neoimperialism, postcolonialism, neocolonialism, or as Empire, its particular temporality continues to function according to the rhythms set in motion with colonialism and slavery.

22 Discussing Fanon's encounter with *Home of the Brave*, Marriott claims that "the film misses, or dismisses, Moss's furious, and paralyzing, encounter with the Black imago apparent in his friend's speech: 'You yellow bellied nig' " (*On Black Men*, 78). It is the fury and the anger, dismissed by the film but available to Fanon, that authorizes Fanon's refusal of the film's cure for Moss's psychosomatic paralysis and thus of the film's prescription for racial harmony.

23 As an epigraph to the conclusion of *Black Skin, White Masks*, Fanon uses Karl Marx's well-known quotation that begins with "the social revolution . . . cannot draw its poetry from the past, but only from the future" and ends with "before, the expression exceeded the content; now, the content exceeds the expression." Fanon's choice of this quotation substantiates the claim he makes in the conclusion that "the problem considered here is one of time," and it emphasizes his interest in exploding the temporality of the colonial mode of representation of otherness and in revealing the temporality that raises the possibility of the impossible. Fanon, *Black Skin, White Masks*, 223, 226.

24 Derrida cautions that "under the banner—which can also become a slogan—of the unanticipatable or the absolutely new, we can fear seeing return the phantom of the worst, the one we have already identified. We know the 'new' only too well, or in any case the old rhetoric, the demagogy, the psychagogy of the 'new'—and sometimes of the 'new order'—of the surprising, the virginal, and the unanticipatable. We must thus be suspicious of both repetitive memory and the completely other of the absolutely new" (*The Other Heading*, 18–19).

25 As Kobena Mercer points out, "What is common to the representational forms of the three distinct modes of 'othering' that often get simplified as racism, sexism, and homophobia is that in each instance the historical construction of differences of race, gender, and sexuality is reduced to the perception of *visible differences* whose social meaning is taken to be obvious, immediate and intelligible to the naked eye" ("Busy in the Ruins," 201).

167

26 I have placed the phrase "marginalized populations" in quotation marks in order to signal that I consider it to be a problematic term, a signifier without an adequate referent. I rely here on the current common sense understanding of what the term designates.

27 The protests surrounding the release of D. W. Griffith's successful and influential film *Birth of a Nation* stand as probably the best-known example of political demonstrations in the face of racist imagery. See Cripps, *Slow Fade to Black*, 41–69.

28 Spivak's critique focuses on a reading of "Intellectuals and Power: A Conversation between Michel Foucault and Gilles Deleuze."

29 Spivak, "Can the Subaltern Speak?" 70. Regarding Deleuze's pronouncement of the death of representation, the specific statement to which Spivak refers is Deleuze's claim that "there is no more representation; there's nothing but action—action of theory and action of practice which relate to each other as relays and form networks." (Ibid.) According to Spivak, this claim renders transparent the role of the intellectual in the production of knowledge about the subaltern and in the production of the subaltern as an object for knowledge. See Michel Foucault, *Language, Counter-Memory, Practice*, 206–7, as cited in Spivak, "Can the Subaltern Speak?" 70.

30 Spivak, "Can the Subaltern Speak?" 70.

31 Ibid.

32 Quoted in ibid., 71.

33 Ibid., 74. Spivak points out that the relationship between the two senses of *representation* under consideration "has received political and ideological exacerbation in the European tradition at least since the poet and the sophist, the actor and the orator, have both been seen as harmful. In the guise of a post-Marxist description of the scene of power, we thus encounter a much older debate: between representation or rhetoric as tropology and as persuasion. *Darstellen* belongs to the first constellation, *vertreten*—with stronger suggestions of substitution—to the second. Again, they are related, but running them together, especially in order to say that beyond both is where oppressed subjects speak, act and know for themselves, leads to an essentialist, utopian politics" (71).

34 Foucault, *Language, Counter-Memory, Practice*, 212, quoted in Spivak, "Can the Subaltern Speak?" 69.

35 Spivak, "Can the Subaltern Speak?" 74.

36 In "The Chapter on Money" in *Grundrisse*, Marx states that "money is labour time in the form of a general object, or the objectification of general labour time, labour time as a general commodity" (168). My claim concerning images of common sense is that they function as a type of money; they are the objectification of an affectivity performed by a habituated, and thus general, sensory-motor schema (which implies an order of temporality). For a different reading of cinematic images as money, see Beller, "Dziga Vertov and the Film of Money."

37 Dienst, *Still Life in Real Time*, 63.

38 Spivak, "Can the Subaltern Speak?" 104.

39 What I refer to here as "a transformed critical engagement" with cinematic images, Patricia Pisters has called "a camera consciousness," which she holds to be a "new critical consciousness" or a "metacinematic consciousness"—a mode of engagement with images that is consistent with Deleuze's theorization of cinema. Another way to conceive of what images hide within them is to consider the relationship Deleuze posits between "actual" and "virtual" images. Pisters, among other Deleuzian film theorists, explicates Deleuze's distinction. See Pisters, *The Matrix of Visual Culture*, 2–3.

3 Haile Gerima's *Sankofa*

"Wade in the Water" is the title of a traditional Negro Spiritual. It has been recorded by various artists, Sweet Honey in the Rock among them. Sweet Honey in the Rock, *Live at Carnegie Hall* (Flying Fish, 1986).

For the first epigraph, see Hartman, *Scenes of Subjection*, and Douglass, *Narrative*, 25–26; for the second, see Fanon, *Black Skin, White Masks*, 109.

1 I borrow the phrase "common-sense black nationalism" from Wahneema Lubiano. See Lubiano, "Black Nationalism."

2 Ibid., 236.

3 Ibid., 233.

4 Ibid., 234.

5 Ibid. In order to define "common sense," Lubiano conflates it with "ideology," a rhetorical move that initially obscures the way that common sense is a category of struggle and negotiation that serves to enable a group's survival under adverse circumstances over time. Lubiano's description of common sense in terms of ideology brings common sense dangerously close to functioning as an ahistorical category, rather than as a record of a group's "historical becoming." Yet, in actuality, Lubiano's understanding of common sense is nevertheless closer to Gramsci's conceptualization of common sense and "good sense" than it is to Althusser's notion of ideology. Consistent with Gramsci's focus on the practical aspects of subaltern common sense, Lubiano's formulation of common sense insists that it is possible to "see [common-sense black nationalism] (and be critical of it) as a way that people try to intervene in what happens within the group," pointing out that the language of common-sense black nationalism, "implies black historical awareness in order to stave off what is seen as within-the-group suicidal behaviors" (237).

6 Lubiano argues that "the political realities and possibilities of black nationalism as an organizing discourse include: (1) demystification of white racial domination, (2) the transformative effects of new deployments of it—such as the valorization of black nationalist constructions of community against, for example, the capitalist driven logic and aesthetics of the drug trade, and (3) activation as a bridge to international political awareness. Historically this last aspect—international political awareness—has manifested itself as Pan-Africanism. As a bridge discourse, black nationalism can begin the work of radicalizing people unaware of international labor politics, for example, by providing a 'jolt' of 'recognition' of the exploitative politics of global capitalism's effect on Third World labor. None of what I've been describing is *guaranteed* by black nationalism; the proof of its capabilities rests in its deployments" (ibid., 236–37).

7 Ibid., 236.

8 Sylvie Kandé points out that Gerima's translation of *Sankofa* (which I adopt in my reading here) reduces the multiple meanings of the Sankofa bird to a single translation that has become the authoritative one: "Whatever its form, the Sankofa bird plays an important role in the Akan system of symbolic relations. It functions as a kind of visual 'clue' that calls to mind a series of proverbs: *the king sees all; one must not be afraid to redeem one's past mistakes; turn back and fetch it,* etc. Drawing on this visual-semantic complex, Gerima privileges a single translation: *one must return to the past in order to move forward*" ("Look Homeward, Angel," 129).

9 Woolford and Gerima, "Filming Slavery," 90.

10 Cripps, "New Black Cinema."

11 Pye and Myles, *The Movie Brats.*

12 See Cook, "Auteur Cinema."

13 See Pines and Willemen, *Questions of Third Cinema.* Lately there has been a renewed interest in exploring the extent to which the category and political potential of Third Cinema might remain relevant given a transformed sociopolitical landscape and an intensification of Hollywood's hegemony within the cultural forces that attend globalization. Recent scholarly work seeks to complement and complicate the organizing logic, if not the projects, that were characteristic of Third Cinema in the late 1960s and early 1970s, expanding Third Cinema's purview while attempting to define its generic characteristics. See, for instance, Wayne, *Political Film,* and Guneratne and Dissanayake, *Rethinking Third Cinema.*

14 For instance, Gerima's 1976 film *Bush Mama* is both a sustained meditation on the logics and effects of the United States's racist political economy and a call for the formation of a black nationalist subjectivity that might be adequate to challenge the socioeconomic conditions that animate such a political economy. As in *Sankofa,* Gerima inscribes his critique on a black female body in an effort to make that body a vehicle for the production of a revolutionary subjectivity. Yet, *Bush Mama*'s revolutionary subject develops out of a confrontation with the ways that race, gender, and class exploitation coalesce to authorize the violence and oppression of poor black people, while *Sankofa* eschews a critique of gender and class exploitation in order to isolate and privilege racism as the primary logic of the continuing oppression of black people.

15 Neal, "The Black Arts Movement," 29.

16 With regard to questions about the responsibilities of the black artist, I am thinking of works such as Jupiter Hammon's "A Dialogue Intitled the Kind Master and the Dutiful Servant" and Phillis Wheatley's "To the Right Honorable William, Earl of Dartmouth, His Majesty's Secretary of State for North America." In so

170

doing, I am positing slavery as the beginning of that sociocultural historical project now known as "African American." My intent is merely to authorize my access to the writings of slaves as constituting an early existing body of litera-ture understood as African American that is both continuous and discontinuous with the position articulated by Larry Neal about BAM's understanding of the black artist.

I retain only the masculine pronoun throughout my discussion of BAM in order to emphasize BAM's conflation of "the artist" with "the race" with "the heterosexual patriarchal black masculine figure" who is also male. This confla-tion is consistent with Fanon's characterization of "the Negro."

17 One also might point to regional differences among BAM artists. For instance, James Smethurst has pointed out the extent to which the stance taken toward popular culture by BAM artists located in the Northeast differed from those in Chicago and in the South. See Smethurst, "Pat Your Foot."

18 Neal, "The Black Arts Movement," 39. As Phillip Brian Harper points out, "Nearly fifty years before, a black theorist of the Harlem Renaissance made a very similar claim about the nature of that movement." Harper explains further: "In his 1925 article on the contemporary flowering of African-American art, 'Negro Youth Speaks,' Alain Locke insisted that "Our poets have now stopped speaking for the Negro—they speak as Negroes. Where formerly they spoke to others and tried to interpret, they now speak to their own and try to express" (*Are We Not Men?* 46). In addition, Theodore R. Hudson in 1988 called BAM a "sort of second Harlem Renaissance, if you will" ("Activism and Criticism," 90).

19 Neal, "The Black Arts Movement," 39. Surely, the open secret concerning the homosexuality of the primary artists in the Harlem Renaissance plays no small part in BAM's reading of them. Moreover, BAM's rejection of the Harlem Renais-sance can be read also as an assertion of an organic relationship to urban black people, a relationship that the Harlem artists compromised by accepting the sponsorship of whites, rather than relying upon "the community" for support.

Thabiti Asukile discusses the historical roots of black nationalism while con-sidering the validity of Sterling Stuckey's argument that David Walker's *Appeal to the Colored Citizens of the World,* published in 1829, is a progenitor of black nationalism. Asukile points out that "as late as the 1820s most people of Afri-can descent referred to themselves as 'Africans' or 'free Africans'" ("The All-Embracing Black Nationalist Theories of David Walker's Appeal," 18).

20 Neal, "The Black Arts Movement," 29–30. The way that Fanon is invoked here is in tension with my reading of his work and political project. Where Lee (Madhabuti) claims that Fanon advocates for the solidification of black culture, I have pointed out the extent to which he is against solidifying the Black. Lee's use of Fanon to support the elaboration of a black aesthetic is significant, and it draws attention to the extent to which Fanon's work, particularly *The Wretched of the Earth,* has become part of what Lubiano refers to as "commonsense black na-tionalism." While I am not arguing for the discovery of a true historical Fanon, I am arguing for the (re)discovery of a more complex and conflicted Fanon. Such a Fanon might assist me as I mine common-sense black nationalism for the alternatives, now invisible, that it might contain.

21 Neal, "The Black Arts Movement," 30.

22 Ibid., 30–31.

23 Harper demonstrates that "intraracial division is implicit in movement references to the 'black' subject itself" through a presentation of what he calls "the I-you division that underlies the Black Arts concept of African-American community." Further, as he points out in his reading of selected poems by BAM poets, the designation *black* as used by many of the BAM poets already signals a consciousness transformed: "If Baraka is calling 'all black people,' he is already calling only those African Americans whose political consciousness is sufficiently developed for them to subscribe to the designation 'black' in the first place. All others— designated by 'you' in the poems that utilize the pronominal rhetoric—will be considered as 'Negroes,' as in the titles of Giovanni's and Jordan's poems—a term that is pointedly transmuted into 'niggers' in Giovanni's text" (*Are We Not Men?* 47–49). The identities and the affective investments in Africa and in forms of black culture that the revaluation of the term *black* enabled remain in circulation today.

24 Neal, "The Black Arts Movement," 33. Karenga is celebrated in contemporary black popular (mass) culture as the originator of Kwanzaa, an African American cultural expression of the winter-solstice holiday season, which is becoming increasingly commercialized.

Neal's presentation of "Negro" as a "set of reactions to white people" draws attention to the interdependence of "Negro" and "white," and it troubles Karenga's and BAM's assertions that their creation of "black," insofar as that concept is articulated out of a terrain previously indexed by "Negro" and in contradistinction to "white" and/or "Western," can be effectively autonomous from "Western," "American," or "white" formulations.

25 See Masilela, "The Los Angeles School," and Bambara, "Reading the Signs."

26 According to Masilela, "The Civil Rights Movement, the Women's Movement, the anti-war movement, and activities in America in support of national liberation struggles in Africa, Asia, and Latin America informed the political consciousness of the members of the group" ("The Los Angeles School," 107–8).

27 At the beginning of *Sankofa*, Sankofa instructs Mona "back to [her] source."

28 The primacy that *Sankofa* grants to culture, especially to film images, in the consolidation of black identity and the way that it works through a familiar Hollywood film style are among the reasons for the film's currency within both black nationalist and certain white progressive social formations. My assertion of *Sankofa*'s popularity along these lines is based on what I have observed at black-nationalist-inflected fairs and other gatherings where *Sankofa* was offered for sale and upon the fact that my local young white progressive member-owned bookstore screened *Sankofa* during one of its weekly movie nights. The most widely accessible of Gerima's films, *Sankofa* seems to have gained something of a follow-ing among black nationalists and white progressives.

29 Fanon's hesitations about Negritude provide a relevant context for considering BAM in relation to his thought.

30 Gerima, "Triangular Cinema," 71–72.

31 Ibid., 72.

32 In his theory of triangular cinema Gerima argues that an economically viable and politically transformative African American film community is necessary for "the advancement of visual culture intended for social change," a community that should consist of "1.) the audience/community, 2.) the film-maker/storyteller, and 3.) the activist/critic" ("Triangular Cinema," 68).

33 Ibid., 72.

34 Ibid., 79–80. With this call, Gerima echoes the call made years earlier in Amiri Baraka's poem "Black Art": "We want poems that kill." In that poem Baraka writes that we want

> Assassin poems, Poems that shoot
> guns. Poems that wrestle cops into alleys
> and take their weapons leaving them dead
> with tongues pulled out and sent to Ireland.

He ends "Black Art" with a plea.

> We want a black poem. And a
> Black World.
> Let the world be a Black Poem
> And Let All Black People Speak This Poem
> Silently
> or LOUD.
>
> (BARAKA, *The LeRoi Jones/Amiri Baraka Reader*, 219–20)

35 Gerima, "Triangular Cinema," 79.

36 In an interview with bell hooks, Charles Burnett points out that "Haile Gerima's film *Sankofa* . . . it's very Hollywood. Contentwise it may differ from Hollywood and in standpoint, but in the way it progresses as a story, in the way it highlights certain kinds of violence, particularly sexualized violence, it is very Hollywood. A distinction has to be made between a racist white public that may not want to support this film because of its standpoint—because they don't think it will sell—and the assumptions that [it] radically parts in style and content from the norm" (hooks, *Reel to Real*, 163–64).

37 Deleuze, *Cinema 2*, 161.

38 For information regarding the classical continuity system, see Bordwell, Staiger, and Thompson, *The Classical Hollywood Cinema*, 194–230.

39 In this regard, the film functions in much the same manner as the tours of slave castles described by Saidiya Hartman in her elucidating analysis of African American tourism in Africa: "We are encouraged to see ourselves as the vessels for the captive's return; we stand in the ancestor's shoes. We imaginatively witness the crimes of the past and cry for those victimized—the enslaved, the ravaged, and the slaughtered. And the obliterative assimilation of empathy enables us to cry for ourselves, too. As we remember those ancestors held in the dungeons, we can't but think of our own dishonored and devalued lives and the unrealized aspirations and the broken promises of abolition, reconstruction, and the civil rights movement. The intransigence of our seemingly eternal second-class status propels us to make recourse to stories of origin, unshakable explanatory narratives, and sites of injury—the land where our blood has been spilt—as if some essential ingredient of ourselves can be recovered at the castles and forts that dot the western coast of Africa, as if the location of the wound was itself the cure, or as if the weight of dead generations could alone ensure our progress" ("The Time of Slavery," 767). I thank Daphne Brooks for bringing this essay to my attention (from the deck of the ferry transporting us to Goree Island, off the coast of Dakar, Senegal, West Africa).

40 Gramsci, *Prison Notebooks*.

41 Hartman's reference to emancipation as a "nonevent" underscores my point (*Scenes of Subjection*, 116).

42 Hartman, "The Time of Slavery," 773–74.

43 The cautionary note Spivak issues to Deleuze and Foucault could be directed at
Gerima as well: "However reductionistic an economic analysis might seem, the French intellectuals forget at their peril that this entire overdetermined enterprise was in the interest of a dynamic economic situation requiring that interests, motives (desires) and power (of knowledge) be ruthlessly dislocated. To invoke that dislocation now as a radical discovery that should make us diagnose the economic (conditions of existence that separate out 'classes' descriptively) as a piece of dated analytic machinery may well be to continue the work of that dislocation and unwittingly help in securing 'a new balance of hegemonic relations' " ("Can the Subaltern Speak?" 75).

44 Woolford and Gerima, "Filming Slavery," 92.

45 Writing of the film's simplification of plantation life into a dichotomous relationship between black and white, Kandé critiques *Sankofa*'s inability to think of survival as a viable option for slaves: "The diversity and the specificity of plantation life—for example, the contradictions and alliances within its various constitutive units of economic and cultural production—are erased. Gone is the concept of 'survival'—that capacity to negotiate an existence among the numerous adverse forces of the slave economy and around which, significantly, the slave narratives are constructed" ("Look Homeward, Angel," 137).

46 For a detailed reading of the way that *Sankofa* reinscribes dichotomous racial categories, see Kandé, "Look Homeward, Angel."

47 In the introduction to *Black Skin, White Masks*, Fanon clearly states, "The black is a black man" (8).

48 As Greg Thomas pointed out to me during an informal discussion about *Sankofa*, the theme of death in the film is resituated within an African cosmological frame-work: death is flying to Africa on the back of a buzzard. I do not dispute the film's ability to present a conception of death different from Western notions of it. I am claiming simply that the spectator is provided no such escape from oppression or exploitation, via death, a buzzard, or otherwise, and that even the film's attempt to transform its spectator's consciousness remains locked in Hegel's dialectic.

49 As Kandé reports, people have begun to "act out" *Sankofa*. Kandé makes reference to "the group headed by Kohain Halevi, a black Hebrew from New York, who locked himself in the Elmina dungeon for two days of fasting, in order that 'this sacred ground be protected' " ("Look Homeward, Angel," 114). Kandé's quotation contains a reference to a *Washington Post* article by Stephen Buckley ("U.S., African Blacks Differ on Turning Slave Dungeons into Tourists Attractions," *Washington Post*, 17 April 1995, A10).

50 Hartman, *Scenes of Subjection*, 100.

51 Fanon, *Black Skin, White Masks*, 225.

52 Ibid., 229.

53 Ibid., 232.

4   Black Revolutionary Women

Nina Simone, "Four Women," *Nina Simone Sings Nina* (Verve, 1996).   175

1 As Nikhil Pal Singh puts it, "Perhaps the greatest irony of the post-1968 period, now that the market appears as the global horizon of all human sociality, is that Black aesthetic commodities—'Black performativity,' if you will—is much more prominent within the public sphere, even as 'Black citizenship' is increasingly devalued" ("The Black Panthers," 89).

2 Fanon figures the "disaster" for both the black man and the white man in both spatial and temporal terms, claiming that it lies "somewhere" in the past: "The disaster of the man of color lies in the fact that he was enslaved. The disaster and the inhumanity of the white man lie in the fact that somewhere he has killed a man. And even today they subsist, to organize this dehumanization rationally" (*Black Skin, White Masks*, 231).

3 Deleuze argues that what the time-image "reveals or makes visible is the hidden ground of time, that is, its differentiation into two flows, that of presents which pass and that of pasts which are preserved. Time simultaneously makes the present pass and preserves the past in itself" (*Cinema 2*, 98).

4 As Bergson explains, "What I call 'my present' has one foot in my past and another in my future. In my past, first, because 'the moment in which I am speaking is already far from me'; in my future, next, because this moment is impending over the future: it is to the future that I am tending, and could I fix this indivisible present, this infinitesimal element of the curve of time, it is the direction of the future that it would indicate. The psychical state, then, that I call 'my present,' must be both a perception of the immediate past and a determination of the immediate future. Now the immediate past, in so far as it is perceived is . . . sensation, since every sensation translates a very long succession of elementary vibrations, and the immediate future, in so far as it is being determined, is action or movement. My present, then, is both sensation and movement; since my present forms an undivided whole, then the movement must be linked with the sensation, must prolong it in action. Whence I conclude that my present consists in a joint system of sensation and movements. My present is, in its essence, sensori-motor" (*Matter and Memory*, 138).

5 Fanon, *Black Skin, White Masks*, 231.

6 Ibid.

7 In his "fourth commentary on Bergson," Deleuze explains that Bergson's temporal schema supplies a nonchronological time whose "paradoxical characteristics" are "the pre-existence of a past in general; the co-existence of all the sheets of past; and the existence of a most contracted degree," the latter being the present which exists "only as an infinitely contracted past which is constituted at the extreme point of the already-there" (*Cinema 2*, 98, 99).

8 In *Black Skin, White Masks* Fanon rejects the possibility that Afrocentric historiography will improve the present situation. The spatiotemporal project that emerges out of *Black Skin, White Masks* does not include a call for the creation of a historical narrative that would reconsolidate the black, but differently. Fanon's call is for the liberation of the black from the past to which he is enslaved, held as the Black.

9 Deleuze states, "Memory is not in us; it is we who move in a Being-memory, a world-memory. In short, the past appears as the most general form of an already-there, a pre-existence in general, which our recollections presuppose, even our first recollection if there was one, and which our perceptions, even the first make use of" (*Cinema 2*, 98).

10 Bergson argues that "if there are actions that are really *free*, or at least partly indeterminate, they can only belong to beings able to fix, at long intervals, that becoming to which their own becoming clings, able to solidify it into distinct moments, and so to condense matter and, by assimilating it, to digest it into movements of reaction. . . . Homogeneous space and homogeneous time are then neither properties of things nor essential conditions of our faculty of knowing them: they express, in an abstract form, the double work of solidification and of division which we effect on the moving continuity of the real in order to obtain there a fulcrum for our action, in order to fix within it starting points for our operation, in short to introduce into it real changes" (*Matter and Memory*, 210–11).

11 Seale, *Seize the Time*, 157. The number of Panthers involved in the demonstration varies according to different accounts. Seale states that "there were thirty brothers and sisters. Six sisters and twenty-four brothers. Twenty of the brothers were armed" (157).

12 Newton and Black, *Revolutionary Suicide*, 49–151.

13 Davis, "Black Nationalism," 319.

14 Doss, " 'Revolutionary Art,' " 180.

15 Newton and Blake, *Revolutionary Suicide*, 151.

16 I use the phrase *cinematic appearance* to refer to an image that has been selected, cut, and framed by a "cinematic machine." Cinematic images are made visible according to a subtractive perceptual process, and I refer to film and television as "technological cinematic machines" in order to differentiate their operations from those of living images who similarly function to cut, select, and frame images. My invocation of film as a technological cinematic machine was in reference to the movie cameras, projectors, reels of celluloid, actors, screens, studios, distributors, exhibitors, producers, directors, lights, sets, and so on that contribute to the production and exhibition of film. Relying upon Deleuze's adaptation in the context of cinema of Bergson's theory of real movement, my usage of the term *the cinematic* derives from film's spatial, temporal, and "phenomenological" (if what I describe still deserves that name) particularities, and living beings, no less than film and television, function as cinematic machines.

17 The republication of Panther "classics" such as Bobby Seale's *Seize the Time* and Huey Newton's autobiography *Revolutionary Suicide* and collection of essays *To Die for the People*, the publication of biographical and autobiographical accounts of party members such as Elaine Brown and David Hilliard, and the very recent publication of two scholarly anthologies devoted to "reconsidering" and "representing" the BPP, *The Black Panther Party Reconsidered* and *Liberation, Imagination, and the Black Panther Party*, are part of a response to the resurgence of 177 interest in the Panthers since Newton's death in 1989, particularly among those too young to have been involved with the BPP, but who have romanticized the Panthers' rebellion as a precursor to hip-hop's rebellious style. These publications offer themselves as correctives to a misrepresentation of the Panthers thought to be primarily a function of the mass media's manipulation of the Panthers. As a way of "setting the record straight," these publications provide additional context for the Panthers' appearance, seeking to fill in the holes that still attend their circulation. By doing so, these publications challenge contemporary audiences to recognize the complexity of the Panthers' innovations and the threats they posed to the authority and dominance of the U.S. State. They also, however, retroactively obfuscate aspects of the BPP's cinematic appearance, such as the appearance of "Black Revolutionary Woman" in the "masculine" image "blacks with guns." See Brown, *A Taste of Power*; Charles E. Jones, *The Black Panther Party (Reconsidered)*; Cleaver and Katsiaficas, *Liberation, Imagination, and the Black Panther Party*; Hilliard and Cole, *This Side of Glory*; Newton, *To Die for the People*; Newton and Blake, *Revolutionary Suicide*; and Seale, *Seize the Time*.

18 Newton and Blake, *Revolutionary Suicide*, 149.

19 Ibid., 148.

20 Ibid., 149.

21 Ibid., 149, 150–51.

22 The Panthers themselves had an international impact. Groups referred to by

Michael L. Clemons and Charles E. Jones as "global emulators of the Black Panther Party" formed in England, Bermuda, Israel, Australia, and India. See Clemmons and Jones, "Global Solidarity."

23 The argument I am developing here is consistent in many respects with Nikhil Pal Singh's suggestion that "rather than seeing the Panthers as the vanguard of a visible insurgency in the country, we should understand them as being the practitioners of an insurgent form of visibility, a literal-minded and deadly serious guerrilla theatre in which militant sloganeering, bodily display, and spectacular actions simultaneously signified their possession and real lack of power" ("The Black Panthers," 83).

Yet, my analysis of the Panthers' visibility diverges from Singh's in important respects, most notably on the issue of agency. Relying upon a notion of "performativity," Singh seems to conceive of the Panthers as a group endowed with an ahistorical human agency that it deploys within the confines of its historical situation. While for the sake of clarity I employ language that might suggest that I, too, think of the Panthers as ahistorical agents confined only by their local, historical context, I understand the Panthers' appearance and, hence, their agency to be distributed throughout the cinematic context that enables their appearance. I reject the notion of an ahistorical human agency in favor of an understanding that compelling and multifarious temporal forces provide the conditions within which certain images or events might become commonly perceptible and that cinematic perception itself entails a collective enterprise that is historical, or, at least, profoundly temporal, and dispersed throughout cinematic reality.

24 I am using the term *sovereignty* here in the sense elaborated by Hardt and Negri in their collaborative project *Empire*. They argue that the "imperial sovereignty" characteristic of what they call "Empire" has its basis in the notion, fundamental to the U.S. Constitution, that power is immanent to society, not transcendent. Imperial sovereignty carries as its own internal constraint the project of limiting and controlling those who produce its power. The "American" ideal of unbounded expansion provides a check against this tendency to limit and control. The capacity for expansion includes the United States's ability to "open itself up to" and "include" the powers it faces as it expands by offering "the basis of consensus" as a means to reform its sovereignty. Yet Hardt and Negri qualify their presentation of the imperial aspect of U.S. sovereignty by pointing out that "the North American terrain can be imagined as empty only by willfully ignoring the existence of the Native Americans." The Native Americans thus "existed outside the Constitution as its negative foundation: in other words, their exclusion and elimination were essential conditions of the functioning of the Constitution itself." While Native Americans are outside the Constitution, black slavery presented the conditions for "the first crisis of American liberty" because it "was paradoxically both an exception to and a foundation of the Constitution" that created an internal barrier to the United States's capacity for expansion based on consensus. See Hardt and Negri, *Empire*, 160–82.

178

I embrace Hardt and Negri's conception of U.S. sovereignty, because it grasps the United States's elasticity, its predication on a notion of consensus, and its innate need for and capacity to accommodate reform. Their description of U.S. sovereignty also allows for an understanding of how that sovereignty can reassert itself as "the form of the true" even in the face of the "powers of the false." It does so primarily via asserting, however tenuously, that it is operating according to consensus.

25 Deleuze, *Cinema 2*, 127.

26 Deleuze states that "whether explicitly or not, [truthful] narration always refers to a system of judgment: even when acquittal takes place due to the benefit of the doubt, or when the guilty is so only because of fate" (ibid., 133).

27 Ibid., 131. Deleuze borrows the term *incompossible* from Leibniz's solution to the "paradox of 'contingent futures.'" According to Deleuze, Leibniz devised "the most ingenious, but also the strangest and most convoluted, solution to this paradox." Deleuze explains, "Leibniz says that the naval battle may or may not take place, but that this is not in the same world: it takes place in one world and does not take place in a different world, and these two worlds are possible, but are not 'compossible' with each other. He is thus obliged to forge the wonderful notion of incompossibility (very different from contradiction) in order to resolve the paradox while saving truth: according to him, it is not the impossible, but only the incompossible that proceeds from the possible; and the past may be true without being necessarily true. But the crisis of truth thus enjoys a pause rather than a solution. For nothing prevents us from affirming that incompossibles belong to the same world, that incompossible worlds belong to the same universe" (130–31).

28 Referring to the Panthers' praxis as "performance," Singh claims that "one way to understand the Panthers performance is to recognize how they literally made a spectacle of the state. Within the logic of this spectacle, the excess and escalation of the rhetoric and imagery that the Panthers invented or popularized ('Off the pig,' 'The sky's the limit,' 'Fuck Reagan,' 'Two, three, many Vietnams') worked to continually heighten the anxiety of those charged with the duty of securing the state. In this regard, the police agencies, once they had been verbally attacked and legally outmaneuvered, found as their only recourse the demonstration that their own power was backed by more than words and empty guns. The bind the Panthers presented to the forces of the state was that if their threats were to go unanswered, they would potentially be proved right. The emperor would be shown to have no clothes, and America would be revealed as little more than a mask of power . . . The Panthers, then, were a threat to the state not simply because they were violent but because they abused the state's own reality principle, including its monopoly on the legitimate uses of violence" ("The Black Panthers," 83–84). David E. James makes a similar argument in "Chained to Devilpictures."

29 Clemmons and Jones, "Global Solidarity," 23.

30 J. Edgar Hoover, quoted in Churchill, " 'To Disrupt, Discredit and Destroy,' " 87. For more information on the FBI's effort to destroy the Panthers, see Churchill and Vander Wall, *Agents of Repression*, and Newton, *War against the Panthers*.

31 In her essay " 'The Most Qualified Person' " Angela D. LeBlanc-Ernest cites Bobby Seale's estimate of the percentage of Panther members who were female in 1968; her citation is to Bobby Seale's autobiography, *A Lonely Rage* (177).

32 According to Tracye Matthews, "Black Revolutionary Women" was how Panther women described themselves (" 'No One Ever Asks,' " 286–87).

33 Although not an account of how the Panthers' protest politicized her, Assata Shakur's recollection of her reaction to blacks with guns supports the idea that black females were drawn in by blacks with guns. Shakur states, "The sheer audacity of walking onto the California senate floor with rifles, demanding that Black people have the right to bear arms and the right to self-defense, made me sit back and take a long look at them. And the more political i became, the more i appreciated them" (*Assata*, 203).

34 Jennings, "Why I Joined the Party," 257.

35 Davis, "Black Nationalism," 319–20.

36 Recognizing oneself as the Black involves various and indeterminate manifestations of affect, including desire, abdication, pride, "nausea," and so on depending on the impact of the Black imago on one's sensory-motor schema. I am not discounting the lure of cross-class identification between a black female and her imago, the Black. (I thank Barbara Smith for drawing this aspect of identification and attraction to my attention. In a personal correspondence, she suggested that cross-class attraction might have informed the decisions of some of the more prominent [or, as Joy James would say, "iconic"] Panthers [and Angela Davis] to join the party [or, in Davis's case to affiliate herself with them]. Elaine Brown, Kathleen Cleaver, and Angela Davis, the most iconic women in or associated with the party, were all from middle-class backgrounds.)

Nor am I forgetting that females might have joined or initially considered joining the party based at least in part on their sexual interest in particular men, who were, of course, themselves images. Elaine Brown, for instance, was at first drawn into the BPP by her attraction to various men in the party. According to her autobiography, however, she joined the party on the heels of Martin Luther King Jr.'s assassination and the subsequent uprisings in black ghettos across the United States.

37 See in particular, Carby, *Reconstructing Womanhood*, and Wiegman, *American Anatomies*.

38 The concept of "ungendering" is borrowed from Hortense Spillers's essay "Mama's Baby, Papa's Maybe: An American Grammar Book."

39 Spillers states, "If we can account for an originary narrative and judicial principle that might have engendered a 'Moynihan Report,' many years into the twentieth century, we cannot do much better than look at Goodell's reading of the *partus sequitur ventrum*: the condition of the slave mother is 'forever entailed on all her remotest posterity' " ("Mama's Baby, Papa's Maybe," 79). See Rainwater and

180

Yancey, *The Moynihan Report and the Politics of Controversy* for the full text of the report, a discussion of the political context for its production, and various analyses of its argument and impact.

40 This characterization pertains to aspects of my project here as well.

41 In her discussion of the Anita Hill–Clarence Thomas hearings, Wahneema Lubiano points out the extent to which the findings of the Moynihan Report have become part of prevailing common sense. See Lubiano, "Black Ladies, Welfare Queens, and State Minstrels."

42 Spillers, "Mama's Baby, Papa's Maybe," 79. In this essay what remains unchallenged in hegemonic common-sense understandings of the black woman is a recourse to slavery as the "primal scene" of the contemporary African American, an understanding of the Black and of the black woman as temporally coherent identities and of the ascriptions of modes of subjectivity that rely upon such coherence, and the insistence that a recognizable version of the category "woman" be made applicable to images recognizable as black females.

43 As Robyn Wiegman points out, "To accept, even skeptically, Spillers's reading of the Middle Passage is, in some sense, to encounter the Gordian knot of difference that the importation of slaves in the New World occasioned, since it forces us to recognize how thoroughly saturated is the socio-symbolic structure of sexual difference with the determinants of white racial supremacy. This structure of sexual difference was (and is) not reducible to the 'essential' components of male and female bodies, but refers instead to the processes and practices by which gendered subjectivity defines and inaugurates the modern subject, organizing 'civil' society by scripting it according to highly gendered roles and functions" (*American Anatomies*, 65–66).

44 Ibid., 64.

45 The literature on this point ranges from Trudier Harris's work on lynching (to which Robyn Wiegman's "Anatomy of a Lynching" is indebted) to Eldridge Cleaver's and Amiri Baraka's angry lamentations about the castration of the black man to more mainstream conceptualizations. For academic and theoretical work on this subject, see in particular, Harris, *Exorcising Blackness*; Wiegman, *American Anatomies*, 81–113. For "movement" thinking about the feminization of the black male, see Cleaver, *Soul on Ice*, and Huey Newton's earlier writings, most notably "Fear and Doubt: May 15, 1967."

46 Wiegman, *American Anatomies*, 98–99; and Carby, *Reconstructing Womanhood*.

47 Armstrong, "Modernism's Iconophobia."

48 The "denigrated" forms in which "femininity" had accrued to the black body include that apparent in the Jezebel stereotype. In this context, Jezebel is a lusty black female temptress, an image used to justify raping female slaves that continues to be projected onto black females after slavery. Other examples of "denigrated femininity" include the feminization of black males via castration and lynching, and the denial of black bodies in general into the "masculine" realm of Enlightened democratic citizenship.

49 The Panthers explicitly invoke *The Declaration of Independence* in the "What We

181

Believe" section of point ten of their "Platform and Program," "What We Want, What We Believe." This document is included in many histories and retrospectives of the Panthers. Most recently, it is included in Eds. Cleaver and Katsiaficas, *Liberation, Imagination, and the Black Panther Party,* 285–6.

50 Cited, as "A Black Panther Song," in Foner, *The Black Panthers Speak,* 31. These also are the lyrics to Elaine Brown, "The End of Silence," on the album *Seize the Time* (Vault Records/BMI, 1970). I thank Ken Wissoker for helping me access this album.

51 Although I am unaware of the context for the production of this song, Brown often wrote songs for party males. Indeed, as Joy James points out, Brown's "star text," as it were, provides "complex images of female leadership for radical black feminists to consider and critique" (*Shadowboxing,* 205n11). These include Brown's deployment of physical punishment against African Americans and other aspects of her reign as BPP chairperson that James deems to be "counter-feminist and antirevolutionary" (102). While crucial to an even analysis of women's role in the BPP, the possible misfit between "Elaine Brown" and "feminist" should not discredit my reading of "The End of Silence" as a call to arms directed at the black.

52 In her reading of Harriet Jacobs's *Incidents in the Life of a Slave Girl* Spillers argues, "Though this is barely hinted at on the surface of the text, we might say that Brent, between the lines of her narrative, demarcates a sexuality that is neuter-bound, inasmuch as it represents an open vulnerability to a gigantic sexualized repertoire that may be alternately expressed as male/female" ("Mama's Baby, Papa's Maybe," 77).

53 Although she does not use these terms, this is a version of Tracye Matthews's argument in " 'No One Ever Asks.' "

54 Deleuze, *Cinema 2,* 132. It could be argued convincingly that each of the organizations that appeared to express the political upheavals to which the BPP was tied relied at first on the powers of the false for their legibility and thus for the achievement of consensus regarding their status as representative of the interests expressed by those upheavals. Yet those that were successful in breaking from the forces that had oppressed and exploited them found that maintaining the hegemony they had won required the installation of an organic regime.

55 Lynn Spigel points out that "between the years 1948 and 1955, more than half of all American homes installed a television set and the basic mechanisms of the network oligopoly were set in motion." Spigel, "Installing the Television Set," 11.

56 In his book, *Blacks and White TV: African Americans in Television Since 1948,* J. Fred MacDonald points to "the simultaneous emergence of the civil rights movement and television" (81).

57 Torres, *Black, White, and in Color,* 13.

58 Ibid., 23.

182

59 Muñoz, *Disidentifications*, 187. Torres, *Black, White, and in Color*, 14.

60 Ibid., 14–5.

61 Dienst, *Still Life in Real Time*, 159.

62 Ibid.

63 Ibid.

64 Ibid., 159, 165.

65 This is the way that Wallace depicts black women's participation in "the Black Movement." See Wallace, *Black Macho*.

66 "My name is Peaches!" is the impassioned ending of the Nina Simone song "Four Women." I read Simone's performance as the imposition of a form of femininity, the name Peaches, onto a masculine construction of black womanhood. The song presents brief vignettes of four varieties of black women, with Peaches being the last. By the time she is presented, the listener expects that her vignette, like the three that precede it, will be about a woman. As Fred Moten would say, "Listen to it now."

Joy James gives an analysis of the terms within which particular, iconic Black Revolutionary Women (Angela Davis and Kathleen Cleaver) appear. According to James, the terms of these women's cinematic appearance—their affiliation with militant males and their physical appearance, including their youth and light skin color—work to sexualize them, thereby "deradicalizing" them and enabling their commodification and consumption as "spectacle" and "icon." Although James is concerned with the process whereby radical politics are distilled into commercialized icons she does not question the way that common sense differentiates between male and female bodies by ascribing the notions of masculinity and femininity to them according to each's perceived anatomy. In addition, her argument raises questions regarding the extent to which sexualized bodies could be radical. Nonetheless, her discussion of the context within which black revolutionary females appear provides a crucial foundation for understanding how the image of blacks with guns appears to feminists today. See James, *Shadowboxing*, 93–122.

67 Quoted in Matthews, "No One Ever Asks," 287.

68 Ibid.

69 Wallace's statement at the beginning of "The Myth of the Superwoman" section is telling in this regard. She states, "By the time I was fifteen there was nothing I dreaded more than being like the women in my family. I had been taught to be repelled by them as effectively as I had been taught to avoid women who wore men's trousers and smoked cigars" (*Black Macho*, 89).

70 In her innovative book *Female Masculinity* Judith Halberstam argues that, within the "nonce taxonomy" of female masculinities she develops, the "stone butch manages the discordance between being a woman and experiencing herself as masculine by creating a sexual identity and a set of sexual practices that correspond to and accommodate the disjuncture. The stone butch makes female masculinity possible." Within the cinematic appearance of women according to an American common sense, the black woman, a category which has historically adjudicated between "woman" and "masculinity," might be understood as occupying the position of the "stone butch." However, it is precisely the sexuality that is definitive for the stone butch that is expunged from the Black Revolutionary Woman, because "homosexuality" is understood to be in conflict with that image's status as "revolutionary" and as "woman." As an addendum to Halberstam's argument that "where sex and gender, biology and gender presentation, fail to match . . . , where appearance and reality collide . . . , this is where the stone butch emerges as viable, powerful, and affirmative," it is necessary to add the following exception: in the case of the cinematic appearance of the Black Revolutionary Woman it is precisely the stone butch (or the "bulldagger," to use the derogatory term from within the black vernacular I have been invoking here) who cannot emerge (or appear). See Halberstam, *Female Masculinity*, 126.

71 James, *Shadowboxing*, 102.

72 In a telephone interview in 2000 Barbara Smith recalled to me that she was not drawn to the Panthers because, even though she was not out as a lesbian at the time nor a feminist per se, she knew that she "was not interested in having babies for the movement." Smith recalled that she did not identify with the BPP, although she thought that they were "cool." She continued, "Now, the photograph of Kathleen Cleaver that appeared in Ramparts . . . she was on the cover or inside and there was this full-page picture of her with [her] afro. I thought wow. That was a photograph that I identified with and that was political statement, absolutely a political statement."

73 In my essay "A Homegrown Revolutionary? Tupac Shakur and the Legacy of the Black Panther Party," I consider the way that the circulation of the Panthers' politics in cinematic images provides a context for understanding how the late rap star Tupac Shakur could have been regarded as "the Malcolm X of Generation X."

74 At first glance, Newton's statement "The Women's Liberation and the Gay Liberation Movements: August 15, 1970" seems to refute the Panthers' homophobic embrace of masculinity as the vehicle adequate to liberation. Significantly, Newton speculates that "the homosexual could be the most revolutionary." See ibid., 152, 155. A close reading of this statement and attention to the fact that it appears anthologized in *To Die for the People* under the section heading "White America" reveals, however, that Newton did not conceive of the BPP as including homosexuals (nor did he conceive of it as including women, according to the logic of this statement). Any embrace of Newton's statement today as "evidence" of the Panthers' tolerance toward homosexuality, while potentially efficacious rhetorically and politically, must be critical of Newton's assumption that "the homosexual" and "the woman" are not included in "the Black."

5 Blaxploitation, Surplus, *The L Word*

Nina Simone's version of "O-o-h Child" was originally recorded on 9 February 1971. This song is included on the compact disc *The Essential Nina Simone, Volume 2* (RCA Records/BMG Music, 1994).

1 I have adapted this formulation of the function of technological cinematic machines from Richard Dienst's account of the way that television "consumes our time." Dienst argues, "If we have to talk about consumption at all, it would be more accurate, of course, to say that television consumes our time, producing value and reproducing social relations along the way" (*Still Life in Real Time*, 62). Working with and against Dienst's formulation of television's temporality, I argue that technological cinematic machines require the active (even if habituated, and seemingly passive) participation of its "spectators" in order to (re)produce official common sense.

2 Landy, *The Folklore of Consensus*, xii.

3 Hardt and Negri, *Empire*, 22–23. *Multitude* was released as *The Witch's Flight* was going to press.

4 Ibid., 23–24.

5 I defer to a later project a more sustained and careful consideration of the relationship between media and biopolitics in a globalizing economy and a global division of labor. Yet it is important to the present project to contextualize my construction and analysis of affectivity within the broader discourse on biopower, biopolitics, and the role of immaterial labor (such as affectivity) in their consolidation.

6 Landy, *The Folklore of Consensus*, xii.

7 Dienst, *Still Life in Real Time*, 59.

8 The account of Marx's theory of surplus value that I crystallize here, however briefly, is based on my understanding of Negri's innovative reading of *Grundrisse* in *Marx beyond Marx* (59–104).

9 Writing specifically about the relationship between folklore and melodrama, Landy points out that "the role of affect [in folklore], rather than serving as the servant of meaning and action, and arising from their failure, must be regarded in opposite terms. Affect is in search of a signifier to which it can attach itself. Overriding the limits of signification, the excessive character of melodrama spills over into and is capable of negating sexual and familial conflicts, contaminating narratives ostensibly devoted to the circulation of truisms, 'underlying meanings,' and 'messages'" (*The Folklore of Consensus*, 16).

10 Ferguson, *Aberrations in Black*, 11–18.

11 This is an allusion to Deleuze's analysis of how an image might break through the cliché: "Sometimes it is necessary to restore the lost parts, to rediscover everything that cannot be seen in the image, everything that has been removed to make it 'interesting.' But sometimes, on the contrary, it is necessary to make holes, to introduce voids and white spaces, to rarify the image, by suppressing many things that have been added to make us believe we were seeing everything" (*Cinema 2*, 21).

185

12 There is some debate about when (and whether) to locate the "official" death of "classical Hollywood" and the birth of "the New Hollywood." Most scholars of American film agree that by the 1950s the traditional American film industry characterized by the studio system had come to an end. Many accounts locate the birth of a "New Hollywood Cinema" in the late 1960s with the 1967 release of both *Bonnie and Clyde* and *The Graduate*. Other accounts, like Les Keyser's, describe the 1970s as "a decade that witnessed, according to the consensus of chroniclers, the death of the Old Hollywood and the phoenix-like rebirth of a New Hollywood" (*Hollywood in the Seventies*, 1). For a brief synopsis of this scholarship, see Kramer, "Post-Classical Hollywood."

13 Mark Reid subsumes blaxploitation films into his generic categorizations of "Black Action Film." In doing so, Reid elides blaxploitation's historical specificity, including, importantly, its sociopolitical and economic significance. His discussion primarily focuses on "the action films of the seventies," and his intrageneric differentiation according to characteristics he attributes to three subtypes of the black action film reveals several of the narrative and aesthetic differences between those films. Additionally, by "redefining" those cheaply made, but highly profitable films of the early 1970s in terms of a black action-film genre, Reid performs some foundational work for further explorations of both the continuities and the variations in the constitution of that genre over time. By referring to blaxploitation films as black action films, Reid also provides a series of important insights into the congruity between those films and the film industry's (white) action-film genre. Nonetheless, because Reid's redefinition of blaxploitation films effaces the historical context of their production (a context from which blaxploitation's social function derives), I think that he is mistaken in his refusal of the term *blaxploitation*. See Reid, *Redefining Black Film*.

14 Guerrero, *Framing Blackness*, 91.

15 See Guerrero, *Framing Blackness*, and Rhines, *Black Film, White Money*.

16 The formulation of the audience's "horizon of expectation" originated with Hans Robert Jauss's *Towards an Aesthetic of Reception* and has been accepted by some theorists of genre as a way of understanding one of the functions of Hollywood film genres. See, for example, Neale, "Questions of Genre."

17 The film *Super Fly* itself was made for under $500,000. It grossed $1 million in its first week in two New York City theaters alone and more than $11 million in its first two months of business.

18 It would be interesting to consider the role of the then emergent eight-track-tape technology in the success of these soundtracks because, as is apparent in the case of *Super Fly*, for instance, much of the film's use of music has to do with providing a mobile soundtrack for the film's ghetto milieu that carries a particular affective register.

19 This point is also made in Isaac Julien's documentary about blaxploitation entitled *Baadasssss Cinema* (2002).

20 This critique is available, for instance, in the lyrics to "Little Child Runnin' Wild."

The music itself operates in a different register to multiply the affective value shaken loose by Mayfield's soundtrack. Listen to that song to confirm my point. Curtis Mayfield, *Super Fly* (Curtom, 1972).

21 This is one of the reasons that *The Witch's Flight* has a soundtrack. Find the songs and burn them to disc.

22 Guerrero, *Framing Blackness*, 105.

23 Ferguson, *Aberrations in Black*, 16.

24 Ibid., 12.

25 Ferguson explains, "While capital can only reproduce itself by ultimately transgressing the boundaries of the neighborhood, home, and region, the state positions itself as protector of these boundaries. . . . As the modern nation-state has historically been organized around an illusory universality particularized in terms of race, gender, sexuality, and class, state formations have worked to protect and guarantee this universality. But in its production of surplus populations unevenly marked by a racialized nonconformity with gender and sexual norms, capital constantly disrupts that universality" (*Aberrations in Black*, 17). Ferguson uses the phrase "the multiplications of surplus" to refer to the constitution of these surplus populations coupled with the proliferation of accompanying discourses of gender, class, sexuality, and race.

26 My insights here draw on Matthew Tinkcom's work on gay male camp and his articulation, via a reading of Gayatri Chakravorty Spivak's essay "Scattered Speculations on the Question of Value," of the category "affectively necessary labor" and its relationship to the production of what he calls "camp expression" (*Working Like A Homosexual*, 22–30).

27 Ed Guerrero explains that "following the release of *Superfly*, black civic dissatisfaction with the genre and that film in particular reached a crescendo and contributed to the formation in Los Angeles of the Coalition against Blaxploitation (CAB), made up of several civil rights and black community groups, the most prominent of which were the NAACP, CORE, and the Southern Christian Leadership Conference" (*Framing Blackness*, 101).

28 James, *That's Blaxploitation!*

29 Elizabeth Lapovsky Kennedy and Madeline D. Davis report that "stud broad" was a term used by black butches and femmes in the 1950s as another name for a "butch" (*Boots of Leather*, 7).

30 The practice of producing "lesbian readings" would find much material in this sequence in *Foxy Brown*. For an example of a lesbian reading of another blaxploitation film, *Cleopatra Jones and the Casino of Gold* (1975), see Brody, "The Returns of Cleopatra Jones." Brody considers Grier's blaxploitation films only to differentiate Tamara Dobson's *Cleopatra Jones* (1973, 1975) series from them. That Brody reads Grier's star image as less amenable to "queering" is, I believe, a testament to the efficacy of the operations that Grier's films employ to prevent the butch lesbian from appearing in Grier's characters.

31 The phrase "in the life" within the context that Priscilla uses it refers directly to

187

the life of prostitution and street hustling, but it also connotes homosexuality, often referred to by black homosexuals as being "in the life." The connection between the phrase's two connotations needs to be historicized, possibly as part of a study that presents the genealogy of the street meanings.

32 In "Pam Grier: The Mocha Mogul of Hollywood" Jamaica Kincaid refers to Grier as "the most winning example of a miscegenated person" that Kincaid has ever seen.

According to Kincaid, Grier claims to be "part Caucasian, part Negro (on her father's side), part American Indian, part Asian (on her mother's side). Her skin is the exact color of the pancakes in the Little Black Sambo book. . . . She has the sort of body that press agents like to promote as a sex symbol" (50).

33 See especially Eldridge Cleaver's book *Soul on Ice*.

34 For a discussion of the rhetorical strategies through which black gay men are excluded from constructions of blackness, see McBride, "Can the Queen Speak?"

35 The impact of the effeminization of whiteness in the name of reclaiming black manhood on black male–black female heterosexual relationships is discussed in Michelle Wallace's articulation of the (hetero)sexual politics of common-sense black nationalism, *Black Macho and the Myth of the Superwoman*.

36 In his personal retrospective about blaxploitation films Darius James includes an anecdote that he attributes to the lesbian author Sarah Schulman: "Author-activist Sarah Schulman tells me that every time The Lesbian Avengers advertise a dance using *Coffy*'s clip art—with Pam Grier in halter-top and tight fitting capri pants, holding a sawed-off, double-barreled, 12-gauge shot gun—d'place be packed! 'Why is that?' I asked. 'What could be more appealing to a lesbian?' she answered." The image James describes as "appealing" to lesbians relies upon a mixture of masculine accoutrements (shotgun) and feminine bodily comportment and clothing fashion (tight pants, halter top, "tits and ass"). A queer reading of this image might see it as "a femme lesbian with a gun" (*That's Blaxploitation!* 49).

37 "Someday we'll" is a line from the song that supplies the soundtrack for this chapter, "O-o-h Child," as performed by Nina Simone. This song is included on the compact disc *The Essential Nina Simone, Volume 2* (RCA Records/BMG Music, 1994). Simone's version was originally recorded on 9 February 1971.

38 James, *Shadowboxing*, 102.

39 For a discussion of the sexualization that attends black women's appearance that employs the trope of the "stereotype," see James, *Shadowboxing*, especially chapter 6.

40 This postscript was written at the end of the first season of *The L Word*.

41 Sedgwick, "The L Word."

42 Like much of my thinking throughout this book, my analysis concerning Pam Grier's role in *The L Word* has been informed by Amy Villarejo's considerable contribution to thinking about lesbian visibility. See Villarejo, *Lesbian Rule*.

43 David L. Eng, Judith Halberstam, and José Estaban Muñoz draw attention to these issues, highlighting them as marking primary concerns in the scholarship collected in the issue of *Social Text* they coedited and introduced.

6 Black Lesbian Butch-Femme

The Family Stand, "Ghetto Heaven," *Chain* (Atlantic, 1990).

1 In order to mark *Set It Off*'s affiliation with films made during the early 1990s, set in the United States's predominately black ghettoes, and preoccupied with the violence and machismo they attribute to that setting, I use the category of the "ghetto action film," following S. Craig Watkin's delineation of it, as a generic description of the film. As do many films, however, *Set It Off* defies its generic descriptors, not least by casting four "women" in the lead roles. For Watkin's admittedly fluid, but generic definition of ghetto action films, see Watkins, *Representing*, especially chapters 6 and 7.

2 Jennifer Brody notes the "coincidence" between Cleopatra Jones's name and "Cleopatra Simms," the name of Queen Latifah's character in *Set It Off*: "Is it mere coincidence that Queen Latifah's role as a black lesbian bank robber in F. Gary Gray's film *Set It Off* (1996) is named 'Cleo'?" ("The Returns of Cleopatra Jones," 103).

3 Guerrero, *Framing Blackness*, 182.

4 Watkins, *Representing*, chap. 7.

5 Kelley, "Kickin' Reality," 208–9.

6 See, for example, Carmichael and Hamilton, *Black Power*.

7 Hegemonic common-sense consolidations of blackness preclude a recognition of what is fundamentally new about the ghettocentric realities that gangsta rap and the ghetto action film make visible to official common sense.

8 See, in particular, Watkins, *Representing*, chaps. 6 and 7.

9 Kelley makes this point when he asserts that "the mass media attack on sexism in hip hop has obscured or ignored the degree to which rappers merely represent an extreme version of sexism that pervades daily life, across race and class" (*Race Rebels*, 222).

10 For an insightful assessment of the socioeconomic context of gangsta rap's production and the sociopolitical implications of the worldview it expresses, see Kelley, *Race Rebels*.

11 I borrow the term *female masculinity* from Judith Halberstam. See Halberstam, *Female Masculinity*.

12 The film's efforts to justify the characters' criminal actions were not plausible to some reviewers. For example, in an unfavorable review of the film Ralph Novak writes, "Intellectually bankrupt and not much richer when it comes to principles, this bank-robbery caper is a throwback to the black-vengeance films of the '70s. The catch is that this time the black Americans seeking revenge for various wrongs are four gun-crazy females. Director F. Gary Gray and writers Takashi Bufford and Kate Lanier strive frantically to rationalize the quartet's murderous

rampage, but without much success. Of the women, only Fox . . . has a real ax to grind against 'the system'—she has been unjustly fired from her job as a bank teller. Of the others, Latifah has the weakest case. Her main complaint seems to be that as a lesbian who wants to hang out with her girlfriend, she is an object of derision. Pinkett, meanwhile, has an unlikely romance with Underwood, who picks her up while she cases the bank where he is an officer. Even Underwood's considerable skills can't make his naive character plausible" ("Set It Off").

13 For Stony, the despair her brother's death caused her and her desire to get out of "the hood" provide her rationale for robbing the first bank. After Stony starts dating a rich banker whom she meets while she and Tisean are casing the bank where he works, her good reason for robbing banks is diminished; Keith earns more than enough money to support her. Out of a ghettocentric sense of loyalty to her lifelong friends, her "people," Stony continues to rob banks even after her relationship with Keith begins to look more promising. It is Cleo who voices the ghettocentric principle of loyalty when she reminds Stony (who says she does not want to rob the second bank) that "you been my people for twenty years." Significantly, Stony is the only one of the four still alive by the end of the film.

14 See Debord, *The Society of the Spectacle*.

15 For a formulation of televisual images as images of value in process, see my discussion of television in chapter 2 and Richard Dienst's analysis of television as a Marxian machine (*Still Life in Real Time*, chap. 2). For an articulation of black masculinity as a tendency toward death, hear especially the recordings of Tupac Shakur and see Holland, "Bill T. Jones, Tupac Shakur and the (Queer) Art of Death."

16 Jewelle Gomez addresses some of the stereotypes about femmes, including "femmes are white, blacks are butches. The explicit racism and sexism in this stereotype persists in every lesbian community. It is a defamatory extension of the sexual stereotyping of both African-Americans and of white women" ("Femme Erotic Independence," 107).

17 The title of this section includes a reference to Ma Rainey's song "Prove It on Me Blues." This song, according to Eric Garber, "speaks directly to the issue of lesbianism. In it she admits to her preference for male attire and female companionship, yet dares her audience to 'prove it' on her" ("A Spectacle in Color," 326).

18 See my essay "Joining the Lesbians: Cinematic Regimes of Black Lesbian Visibility" for an argument about the consolidation of the category "lesbian" and the set of exclusions on which it relies.

19 Much of the information I give here about butch-femme is contained in the historical account of a butch-femme community in Buffalo, New York, provided in Kennedy and Davis, *Boots of Leather*. See also "Butch-Femme Relationships: Sexual Courage in the 1950s," in Nestle, *A Restricted Country*, 100–109; Feinberg, *Stone Butch Blues*; and Lorde, *Zami*.

20 References to black butches ("bulldaggers") frequently were made in the cultural productions of the Harlem Renaissance, especially in the blues songs of Ma

Rainey, Bessie Smith, and Lucille Bogan. But I have found few historical narratives detailing the forms of community that "B.D." (bulldagger) women contributed to making. "B.D. Women Blues" is the name of a song recorded by Bessie Jackson (Lucille Bogan). For an account of the prevalence of lesbians and gays during the Harlem Renaissance, see Garber, "A Spectacle in Color."

21 For a discussion of the 1970s lesbian feminist stance against butch-femme, see Roof, "1970s Lesbian Feminism Meets 1990s Butch-Femme." Most relevant to the present discussion is an essay written by Anita Cornwell, whom Roof refers to as "one of the few black lesbian feminists publishing essays in a predominantly white media during [the late 1960s and early 1970s]." In "Three for the Price of One: Notes from a Gay Black Feminist," Cornwell laments being mistaken for "a stud" by a "Black lesbian" friend and attributes the fact that butch-femme persists among black lesbians to the racism of the women's movement. Writing in the late 1970s, Cornwell asserts, "Not surprisingly, fear of encountering racism seems to be one of the main reasons that so many Black womyn refuse to join the Womyn's Movement. This is especially unfortunate for the Black lesbians because, unless they have come across Feminist ideas from somewhere, they are apt to remain in the old rut of sexual role playing that apparently affects all traditional Lesbian circles" (*Black Lesbian in White*, 12).

22 In her novel *Stone Butch Blues* Leslie Feinberg writes, "We thought we'd won the war of liberation when we embraced the word gay. Then suddenly there were professors and doctors and lawyers coming out of the woodwork telling us that meetings should be run with Roberts Rules of Order. . . . They drove us out, made us feel ashamed of how we looked. They said we were male chauvinist pigs, the enemy. It was women's hearts they broke. We were not hard to send away, we went quietly" (11).

23 See chapter 2 herein for a discussion of Gilles Deleuze's formulation of "the powers of the false." See also Deleuze, *Cinema 2*, chap. 6.

24 Deleuze, *Cinema 1*, 16.

25 Ibid.

26 Ibid., 17.

27 Ibid.

7 Reflections on Black Femme

"On and On" is the title of a song on Erykah Badu's breakthrough neosoul album, *Baduizm* (Universal Records, 1997).

1 Discussing the way that the powers of the false supercede the regime of the true, Deleuze explains that "if the ideal of truth crumbles, the relations of appearance will no longer be sufficient to maintain the possibility of judgement" (*Cinema 2*, 139).

2 Deleuze, *Cinema 1*, 16–17.

3 Ibid., 16.

191

4 Ibid., 17.

5 Ibid.

6 Deleuze's discussion of "the problem" and its relationship to the time-image informs my discussion here. My comment that my work is vulnerable to debates about choices I have made in my framing of the black femme is informed by Deleuze's assertion that "it is characteristic of the problem that it is inseparable from a choice" (*Cinema 2*, 176).

7 In the context of a discussion of the role of the interstice between images in establishing "the whole" as "the outside," Deleuze claims that "film ceases to be 'images in a chain . . . an uninterrupted chain of images each one the slave of the next' and whose slave we are. It is the method of BETWEEN, 'between two images,' which does away with all cinema of the One. It is the method of AND, 'this and then that,' which does away with all the cinema of Being=is" (*Cinema 2*, 180).

8 Barbara Smith's scholarly work—including the collection she coedited with Gloria T. Hull and Patricia Bell Scott, *All the Women Are White, All the Blacks Are Men, But Some of Us Are Brave: Black Women's Studies*—gave expression to a critique of the projects of "black identity" and of "women" whose accessible pasts include, among other black feminist critiques, Sojourner Truth's scathing challenge to the exclusionary project "women": Ain't I a Woman?" Though Smith's work does not question identity politics per se, it does valorize identity formations (such as "black women") that particular conceptions of collective identity (for instance, "black" and "women") exclude. By doing so, it reveals that identity itself is problematic.

9 Insofar as I have argued against identity-based movements in general, I do not expect this project to be so directed.

10 Within Deleuze's theory of cinema, with the advent of the time-image, as the whole becomes the outside, "modern cinema develops new relations with thought from three points of view: the obliteration of a whole or of a totalization of images, in favour of an outside which is inserted between them; the erasure of the internal monologue as whole of the film, in favour of a free indirect discourse and vision; the erasure of the unity of man and the world, in favour of a break which now leaves us with only a belief in this world" (*Cinema 2*, 187–88).

11 Davis, "Reflections," 7.

12 Hardt and Negri, *Empire*, 293. Hardt and Negri point out that affective labor produces "social networks, forms of community."

13 Saidiya Hartman's description of the formation of community among slaves is an important one to keep in mind throughout the discussion that follows because it underscores the primacy of affect, rather than identity, in the formation of community. Hartman states, "It cannot be assumed that the conditions of domination alone were sufficient to create a sense of common values, trust, or collective identification. The commonality constituted in practice depends less on presence or sameness than upon desired change—the abolition of bondage. Thus, contrary to identity providing the ground of community, identity is figured as the desired negation of the very set of constraints that create commonality—that is, the yearning to be liberated from the condition of enslavement facilitates the networks of affiliation and identification" (*Scenes of Subjection*, 59).

14 Davis, *Women, Race, and Class*, chap. 1.

15 Davis, "Reflections," 6.

16 Moten, *In the Break*, 1.

17 As Davis says at the beginning of her essay, "Initially, I did not envision this paper as strictly confined to the era of slavery. Yet, as I began to think through the issue of the black matriarch, I came to the conclusion that it had to be refuted at its *presumed* historical inception" ("Reflections," 3; emphasis added).

18 By pointing out that the black female slave is the presumed historical origin of the black woman," Davis is critical about reinscribing "slavery" as the originary site of black subjectivity, even though that is, in effect, what she does in "Reflections."

19 Marx, *Grundrisse*, 489. Also quoted in Davis, "Reflections," 114.

20 Roberts, "As Vid Mart Matures," A12.

21 Ibid.

22 Price recalls, "We had little marketing money and threw it at the feet of the critics and said, 'Here, it's an art film.' Thank God they agreed" (ibid., A13).

23 One reviewer of *Eve's Bayou* ended his enthusiastic recommendation of the film with the statement: "Avoiding the clichés of recent African American cinema, *Eve's Bayou* is a complex, exciting film that builds confidently to an inevitable explosion" (Joseph Cunneen, "Eve's Bayou," in Movie Reviews section of the *National Catholic Reporter*, 19 December 1997, 20).

24 Roberts, "As Vid Mart Matures," A12.

25 bell hooks explains how "audiences who watched *Daughters of the Dust* (which merges the conventional and the unconventional) at an early screening witnessed resisting spectatorship. To a grave extent the film had to be positioned aesthetically before many viewers could see it and appreciate it on its own terms. When viewers came looking for conventional cinema and did not find it, many were disappointed and enraged" (*Reel to Real*, 105).

26 For a discussion of the relationship between "thought" and "the unthought" in the regime of the time-image, see Deleuze, *Cinema 2*, chap. 7.

27 During an insightful and creative meditation on *Eve's Bayou*'s revision of Freudian-Lacanian psychoanalysis, D. Soyini Madison explains that "most everyone who saw [*Eve's Bayou*], whether they loved it or hated it, wants to know if the father is lying or if it was the daughter" ("Oedipus Rex at *Eve's Bayou*," 312).

28 By dropping hints to Mr. Meraux that her dad and Mrs. Meraux are having an affair and by bringing a lock of her father's hair to Elzora, a voodoo practitioner, Eve sets in motion a chain of events that lead to Mr. Meraux murdering her father.

29 "Samuel L. Jackson and Lynn Whitfield," 64.

30 Roberts, "As Vid Mart Matures," A13.

31 Ibid.

32 The article provided no information about Trimark's data-collection methods.

193

33 After Louis's death, Mozelle tells a grieving Eve, "Last night I had a dream that I was flying. It was such a fine feeling. From the corner of my eye I saw a woman drowning in the very same air that was keeping me afloat and I knew without looking that it was me. Should I save her? And I heard Louis's voice saying 'Don't look back.' So, I kept on flying and I let her drown. When I woke up, I told Julian I would marry him." Based on her brother's instructions, Mozelle decides to continue a habituated movement rather than hold herself open to what might be revealed in the space-time of herself drowning. Instead of lingering in the image of herself drowning, an image that might rupture "the very same air that was keeping" her afloat and open onto something new or, at least, different, she reproduces the hegemonic institution of marriage in spite of the fact that marriage is, for her, a form of sociality that consistently fails to meet her needs and that has meant death for each of her husbands. Reproducing hegemonic institutions and relations is the risk of valorizing survival within cinematic reality. Are "marriage" and "drowning" the only possibilities within an air in which one might fly and drown simultaneously? What (im)possibilities persist therein?

Armstrong, Nancy. "Modernism's Iconophobia and What It Did to Gender." *Modernism/Modernity* 5, no. 2 (1998): 47–75.

Asukile, Thabiti. "The All-Embracing Black Nationalist Theories of David Walker's Appeal." *Black Scholar* 29, no. 4 (1999): 16–24.

Bambara, Toni Cade. "Reading the Signs, Empowering the Eye: *Daughters of the Dust* and the Black Independent Cinema Movement." In *Black American Cinema*, edited by Manthia Diawara, 118–44. New York: Routledge, 1993.

Baraka, Amiri. *The LeRoi Jones/Amiri Baraka Reader*, edited by William J. Harris and Amiri Baraka. 2nd ed. New York: Thunder's Mouth Press, 2000.

Beller, Jonathan L. "Dziga Vertov and the Film of Money." *boundary 2* 26, no. 3 (1999): 151–99.

Benjamin, Walter. "The Work of Art in the Age of Mechanical Reproduction." In *Illuminations: Essays and Reflections*, edited by Hannah Arendt, 217–52. New York: Schocken Books, 1968.

Bergson, Henri. *Creative Evolution*. Translated by Arthur Mitchell. Mineola, N.Y.: Dover, 1998.

——. *Matter and Memory*. Translated by Nancy Margaret Paul and W. Scott Palmer. New York: Zone Books, 1990.

Bordwell, David, Janet Staiger, and Kristin Thompson. *The Classical Hollywood Cinema: Film Style and Mode of Production to 1960*. New York: Columbia University Press, 1985.

Brody, Jennifer DeVere. "The Returns of Cleopatra Jones." *Signs* 25, no. 1 (1999): 91–121.

Brown, Elaine. *A Taste of Power: A Black Woman's Story*. New York: Pantheon Books, 1992.

Buck-Morss, Susan. "Aesthetics and Anaesthetics: Walter Benjamin's Artwork Essay Reconsidered." *October* 62 (1992): 3–41.

——. "The Dream World of Mass Culture: Walter Benjamin's Theory of Modernity and the Dialectics of Seeing." In *Modernity and the Hegemony of Vision*, edited by David Michael Levin, 309–38. Berkeley: University of California Press, 1993.

Carby, Hazel V. *Reconstructing Womanhood: The Emergence of the Afro-American Woman Novelist*. New York: Oxford University Press, 1987.

Carmichael, Stokely, and Charles V. Hamilton. *Black Power: The Politics of Liberation in America*. New York: Random House, 1967.

Churchill, Ward. " 'To Disrupt, Discredit and Destroy': The FBI's Secret War against the Black Panther Party." In *Liberation, Imagination, and the Black Panther Party: A New Look at the Panthers and Their Legacy*, edited by Kathleen Cleaver and George Katsiaficas, 78–117. New York: Routledge, 2001.

Churchill, Ward, and Jim Vander Wall. *Agents of Repression: The* FBI's Secret Wars against the Black Panther Party and the American Indian Movement. Boston: South End Press, 1990.

Cleaver, Eldridge. *Soul on Ice.* New York: Dell Publishing, 1968.

Cleaver, Kathleen, and George Katsiaficas, eds. *Liberation, Imagination, and the Black Panther Party: A New Look at the Panthers and Their Legacy.* New York: Routledge, 2001.

Clemmons, Michael L., and Charles E. Jones. "Global Solidarity: The Black Panther Party in the International Arena." In *Liberation, Imagination, and the Black Panther Party: A New Look at the Panthers and Their Legacy,* edited by Kathleen Cleaver and George Katsiaficas, 20–39. New York: Routledge, 2001.

Cook, David A. "Auteur Cinema and the 'Film Generation' in 1970s Hollywood." In *The New American Cinema,* edited by Jon Lewis, 11–37. Durham, N.C.: Duke University Press, 1998.

Cooper, Anna Julia. *A Voice from the South.* Edited by Henry Louis Gates Jr. New York: Oxford University Press, 1988.

Cornwell, Anita. *Black Lesbian in White America.* Minneapolis: Naiad Press, 1983.

Cripps, Thomas. "New Black Cinema and Uses of the Past." In *Black Cinema Aesthetics: Issues in Independent Black Filmmaking,* edited by Gladstone Yearwood. Athens: Ohio University Center for Afro-American Studies, 1982.

——. *Slow Fade to Black: The Negro in American Film, 1900–1942.* New York: Oxford University Press, 1993.

Davis, Angela. "Black Nationalism: The Sixties and the Nineties." In *Black Popular Culture,* edited by Gina Dent, 317–24. Seattle: Bay Press, 1992.

——. "Reflections on the Black Woman's Role in the Community of Slaves." In *The Angela Y. Davis Reader,* edited by Joy James, 111–28. New York: Blackwell, 1998.

——. *Women, Race, and Class.* New York: Random House, 1983.

Debord, Guy. *The Society of the Spectacle.* Translated by Donald Nicholson-Smith. New York: Zone Books, 1995.

Deleuze, Gilles. *Cinema 1: The Movement-Image.* Translated by Hugh Tomlinson and Barbara Hammerjam. Minneapolis: University of Minnesota Press, 1991.

——. *Cinema 2: The Time-Image.* Translated by Hugh Tomlinson and Robert Galeta. 1985. Reprint, Minneapolis: University of Minnesota Press, 1994.

——. *Difference and Repetition.* Translated by Paul Patton. New York: Columbia University Press, 1994.

——. *Negotiations, 1972–1990.* Translated by Martin Joughin. New York: Columbia University Press, 1995.

Deleuze, Gilles, and Felix Guattari. *What Is Philosophy?* Translated by Hugh Tomlinson and Graham Burchall. New York: Columbia University Press, 1994.

Derrida, Jacques. *Aporias.* Translated by Thomas Dutoit. Palo Alto, Calif.: Stanford University Press, 1993.

——. *The Other Heading: Reflections on Today's Europe.* Translated by Pascale-Anne Brault and Michael B. Naas. Bloomington: Indiana University Press, 1992.

Diawara, Manthia, ed. *Black American Cinema.* New York: Routledge, 1993.

Dienst, Richard. *Still Life in Real Time: Theory after Television*. Durham, N.C.: Duke University Press, 1994.

Doss, Erika. " 'Revolutionary Art Is a Tool for Liberation': Emory Douglas and Protest Aesthetics at the *Black Panther*." In *Liberation, Imagination, and the Black Panther Party: A New Look at the Panthers and Their Legacy*, edited by Kathleen Cleaver and George Katsiaficas, 175–87. New York: Routledge, 2001.

Douglass, Frederick. *My Bondage and My Freedom*. New York: Washington Square Press, 2003.

——. *Narrative of the Life of Frederick Douglass, an American Slave, Written by Himself*. New York: New American Library, 1968.

Du Bois, W. E. B. *The Souls of Black Folk*. New York: Penguin Classics, 1996.

Dyer, Richard. *White*. New York: Routledge, 1997.

Eng, David L., Judith Halberstam, and José Esteban Muñoz. "Introduction: What's Queer about Queer Studies Now?" *Social Text* 84–85 (2005): 1–17.

Fanon, Frantz. *Black Skin, White Masks*. Translated by Constance Farrington. New York: Grove Press, 1968.

Feinberg, Leslie. *Stone Butch Blues*. Ithaca, N.Y.: Firebrand Books, 1993.

Ferguson, Roderick A. *Aberrations in Black: Toward a Queer of Color Critique*. Minneapolis: University of Minnesota Press, 2004.

Flaxman, Gregory, ed. *The Brain Is the Screen: Deleuze and the Philsophy of Cinema*. Minneapolis: University of Minnesota Press, 2000.

Foner, Philip, ed. *The Black Panthers Speak*. New York: Da Capo Press, 1995.

Foucault, Michel. *Language, Counter-Memory, Practice: Selected Essays and Interviews*. Translated by Donald F. Bouchard and Sherry Simon. Ithaca, N.Y.: Cornell University Press, 1977.

Garber, Eric. "A Spectacle in Color: The Lesbian and Gay Subculture of Jazz Age Harlem." In *Hidden from History: Reclaiming the Gay and Lesbian Past*, edited by Martin Duberman, Martha Vicinus, and George Chauncey Jr., 318–31. New York: Penguin Books, 1989.

Gerima, Haile. "Triangular Cinema, Breaking Toys, and Dinknesh vs Lucy." In *Questions of Third Cinema*, edited by Jim Pines and Paul Willeman, 65–89. London: British Film Institute, 1989.

Gomez, Jewelle. "Femme Erotic Independence." In *Butch/Femme: Inside Lesbian Gender*, edited by Sally Munt, 101–8. London: Cassell, 1998.

Gordon, Avery. *Ghostly Matters: Haunting and the Sociological Imagination*. Minnesota: University of Minnesota Press, 1997.

Gordon, Lewis R. "The Black and the Body Politic: Fanon's Existential Phenomenological Critique of Psychoanalysis." In *Fanon: A Critical Reader*, edited by Lewis R. Gordon, T. Denean Sharpley-Whiting, and Renee T. White, 74–84. Cambridge, Mass.: Blackwell, 1996.

Gordon, Lewis R., T. Denean Sharpley-Whiting, and Renee T. White, eds. *Fanon: A Critical Reader*. Cambridge, Mass.: Blackwell, 1996.

Gramsci, Antonio. *Selections from the Prison Notebooks*. Translated by Quintin Hoare and Geoffrey Nowell-Smith. New York: International Publishers, 1992.

Guerrero, Ed. *Framing Blackness: The African American Image in Film.* Philadelphia: Temple University Press, 1993.

Guneratne, Anthony R., and Wimal Dissanayake, eds. *Rethinking Third Cinema.* New York: Routledge, 2003.

Halberstam, Judith. *Female Masculinity.* Durham, N.C.: Duke University Press, 1998.

Hammonds, Evelynn. "Black (W)Holes and the Geometry of Black Female Sexuality." *Differences* 6, nos. 2–3 (1994): 126–45.

Hansen, Miriam Bratu. "Benjamin and Cinema: Not a One Way Street." *Critical Inquiry* 25, no. 2 (1999): 306–43.

——. "The Mass Production of the Senses: Classical Cinema and Vernacular Modernism." *Modernism/Modernity* 6, no. 2 (1999): 59–77.

Hardt, Michael, and Antonio Negri. *Empire.* Cambridge, Mass.: Harvard University Press, 2000.

Harper, Phillip Brian. *Are We Not Men? Masculine Anxiety and the Problem of African-American Identity.* New York: Oxford University Press, 1996.

Harris, Trudier. *Exorcising Blackness: Historical and Literary Lynching and Burning Rituals.* Bloomington: Indiana University Press, 1984.

Hartman, Saidiya. *Scenes of Subjection: Terror, Slavery, and Self-Making in Nineteenth-Century America.* New York: Oxford University Press, 1997.

——. "The Time of Slavery." *South Atlantic Quarterly* 101, no. 4 (2002): 757–77.

Hegel, G. W. F. *Phenomenology of Spirit.* Translated by A. V. Miller. New York: Oxford University Press, 1977.

Hilliard, David, and Lewis Cole. *This Side of Glory: The Autobiography of David Hilliard and the Story of the Black Panther Party.* Boston: Little, Brown, 1993.

Holland, Sharon Patricia. "Bill T. Jones, Tupac Shakur and the (Queer) Art of Death." *Callaloo* 23, no. 1 (2000): 384–93.

hooks, bell. *Reel to Real: Race, Sex, and Class at the Movies.* New York: Routledge, 1996.

Hudson, Theodore R. "Activism and Criticism during the Black Arts Movement." In *Connections: Essays on Black Literatures,* edited by Emmanuel S. Nelson, 89–99. Canberra, Australia: Aboriginal Studies Press, 1988.

James, Darius. *That's Blaxploitation! Roots of the Baadasssss 'Tude (Rated X by an All-Whyte Jury).* New York: St. Martin's Press, 1995.

James, David E. "Chained to Devilpictures: Cinema and Black Liberation in the Sixties." In *The Year Left 2: An American Socialist Yearbook,* edited by Mike Davis, Manning Marable, Fred Pfeil, and Michael Sprinker, 125–38. London: Verso, 1987.

James, Joy. *Shadowboxing: Representations of Black Feminist Politics.* New York: St. Martin's Press, 1999.

Jauss, Hans Robert. *Towards an Aesthetic of Reception.* Brighton, U.K.: Harvester Press, 1982.

Jennings, Regina. "Why I Joined the Party: An Africana Womanist Reflection." In *The Black Panther Party (Reconsidered),* edited by Charles E. Jones, 257–66. Baltimore: Black Classic Press, 1998.

Jones, Charles E., ed. *The Black Panther Party (Reconsidered).* Baltimore: Black Classic Press, 1998.

Judy, Ronald A. T. "Fanon's Body of Black Experience." In *Fanon: A Critical Reader*, edited by Lewis R. Gordon, T. Denean Sharpley-Whiting, and Renee T. White, 53–73. Cambridge, Mass.: Blackwell, 1996.

Kandé, Sylvie. "Look Homeward, Angel: Maroons and Mulattos in Haile Gerima's *Sankofa*." *Research in African Literatures* 29, no. 2 (1998): 128–46.

Kawash, Samira. "Terrorists and Vampires: Fanon's Spectral Violence of Decolonization." In *Frantz Fanon: Critical Perspectives*, edited by Anthony C. Alessandrini, 235–57. New York: Routledge, 1999.

Keeling, Kara. "A Homegrown Revolutionary? Tupac Shakur and the Legacy of the Black Panther Party." *Black Scholar* 29, nos. 2–3 (1999): 59–63.

——. "In the Interval: Frantz Fanon and the 'Problems' of Visual Representation." *Qui Parle* 13, no. 2 (2003): 91–117.

——. "Joining the Lesbians: Cinematic Regimes of Black Lesbian Visibility." In *Black Queer Studies: A Critical Anthology*, edited by E. Patrick Johnson and Mae G. Henderson, 213–77. Durham, N.C.: Duke University Press, 2005.

Kelley, Robin D. G. "Kickin' Reality, Kickin' Ballastics: 'Gangsta Rap' and Post-industrial Los Angeles." In *Race Rebels: Culture, Politics, and the Black Working Class*, by Robin D. G. Kelley, 183–228. New York: Free Press, 1996.

——. *Race Rebels: Culture, Politics, and the Black Working Class.* New York: Free Press, 1996.

Kennedy, Elizabeth Lapovsky, and Madeline D. Davis. *Boots of Leather, Slippers of Gold: The History of a Lesbian Community.* New York: Penguin, 1994.

Keyser, Les. *Hollywood in the Seventies.* 1st ed. New York: A. S. Barnes, 1981.

Kincaid, Jamaica. "Pam Grier: The Mocha Mogul of Hollywood." *Ms.*, August 1975, 49–53.

Kramer, Peter. "Post-Classical Hollywood." In *American Cinema and Hollywood: Critical Approaches*, edited by John Hill and Pamela Church Gibson, 63–83. New York: Oxford University Press, 2000.

Landy, Marcia. *Film, Politics, and Gramsci.* Minneapolis: University of Minnesota Press, 1994.

——. *The Folklore of Consensus: Theatricality in Italian Cinema, 1930–1943.* Albany: State University of New York Press, 1998.

LeBlanc-Ernest, Angela D. " 'The Most Qualified Person to Handle the Job': Black Panther Party Women, 1966–1982." In *The Black Panther Party (Reconsidered)*, edited by Charles E. Jones, 305–34. Baltimore: Black Classic Press, 1998.

Lewis, Jon, ed. *The New American Cinema.* Durham, N.C.: Duke University Press, 1998.

Lipsitz, George. "The Struggle for Hegemony." *Journal of American History* 75, no. 1 (1988): 146–50.

Lorde, Audre. *Zami: A New Spelling of My Name.* Freedom, Calif.: Crossing Press, 1997.

Lowe, Lisa, and David Lloyd, eds. *The Politics of Culture in the Shadow of Capital.* Durham, N.C.: Duke University Press, 1997.

Lubiano, Wahneema. "Black Ladies, Welfare Queens, and State Minstrels: Ideological

199

War by Narrative Means." In *Race-Ing Justice, En-Gendering Power: Essays on Anita Hill, Clarence Thomas, and the Construction of Social Reality*, edited by Toni Morrison, 323–63. New York: Pantheon Books, 1992.

——. "Black Nationalism and Black Common Sense: Policing Ourselves and Others." In *The House that Race Built: Black Americans, U.S. Terrain*, edited by Wahneema Lubiano, 232–52. New York: Pantheon Books, 1997.

MacDonald, J. Fred. *Blacks and White TV: African Americans in Television since 1948*. Chicago: Nelson Hall, 1992.

Madison, D. Soyini. "Oedipus Rex at *Eve's Bayou* or the Little Black Girl Who Left Sigmund Freud in the Swamp." *Cultural Studies* 14, no. 2 (2000): 311–40.

Marriott, David. *On Black Men*. New York: Columbia University Press, 2000.

Marx, Karl. *Economic and Philosophic Manuscripts of 1844*. Translated by Martin Milligan. New York: International Publishers, 1993.

——. *Grundrisse: Foundations of the Critique of Political Economy*. Translated by Martin Nicolaus. New York: Penguin Books, 1993.

Masilela, Ntongela. "The Los Angeles School of Black Filmmakers." In *Black American Cinema*, edited by Manthia Diawara, 107–17. New York: Routledge, 1993.

Matthews, Tracye. " 'No One Ever Asks, What a Man's Role in the Revolution Is': Gender and the Politics of the Black Panther Party, 1966–1971." In *The Black Panther Party (Reconsidered)*, edited by Charles E. Jones, 267–304. Baltimore: Black Classic Press, 1998.

McBride, Dwight A. "Can the Queen Speak? Racial Essentialism, Sexuality and the Problem of Authority." *Callaloo* 21, no. 2 (1998): 363–79.

Mercer, Kobena. "Busy in the Ruins of a Wretched Phantasia." In *Frantz Fanon: Critical Perspectives*, edited by Anthony C. Alessandrini, 195–218. New York: Routledge, 1999.

Morrison, Toni. *Playing in the Dark: Whiteness and the Literary Imagination*. New York: Vintage Books, 1993.

Moten, Fred. *In the Break: The Aesthetics of the Black Radical Tradition*. Minneapolis: University of Minnesota Press, 2003.

Muñoz, José Esteban. *Disidentifications: Queers of Color and the Performance of Politics*. Minneapolis: University of Minnesota Press, 1999.

Neal, Larry. "The Black Arts Movement." *Drama Review* 12, no. 4 (1968): 28–39.

Neale, Steve. "Questions of Genre." *Screen* 31, no. 1 (1990): 45–66.

Negri, Antonio. *Marx beyond Marx: Lessons on the Grundrisse*. Translated by Harry Cleaver, Michael Ryan, and Maurizio Viano. Brooklyn: Autonomedia, 1991.

Nestle, Joan. *A Restricted Country: Essays and Short Stories*. London: Sheba Feminist Publishers, 1988.

Newton, Huey P. "Fear and Doubt: May 15, 1967." In *To Die for the People: The Writings of Huey P. Newton*, 79–81. New York: Random House, 1972.

——. *To Die for the People: The Writings of Huey P. Newton*. New York: Random House, 1972.

——. *War against the Panthers: A Study of Repression in America*. New York: Writers and Readers, 1996.

——. "The Women's Liberation and the Gay Liberation Movements: August 15, 1970." In *To Die for the People: The Writings of Huey P. Newton*, 152–55. New York: Random House, 1972.

Newton, Huey P., and J. Herman Black. *Revolutionary Suicide*. New York: Writers and Readers, 1995.

Novak, Ralph. "Set It Off." *People* 46, no. 20 (1996).

Nun, Jose. "Elements for a Theory of Democracy: Gramsci and Common Sense." *boundary 2* 14, no. 3 (1986): 197–229.

Pines, Jim, and Paul Willemen, eds. *Questions of Third Cinema*. London: British Film Institute, 1989.

Pisters, Patricia. *The Matrix of Visual Culture: Working with Deleuze in Film Theory*. Stanford, Calif.: Stanford University Press, 2003.

Pye, Michael, and Linda Myles. *The Movie Brats: How the Film Generation Took Over Hollywood*. New York: Holt, Rinehart, and Winston, 1979.

Rainwater, Lee, and William L. Yancey, eds. *The Moynihan Report and the Politics of Controversy*. Cambridge, Mass.: MIT Press, 1967.

Reid, Mark A. *Redefining Black Film*. Berkeley: University of California Press, 1993.

Rhines, Jesse Algeron. *Black Film, White Money*. New Brunswick, N.J.: Rutgers Univesity Press, 1996.

Roberts, Jerry. "As Vid Mart Matures, Indies Go Upscale to Find Niche Biz." *Variety*, 23 February 1998, A12–A13.

Roof, Judith. "1970s Lesbian Feminism Meets 1990s Butch-Femme." In *Butch/Femme: Inside Lesbian Gender*, edited by Sally Munt, 27–36. Herndon, Va.: Cassell, 1998.

"Samuel L. Jackson and Lynn Whitfield Star in Movie about Success and Secrets of Louisiana Family (*Eve's Bayou*)." *Jet*, 10 November 1997, 60–64.

Seale, Bobby. *A Lonely Rage: The Autobiography of Bobby Seale*. New York: Times Books, 1977.

——. *Seize the Time: The Story of the Black Panther Party and Huey P. Newton*. New York: Random House, 1970.

Sedgwick, Eve Kosofsky. "*The L Word*: Novelty in Normalcy." *Chronicle of Higher Education*, 16 January 2004, B10–B12.

Shakur, Assata. *Assata: An Autobiography*. Westport, Conn.: Lawrence Hill, 1987.

Singh, Nikhil Pal. "The Black Panthers and the 'Undeveloped Country' of the Left." In *The Black Panther Party (Reconsidered)*, edited by Charles E. Jones, 57–105. Baltimore: Black Classic Press, 1998.

Smethurst, James. "Pat Your Foot and Turn the Corner: Amiri Baraka, the Black Arts Movement, and the Poetics of a Popular Avant-Garde." *African American Review* 37, nos. 2–3 (2003): 261–70.

Smith, Barbara, Gloria T. Hull, and Patricia Bell Scott, eds. *All the Women Are White, All the Blacks Are Men, but Some of Us Are Brave: Black Women's Studies*. New York: Feminist Press, 1982.

Smythe, Dallas. *Dependency Road: Communications, Capitalism, Consciousness, and Canada*. Norwood, N.J.: Ablex, 1981.

Sobchack, Vivian. "The Insistent Fringe: Moving Images and Historical Consciousness." *History and Theory* 36, no. 4 (1997): 4–20.

Spigel, Lynn. "Installing the Television Set: Popular Discourses on Television and
Domestic Space, 1948–1955." *Camera Obscura* 16 (1988): 11–46.

Spillers, Hortense J. "Mama's Baby, Papa's Maybe: An American Grammar Book."
diacritics 17, no. 2 (1987): 65–81.

Spivak, Gayatri Chakravorty. "Can the Subaltern Speak?" In *Colonial Discourse and
Post-Colonial Theory: A Reader*, edited by Patrick Williams and Laura Chrisman,
66–111. New York: Columbia University Press, 1994.

Tinkcom, Matthew. *Working Like a Homosexual: Camp, Capital, Cinema.* Durham,
N.C.: Duke University Press, 2002.

Torres, Sasha. *Black, White, and in Color: Television and Black Civil Rights.* Princeton:
Princeton University Press, 2003.

Villarejo, Amy. *Lesbian Rule: Cultural Criticism and the Value of Desire.* Durham, N.C.:
Duke University Press, 2003.

Wallace, Michele. *Black Macho and the Myth of the Superwoman.* New York: Dial Press,
1978.

Watkins, S. Craig. *Representing: Hip Hop Culture and the Production of Black Cinema.*
Chicago: University of Chicago Press, 1998.

Wayne, Mike. *Political Film: The Dialectics of Third Cinema.* Sterling, Va.: Pluto Press,
2001.

White, Armond. *Rebel for the Hell of It: The Life of Tupac Shakur.* New York: Thunder's
Mouth Press, 1997.

Wiegman, Robyn. *American Anatomies: Theorizing Race and Gender.* Durham, N.C.:
Duke University Press, 1995.

Woolford, Pamela, and Haile Gerima. "Filming Slavery: A Conversation with Haile
Gerima." *Transition* no. 64 (1994): 90–104.

Index

208

Kara Keeling is an assistant professor of critical studies in the School of Cinematic Arts and of African American studies in the American studies and ethnicity department at the University of Southern California. She is the coeditor (with Cornel West and Colin MacCabe) of *Racist Traces and Other Writings: European Pedigrees/African Contagions* by James A. Snead (2003).

Library of Congress Cataloging-in-Publication Data

Keeling, Kara
The witch's flight : the cinematic, the Black femme,
and the image of common sense / Kara Keeling.
p. cm. — (Perverse modernities)
Includes bibliographical references and index.
ISBN-13: 978-0-8223-4013-3 (cloth : alk. paper)
ISBN-13: 978-0-8223-4025-6 (pbk. : alk. paper)
1. Lesbians in motion pictures.
2. Lesbianism in motion pictures.
3. African American women in motion pictures. I. Title.
PN1995.9.L48K44 2007
791.43'6526643—dc22   2007014053